ATS-13   ADMISSION TEST SERIES

This is your
PASSBOOK for...

Law School Admission Test (LSAT)

Test Preparation Study Guide
Questions & Answers

NATIONAL LEARNING CORPORATION®

COPYRIGHT NOTICE

This book is SOLELY intended for, is sold ONLY to, and its use is RESTRICTED to individual, bona fide applicants or candidates who qualify by virtue of having seriously filed applications for appropriate license, certificate, professional and/or promotional advancement, higher school matriculation, scholarship, or other legitimate requirements of education and/or governmental authorities.

This book is NOT intended for use, class instruction, tutoring, training, duplication, copying, reprinting, excerption, or adaptation, etc., by:

1) Other publishers
2) Proprietors and/or Instructors of "Coaching" and/or Preparatory Courses
3) Personnel and/or Training Divisions of commercial, industrial, and governmental organizations
4) Schools, colleges, or universities and/or their departments and staffs, including teachers and other personnel
5) Testing Agencies or Bureaus
6) Study groups which seek by the purchase of a single volume to copy and/or duplicate and/or adapt this material for use by the group as a whole without having purchased individual volumes for each of the members of the group
7) Et al.

Such persons would be in violation of appropriate Federal and State statutes.

PROVISION OF LICENSING AGREEMENTS – Recognized educational, commercial, industrial, and governmental institutions and organizations, and others legitimately engaged in educational pursuits, including training, testing, and measurement activities, may address request for a licensing agreement to the copyright owners, who will determine whether, and under what conditions, including fees and charges, the materials in this book may be used them. In other words, a licensing facility exists for the legitimate use of the material in this book on other than an individual basis. However, it is asseverated and affirmed here that the material in this book CANNOT be used without the receipt of the express permission of such a licensing agreement from the Publishers. Inquiries re licensing should be addressed to the company, attention rights and permissions department.

All rights reserved, including the right of reproduction in whole or in part, in any form or by any means, electronic or mechanical, including photocopying, recording, or by any information storage and retrieval system, without permission in writing from the Publisher.

Copyright © 2024 by
National Learning Corporation

212 Michael Drive, Syosset, NY 11791
(516) 921-8888 • www.passbooks.com
E-mail: info@passbooks.com

PUBLISHED IN THE UNITED STATES OF AMERICA

PASSBOOK® SERIES

THE *PASSBOOK® SERIES* has been created to prepare applicants and candidates for the ultimate academic battlefield – the examination room.

At some time in our lives, each and every one of us may be required to take an examination – for validation, matriculation, admission, qualification, registration, certification, or licensure.

Based on the assumption that every applicant or candidate has met the basic formal educational standards, has taken the required number of courses, and read the necessary texts, the *PASSBOOK® SERIES* furnishes the one special preparation which may assure passing with confidence, instead of failing with insecurity. Examination questions – together with answers – are furnished as the basic vehicle for study so that the mysteries of the examination and its compounding difficulties may be eliminated or diminished by a sure method.

This book is meant to help you pass your examination provided that you qualify and are serious in your objective.

The entire field is reviewed through the huge store of content information which is succinctly presented through a provocative and challenging approach – the question-and-answer method.

A climate of success is established by furnishing the correct answers at the end of each test.

You soon learn to recognize types of questions, forms of questions, and patterns of questioning. You may even begin to anticipate expected outcomes.

You perceive that many questions are repeated or adapted so that you can gain acute insights, which may enable you to score many sure points.

You learn how to confront new questions, or types of questions, and to attack them confidently and work out the correct answers.

You note objectives and emphases, and recognize pitfalls and dangers, so that you may make positive educational adjustments.

Moreover, you are kept fully informed in relation to new concepts, methods, practices, and directions in the field.

You discover that you are actually taking the examination all the time: you are preparing for the examination by "taking" an examination, not by reading extraneous and/or supererogatory textbooks.

In short, this PASSBOOK®, used directedly, should be an important factor in helping you to pass your test.

LAW SCHOOL ADMISSION TEST

Preparing for the LSAT

Most law school applicants familiarize themselves with test directions and question types, practice on sample tests, and study the information available on test-taking techniques and strategies. Although it is difficult to say when you are sufficiently prepared for the LSAT, very few people achieve their full potential without some preparation. You should be so familiar with the instructions and question types that nothing you see on the test can delay or distract you from thinking about how to answer a question. At a minimum, you should review the descriptions of the question types (below) and simulate the day of the test by taking, under actual time constraints, a practice test that includes a writing sample. Taking a practice test under timed conditions helps you to estimate the amount of time you can afford to spend on each question in a section and to determine the question types for which you may need additional practice.

The five multiple-choice sections of the test contain three different question types. The following pages present a general discussion of the nature of each question type and some strategies that can be used in answering them. Directions for each question type, sample questions, and a discussion of the answers are also included. When possible, explanations of the sample questions indicate their comparative level of difficulty.

Next, the writing sample is described, including directions and example prompts.

The following descriptive materials reflect the general nature of the test. It is not possible or practical to cover the full range of variation that may be found in questions on the LSAT. Be aware that material may appear in the test that is not described in the discussion of question types found here. For additional practice,

The Three LSAT Multiple-Choice Question Types

■ Reading Comprehension Questions

The purpose of reading comprehension questions is to measure your ability to read, with understanding and insight, examples of lengthy and complex materials similar to those commonly encountered in law school work. The reading comprehension section of the LSAT contains four sets of reading questions, each consisting of a selection of reading material followed by five to eight questions. The reading selection in three of the four sets consists of a single reading passage of approximately 450 words in length. The other set contains two related shorter passages. Sets with two passages are a new variant of reading comprehension, called comparative reading, which will be introduced into the reading comprehension section starting in June 2007. See the box on page 2 for more information.

Reading selections for reading comprehension questions are drawn from subjects such as the humanities, the social sciences, the biological and physical sciences, and issues related to the law. Reading comprehension questions require you to read carefully and accurately, to determine the relationships among the various parts of the reading selection, and to draw reasonable inferences from the material in the selection. The questions may ask about the following characteristics of a passage or pair of passages:

- the main idea or primary purpose;
- the meaning or purpose of words or phrases used;
- information explicitly stated;
- information or ideas that can be inferred;
- the organization or structure;
- the application of information in a passage to a new context; and
- the author's attitude as it is revealed in the tone of a passage or the language used.

Suggested Approach

Since reading selections are drawn from many different disciplines and sources, you should not be discouraged if you encounter material with which you are not familiar. It is important to remember that questions are to be answered exclusively on the basis of the information provided in the selection. There is no particular knowledge that you are expected to bring to the test, and you should not make inferences based on any prior knowledge of a subject that you may have. You may, however, wish to defer working on a set of questions that seems particularly difficult or unfamiliar until after you have dealt with sets you find easier.

Strategies. In preparing for the test, you should experiment with different strategies and decide which work most effectively for you. These include:

- reading the selection very closely and then answering the questions;
- reading the questions first, reading the selection closely, and then returning to the questions; or
- skimming the selection and questions very quickly, then rereading the selection closely and answering the questions.

Remember that your strategy must be effective for you under timed conditions.

Comparative Reading

Starting with the June 2007 administration, LSAC is introducing a new variant of reading comprehension, called comparative reading, as one of the four sets in the LSAT reading comprehension section. In general, comparative reading questions are similar to traditional reading comprehension questions, except that comparative reading questions are based on two shorter passages instead of one longer passage. The two passages together are of roughly the same length as one reading comprehension passage, so the total amount of reading in the reading comprehension section will remain essentially the same. A few of the questions that follow a comparative reading passage pair might concern only one of the two passages, but most will be about both passages and how they relate to each other.

Comparative reading questions reflect the nature of some important tasks in law school work, such as understanding arguments from multiple texts by applying skills of comparison, contrast, generalization, and synthesis to the texts. The purpose of comparative reading is to assess this important set of skills directly.

What comparative reading looks like

The two passages in a comparative reading set—labeled "**Passage A**" and "**Passage B**"—discuss the same topic or related topics. The topics fall into the same academic categories traditionally used in reading comprehension: humanities, natural sciences, social sciences, and issues related to the law. Like traditional reading comprehension passages, comparative reading passages are complex and generally involve argument. The two passages in a comparative reading pair are typically adapted from two different published sources written by two different authors. They are usually independent of each other, with neither author responding directly to the other.

As you read the pair of passages, it is helpful to try to determine what the central idea or main point of each passage is, and to determine how the passages relate to each other. The passages will relate to each other in various ways. In some cases, the authors of the passages will be in general agreement with each other, while in others their views will be directly opposed. Passage pairs may also exhibit more complex types of relationships: for example, one passage might articulate a set of principles, while the other passage applies those or similar principles to a particular situation.

Questions that are concerned with only one of the passages are essentially identical to traditional reading comprehension questions. Questions that address both passages test the same fundamental reading skills as traditional reading comprehension questions, but the skills are applied to two texts instead of one. You may be asked to identify a main purpose shared by both passages, a statement with which both authors would agree, or a similarity or dissimilarity in the structure of the arguments in the two passages. The following are additional examples of comparative reading questions:

- Which one of the following is the central topic of each passage?

- Both passages explicitly mention which one of the following?

- Which one of the following statements is most strongly supported by both passages?

- Which one of the following most accurately describes the attitude expressed by the author of passage B toward the overall argument in passage A?

- The relationship between passage A and passage B is most analogous to the relationship in which one of the following?

This is not a complete list of the sorts of questions you may be asked in a comparative reading set, but it illustrates the range of questions you may be asked.

Reading the selection. Whatever strategy you choose, you should give the passage or pair of passages at least one careful reading before answering the questions. Try to distinguish main ideas from supporting ideas, and opinions or attitudes from factual, objective information. Note transitions from one idea to the next and examine the relationships among the different ideas or parts of a passage, or between the two passages in comparative reading sets. Consider how and why an author makes points and draws conclusions. Be sensitive to implications of what the passages say.

You may find it helpful to mark key parts of passages. For example, you might underline main ideas or important arguments, and you might circle transitional words—"although," "nevertheless," "correspondingly," and the like—that will help you map the structure of a passage. Moreover, you might note descriptive words that will help you identify an author's attitude toward a particular idea or person.

Answering the Questions

- Always read all the answer choices before selecting the best answer. The best answer choice is the one that most accurately and completely answers the question being posed.

- Respond to the specific question being asked. Do not pick an answer choice simply because it is a true statement. For example, picking a true statement might yield an incorrect answer to a question in which you are asked to identify an author's position on an issue, since here you are not being asked to evaluate the truth of the author's position but only to correctly identify what that position is.

- Answer the questions only on the basis of the information provided in the selection. Your own views, interpretations, or opinions, and those you have heard from others, may sometimes conflict with those expressed in a reading selection; however, you are expected to work within the context provided by the reading selection. You should not expect to agree with everything you encounter in reading comprehension passages.

Fourteen Sample Reading Comprehension Questions and Explanations

The sample questions on the following pages are typical of the reading comprehension questions you will find on the LSAT. Three traditional reading comprehension passages are included, but they are followed by only two or three sample questions each, whereas each passage in the actual LSAT is followed by five to eight questions. In contrast, since comparative reading is a new variant of reading comprehension, the comparative reading set below includes seven questions and explanations for familiarization purposes. (Note: There is also a comparative reading set in the sample LSAT included in this book.)

Directions: Each set of questions in this section is based on a single passage or a pair of passages. The questions are to be answered on the basis of what is stated or implied in the passage or pair of passages. For some of the questions, more than one of the choices could conceivably answer the question. However, you are to choose the best answer; that is, the response that most accurately and completely answers the question, and blacken the corresponding space on your answer sheet.

Passage for Questions 1 and 2

For many African American writers, history and personal experience have reflected not diversity of opportunity, but limitation of opportunity. Their writings consequently demonstrate their
(5) sense that literature should provide a unified, cultural identity in forceful opposition to that limitation. For Ralph Ellison and some younger contemporary novelists such as Charles Johnson, Leon Forrest, and John Wideman,
(10) however, the problem seems the reverse. With African American life offering multiple perspectives and possibilities to these writers, how can one pattern of unification explain all? And if one pattern cannot, what identities are
(15) available to their characters?
In *Invisible Man*, Ellison's protagonist, like Ellison in his early life, experiments with a variety of roles. As he assumes new roles, each a result of racial pressure, he realizes
(20) paradoxically that while his options should be decreasing, they are actually increasing. Most frightening to him is the prospect that there might be innumerable roles for him to play, that the perception of "infinite possibilities" would
(25) become the terrifying perception of chaos; he might, in other words, be without any permanent "form." Ellison's protagonist's problem is the same epistemological problem as that of Herman Melville's character Ishmael in
(30) *Moby-Dick* (1851): how to make definitions, especially of one's self. The only "plan" that Ellison's protagonist finds capable of shielding him from the chaos of living is a personal aesthetic plan for an individual rather than for a
(35) people. As the novel progresses, the Invisible Man perceives that actively creating a personal style makes survival possible; as a style for himself he adopts the attitudes of traditional blues.
(40) Johnson, Forrest, and Wideman, however, cannot rest easy with even such a hard-won solution as the blues, if that solution is used to serve only an isolated individual. For them, the blues are chiefly a triumphant and lasting part of
(45) African American culture, rather than a solution to the problem of defining identity. In their novels, the individual, that archetypal figure of Western myth and fiction, often journeys forth from a rural Southern community to the urban
(50) North, seeking to know himself and give form to his life. Eventually the reader realizes that this journey is, as Ellison explicitly states about the journey of his protagonist, cyclical. Yet it should be noted that, whereas Ellison's
(55) protagonist concludes his quest as a lone individual once again, the protagonists of these other

novels reconfirm their identity as members of the African American community. No character like Ras the Exhorter, who attempts in *Invisible Man* to
(60) unify the African American community, triumphs in these novels, as many of Ellison's critics think should have happened in *Invisible Man*; but their protagonists do not end underground, companioned alone with their thoughts.

Question 1

It can be inferred from the passage that some of the protagonist's actions in *Invisible Man* are most likely to have been modeled on the

(A) actions of Ishmael in Melville's *Moby-Dick*
(B) most recurrent situations in Western myth and fiction
(C) author's personal experiences before he wrote the novel
(D) actions of those African American literary characters who question traditional blues attitudes
(E) actions of those African American literary characters who work to establish a single African American identity

Explanation for Question 1

This question requires the examinee to draw from the information presented in the passage an inference about what most likely is the case.

The credited response is (C). The author implies that Ellison's personal experiences provided the model for his protagonist: "In *Invisible Man*, Ellison's protagonist, like Ellison in his early life, experiments with a variety of roles" (lines 16–18). It is also indicated (in the first paragraph) that Ellison's personal experience provided the diversity of opportunity needed for such experimentation, and that these "multiple perspectives and possibilities" (lines 11–12) are reflected in his writing.

Response (A) is incorrect, because, although the author compares *Invisible Man* to *Moby-Dick* in lines 27–31, response (A) mistakes the author's purpose in referring to Melville's novel. The author of the passage is making a very limited comparison between the respective protagonists of both novels. The author of the passage merely points out that both novels have protagonists who face the same epistemological question and who attempt "to make definitions, especially of one's self." This is nothing more than an observation that the author of the passage makes. There is no suggestion that Ellison used Melville's work as a model.

Response (B) is incorrect because it confuses the context in which the author refers to recurrent situations in Western myth and fiction. The second paragraph examines the work of Ellison. The third contrasts that author with Johnson, Forrest, and Wideman, whose novels are said to deal with the individual as "that archetypal figure of Western myth and fiction" (lines 47–48). There is no basis in the passage for assuming that this archetype is the model for Ellison's protagonist. If anything, there is a slight suggestion in lines 53–58, where the author of the passage contrasts Ellison's protagonist with those of Johnson, Forrest, and Wideman, that Ellison's protagonist is unlike this archetype.

Response (D) is incorrect because it distorts information in the passage. Ellison's character "adopts the attitudes of traditional blues" (lines 38–39). The writers Johnson, Forrest, and Wideman are said to see the blues as an aspect of African American culture, "rather than a solution to the problem of defining identity" (lines 45–46). The passage never refers to literary characters who question traditional blues attitudes.

Response (E) is incorrect. It refers to the work of those African American writers mentioned in the first sentences of the passage whose work deals with the problem of creating "a unified, cultural identity" (lines 5–6). This is the point of departure for the author's discussion of Ellison and the other younger writers for whom "the problem seems the reverse" (line 10). Therefore, since the author establishes a clear distinction between these writers and Ellison, it would be very odd to say that Ellison modeled his protagonist on the actions of characters typical of the other group. Moreover, although the character Ras the Exhorter in *Invisible Man* is said to attempt to unify the African American community, there is every indication that Ras the Exhorter is not *Invisible Man's* protagonist (for example, see lines 31–35).

This question was answered correctly by 47 percent of test takers, making it a "middle difficulty" question.

Question 2

Which one of the following terms could best be substituted for the word "chaos" (line 25) without changing the author's meaning?

(A) racial pressure
(B) literary incoherence
(C) contradictory roles
(D) limited identity
(E) unstable identity

Explanation for Question 2

This question requires the examinee to understand from context the meaning of the word "chaos," which is used by the author in an interesting way.

The credited response is (E). Ellison's protagonist, faced with the prospect of a life of innumerable roles, of "infinite possibilities" (line 24), becomes terrified at the thought of the chaos that would leave him no "permanent 'form'" (line 27). Any word that replaces the word "chaos" without changing the author's meaning, must denote something that leads to a lack of permanent form. "Unstable identity" does this best in that it suggests that one's identity never remains the same, that it is always changing, and thus leaves one with no permanent form.

Response (A) is incorrect. Although each of the roles played by Ellison's protagonist is the result of racial pressure, it is not the pressures themselves that the protagonist equates with chaos.

Response (B) is incorrect. Nothing in the passage suggests that the problem of "chaos" faced by Ellison's protagonist is a literary problem for the character or Ellison.

Response (C) is incorrect. The protagonist fears innumerable roles—that is, the perception of "infinite possibilities" (line 24). So, the passage suggests that it is a consequence of the number of roles, rather than the contradictions among them, that would positively terrify Ellison's protagonist.

Response (D) is incorrect. Substituting "limited identity" for "chaos" would make the perception incongruent with the perception of "infinite possibilities" mentioned in line 24. These contradictory concepts would make the resulting sentence incoherent. Furthermore, in the second paragraph, the author is examining the phenomenon of "increasing" options, not limiting ones.

This is considered an "easy" question. Sixty-eight percent of test takers answered this question correctly.

Passage for Questions 3 and 4

The auction is a market mechanism. It consists of unique transactions between willing sellers and eager buyers who have been brought together by the auctioneer to determine a price at which the
(5) items for sale will be sold. As a method for determining price, auctions are easy, accurate, and fair. However, auctions are occasionally marred by certain bidding practices that conflict with fairness and openness in business deals. Some of these
(10) practices involve negotiations behind the scenes.

Two of the more common types of illegal bidding practices in auction circuits are "puffing" and "stifling competition." The objective of "puffing" is to buoy the price of the item for sale. Two puffing
(15) practices are common: having the seller, or the seller's agent, bid on an item the seller himself has put up for sale; or having the seller in some way exempt the person bidding from being held responsible for the full amount of the bid. Sellers bid
(20) on their own property because they want to get the highest price possible; they do not want the property to be sacrificed.

When puffing is suspected, it is important to establish whether the person suspected of puffing is
(25) indeed the seller of the item. Ownership interests may be divided among several persons, each of whom must agree to the sale. Those persons, as a group, then constitute the seller. An individual with ownership interests can bid as an individual without being a
(30) puffer so long as the seller—that is, the group as a whole—can hold that person responsible for the full amount of the bid. If the person bidding is even partially immunized by the seller from being held responsible for the full amount of the bid, puffing
(35) has occurred.

Buyers engage in "stifling competition," the other common illegal bidding practice, to dampen competition so that they can purchase an item for less than the amount it would have brought in an
(40) auction uninfluenced by such conduct. Stifling competition can take several forms: agreements among prospective buyers not to bid, words or actions that are meant to discourage others from bidding, or bidding techniques that diminish the
(45) price ultimately paid for the item being auctioned.

Puffing and stifling competition are opposite sides of the same coin. When they occur, buyers and sellers, respectively, complain that the other's conduct has prevented the auction from being fair
(50) and open. In those instances when the complaints have been found to be justified, the courts have held puffing to be a fraud on the buyers and stifling competition to be a fraud on the sellers. Both practices are fraudulent because they undermine
(55) the fair, open, and competitive determination of price that is meant to be the distinguishing characteristic of auctions as market mechanisms.

Question 3

According to the information in the passage, each of the following is an accurate statement about auctions EXCEPT:

(A) Puffing is considered an illegal practice at auctions.
(B) Ideally, auctions are a fair method for determining the price of an item.
(C) Sellers are generally able to get higher prices through auctions than through other market mechanisms.
(D) The prices paid at a fair auction are the result of competition among buyers.
(E) The price that is determined at a fair auction is not always acceptable to the seller.

Explanation for Question 3

This question requires the examinee to identify what information about auctions the passage does and does not contain. Note that the question says, "According to the information in the passage, each of the following is an accurate statement about auctions *EXCEPT*." The correct response, in this case, is one that the passage *does not* support as accurate.

(C) is the credited response because the passage does not discuss "other market mechanisms," and nowhere does it suggest that sellers could do better through auctions than such mechanisms. Therefore, (C) correctly answers the question asked because the information given in the passage does not support it as an accurate statement about auctions.

Response (A) is incorrect because the passage clearly states that "*puffing*" is considered an illegal bidding practice at auctions. Paragraph two begins by saying, "*Two of the more common types of illegal bidding practices in auction circuits are 'puffing' and 'stifling competition.'*" Therefore, based on the information in the passage, response (A) is an accurate statement about auctions.

Response (B) is incorrect because the first paragraph of the passage establishes that "ideally, auctions are a fair method for determining the price of an item." It says, *"As a method for determining price, auctions are easy, accurate, and fair."* The final paragraph also provides information supporting response (B). It says, *"the fair, open, and competitive determination of price...is meant to be the distinguishing characteristic of auctions as market mechanisms."* Therefore, response (B) is an accurate statement about auctions, given the information in the passage.

Response (D) is incorrect because the fourth paragraph of the passage, which discusses the illegal bidding practice of *"stifling competition,"* makes it clear that when competition is stifled, an auction is no longer fair. Thus, the passage does provide information to support the statement, "The prices paid at a fair auction are the result of competition among buyers."

Response (E) is incorrect because the passage contains information to support the statement that the price "determined at a fair auction is not always acceptable to the seller." The practice of *"puffing,"* described in paragraph two, is an attempt on the seller's part to get the best possible price for whatever is being auctioned. If the price determined at a fair auction were always acceptable to the seller, there would be no need for a practice such as *"puffing."* Therefore, information in the passage provides support for response (E) as an accurate statement about auctions.

This is considered an "easy" question, answered correctly by 86 percent of test takers. Although small numbers of test takers chose each of the other responses, the overwhelming majority answered this question correctly.

Question 4

Which one of the following statements about competition in auctions is best supported by the information in the passage?

(A) Competition among buyers sometimes becomes excessive.
(B) Competition among buyers that results from puffing is artificial.
(C) Competition among sellers can be undermined by the practice of puffing.
(D) Competition among sellers is more likely in auctions than in other market mechanisms.
(E) Competition among sellers is the critical element in the determination of a fair price.

Explanation for Question 4

This question requires the examinee to see the logical implications following from the passage in order to identify which response is best supported by the information in the passage.

The credited response is (B). *"Puffing"* is an artificial way of determining price in an auction because it is an attempt on the seller's part to *"buoy the price of an item for sale"* illegally. The seller or the seller's agent interferes with the fair auction market mechanism by stimulating more competition than would naturally occur. Therefore, "Competition among buyers that results from puffing is artificial." Response (B) is clearly supported by information in the passage.

Response (A) is incorrect because the passage does not discuss the intensity of competition among buyers.

Response (C) is incorrect because, according to the passage, the practice of *"puffing"* artificially increases competition among buyers. The passage does not discuss "competition among sellers," nor how such competition might be undermined.

Response (D) is incorrect because the passage does not discuss "competition among sellers," nor does it compare auctions to other market mechanisms.

Response (E) is incorrect because the passage suggests that competition among buyers, not among sellers, is important to a determination of fair price. The passage never discusses competition among sellers, let alone suggests that such competition, as opposed to other factors, is critical to determining fair price.

This is considered a "middle-difficulty" question, answered correctly by approximately 56 percent of test takers. About 23 percent of test takers chose response (C), and about 10 percent chose response (E).

Passage for Questions 5, 6, and 7

During the past 25 years, there has been much discussion of "black capitalism." Many people have debated fruitlessly about the meaning of this term and the values of the philosophy it supposedly
(5) describes. However, there is no such thing as black capitalism. In the United States capitalism, like socialism, is an economic and political philosophy that describes the experience of Europeans and their descendants—white Americans. Blacks must
(10) therefore create a new economic ideology that may include elements of capitalism, elements of socialism, or elements of neither. What matters is that the new economic ideology be created to suit our economic goals, the chief of which is the
(15) creation and acquisition of capital-producing instruments. What sort of economic entity might result were the new economic ideology put into practice? Although I am not interested in defining styles of ownership in absolute terms, I imagine
(20) that the HCC (Harlem Commonwealth Council) very much resembles such an entity.

The HCC, which was the first group in the United States to formalize the advance of black-owned business beyond the risky "Mom and Pop"
(25) businesses financed and managed by a single individual or family, is a nonprofit, tax-exempt corporation that invests in profit-making businesses and uses the accumulated capital to reinvest in black-owned or black-managed businesses. The
(30) HCC's first brochure, issued in the 1960s, noted that Harlem's half million people spend over half a billion dollars for consumer goods each year—a

sum larger than the gross national product of many
newly industrialized nations. Yet the brochure also
(35) noted that most of this money is siphoned off from
the community by outsiders who control 80 percent
of Harlem's business volume. Thus the HCC
concluded that the major economic problem of
Harlem is that the community is prevented from
(40) accumulating the capital required to make investments
(and thus earn revenue on those investments) and to
finance the industry necessary for the creation of jobs
for members of the community. Accordingly, the
goal of the HCC has been to develop Harlem's
(45) capital resources, thereby restoring to Harlem the
internal economic vitality that is inseparable from
the acquisition of political power.

To accomplish its goal, the HCC set up, during
the 1960s, a community-based board of directors to
(50) evaluate opportunities for investment. The directors
first invested in those businesses that would meet a
community need (e.g., a 24-hour pharmacy selling
prescription medicines by their generic names, thus
permitting prices considerably lower than those for
(55) brand-name medicines) and those businesses that
could take advantage of Harlem's location in
Manhattan.

The HCC, then, is not confined by the
restrictions either of capitalism (financial
(60) risk-taking by the entrepreneur) or of socialism
(financial risk-taking by the state); rather, it
combines elements of both in its pursuit of
tomorrow's opportunities.

Question 5

The author most probably refers to "the gross national product of many newly industrialized nations" (lines 33-34) in order to

(A) compare economic conditions in other countries to the economic conditions in the United States
(B) provide an example of the type of economic entity sought by the advocates of the new economic ideology
(C) clarify the meaning of the phrase "capital-producing instruments"
(D) emphasize the enormous economic benefits that Harlem would derive from the acquisition of greater political power
(E) suggest the magnitude of Harlem's potential for accumulating capital

Explanation for Question 5

This question requires the examinee to identify from the context what the author intends to accomplish or convey by using the phrase "the gross national product of many newly industrialized nations."

The credited response is (E). The phrase is used parenthetically immediately following reference in the passage to *the over half a billion dollars residents of Harlem spend each year on consumer goods*. The passage then goes on to say that most of this money is *"siphoned off from the community by outsiders,"* and that this is why Harlem has trouble accumulating capital for making investments within the community. These statements imply that, if over half a billion dollars can be spent in Harlem on consumer goods—a sum as great as the gross national product of many newly industrialized nations—there is potential for generating capital for investment within the Harlem community of a magnitude comparable to that generated in entire newly industrialized nations, if only that money could be directed to investment within the Harlem community instead of being siphoned off by outsiders who control most of Harlem's business volume.

Response (A) is incorrect. Nowhere in the passage does the author compare economic conditions in other countries to those in the United States. The reference to *the gross national product of other countries* is intended to make a point about economic conditions in Harlem.

Response (B) is incorrect because the author uses the HCC, not newly industrialized nations, as an example of the type of economic entity sought by advocates of "the new economic ideology."

Response (C) is incorrect. The phrase *"capital producing instruments"* occurs earlier, in the first paragraph of the passage, and there is no language in the passage linking it with *"the gross national product of many newly industrialized nations."* So, there is nothing in the passage to suggest that the latter is intended to clarify the meaning of the former.

Response (D) is also incorrect. While the passage does relate economic vitality and political power, response (D) misstates the relationship described in the passage. The passage states that *internal economic vitality is necessary for the acquisition of political power*, while response (D) states that enormous economic benefits could be realized from the acquisition of greater political power. So, response (D) describes a relationship which is the reverse of the one being stressed in the passage. Moreover, the reference to the *gross national product of other countries* is not related in the passage to the relationship between economic vitality and political power.

Question 6

The primary purpose of the passage is to

(A) contend that black capitalism has failed and urge that the techniques of capitalism and socialism be combined by black entrepreneurs
(B) summarize the old economic ideology espoused by many theorists of black economics and then explain the new economic ideology
(C) argue for the creation of a new economic ideology and explain how it can be put into practice
(D) outline the economic goals of Harlem and provide examples of the ways in which some of those goals can be achieved

(E) point out that the HCC has been an effective organization and suggest that the HCC expand the scope of its activities

Explanation for Question 6

This question requires the examinee to look at the passage as a whole and determine its primary purpose.

(C) is the credited response because it most accurately and completely reflects the purpose of the passage as a whole. The first paragraph of the passage argues for the creation of *"a new economic ideology,"* one which, the author says, *"may include elements of capitalism, elements of socialism, or elements of neither,"* so long as it suits certain economic goals, *"the chief of which is the creation and acquisition of capital-producing instruments."* The remainder of the passage then explains, by using the HCC as an example, how this ideology "can be put into practice." At the end of paragraph one, the author says, *"Although I am not interested in defining styles of ownership in absolute terms, I imagine that the HCC (Harlem Commonwealth Council) very much resembles such an entity."*

Response (A) is incorrect because the passage does not contend that "black capitalism has failed," nor does it "urge that the techniques of capitalism and socialism be combined by black entrepreneurs." In fact, the passage says that *"there is no such thing as black capitalism,"* and it suggests that black entrepreneurs create a *"new economic ideology" that may or may not use elements of capitalism and socialism.*

Response (B) is incorrect because, although the passage does explain a "new economic ideology," it does not contain a summary of "the old economic ideology espoused by many theorists of black economics." It makes brief mention of *"black capitalism,"* but it does not summarize this ideology.

Response (D) is incorrect because, although the passage discusses "the economic goals of Harlem" and "ways in which some of those goals can be achieved," it does so in order to illustrate the operation of the HCC, which is an example of the *"new economic ideology"* in practice. This *"new economic ideology,"* not "the economic goals of Harlem," is the passage's primary focus.

Response (E) is incorrect. Although the passage points out that the HCC has been an effective organization, it says nothing about expanding "the scope of its activities." Moreover, while pointing out the effectiveness of the HCC is one purpose of the passage, it is not the primary purpose, which is established in the first paragraph.

Question 7

The author suggests which one of the following about the debate over black capitalism?

(A) The usefulness of the debate has been negligible because black-controlled businesses should not be guided solely by the values of capitalism.
(B) The debate has been worthless because capitalism is both a self-contradictory and an evolving philosophy.
(C) The questions raised by the debate remain unanswered because the people taking part have accepted incompatible definitions of economic growth.
(D) The debate will soon become more helpful than it has been in the past because of the activities of the HCC.
(E) The people taking part in the debate have not adequately distinguished the values of capitalism from the values of socialism.

Explanation for Question 7

This question requires the examinee to identify an idea suggested in the passage.

The credited response is (A), because it summarizes an argument that the author makes in the passage. "The usefulness of the debate has been negligible" is implied by the author's assertion in the first paragraph that people have debated *"fruitlessly"* about the meaning of *"black capitalism."* Moreover, the statement that "black-controlled businesses should not be guided solely by the values of capitalism" is implied by the author's argument that both capitalism and socialism reflect European and white American, not black, economic reality, and that blacks must create their own synthesis of these and other models.

Response (B) is incorrect because the author never suggests in the passage that capitalism is "a self-contradictory and an evolving philosophy." Nor is this given as a reason for believing that the debate over black capitalism has been *"fruitless."*

Similarly, response (C) is incorrect because "incompatible definitions of economic growth" held by participants in the debate over black capitalism is not a reason given by the author for feeling that the debate has been *"fruitless."*

Response (D) is incorrect because, while the author describes the HCC approvingly as a model of the *"new economic ideology"* that blacks need to develop, the passage does not imply that the debate will "soon become more helpful than it has been in the past," or indeed, that the HCC will affect the debate over black capitalism one way or another. The debate is briefly mentioned in the first paragraph only to provide a context for the author's discussion of the HCC, then is dismissed as *"fruitless"* and not mentioned again.

Response (E) is incorrect because the problem with the debate is not that "the people taking part have not adequately distinguished the values of capitalism from the values of socialism." The author makes a different argument: that the debate has focused (*"fruitlessly"*) on capitalism, when in fact capitalism is irrelevant to blacks. What is needed, according to the author, is *"a new economic ideology that may include elements of capitalism, elements of socialism, or elements of neither."*

This question is classified as "very difficult," answered correctly by only 38 percent of test takers on the LSAT. Most people were drawn to responses (B) and (C), which attribute to the author particular arguments that were not made in the passage. Many "difficult" reading comprehension questions, like this one, require close attention to modifying words, such as "self-contradictory" and "evolving," and a careful search of the text to determine if the author actually is suggesting the relationships implied by these words.

Passage Pair for Questions 8-14

For the following comparative reading set, difficulty information is not available.

The following passages were adapted from articles published in the mid-1990s.

Passage A
In January 1995 a vast section of ice broke off the Larsen ice shelf in Antarctica. While this occurrence, the direct result of a regional warming trend that began in the 1940s, may be the most spectacular
(5) manifestation yet of serious climate changes occurring on the planet as a consequence of atmospheric heating, other symptoms—more intense storms, prolonged droughts, extended heat waves, and record flooding—have been emerging around the
(10) world for several years.
According to scientific estimates, furthermore, sea-level rise resulting from global warming will reach 3 feet (1 meter) within the next century. Such a rise could submerge vast coastal areas, with
(15) potentially irreversible consequences.
Late in 1995 the Intergovernmental Panel on Climate Change (IPCC) reported that it had detected the "fingerprint" of human activity as a contributor to the warming of the earth's atmosphere. Furthermore,
(20) panel scientists attributed such warming directly to the increasing quantities of carbon dioxide released by our burning of fossil fuels. The IPCC report thus clearly identifies a pattern of climatic response to human activities in the climatological record, thereby
(25) establishing without doubt that global warming can no longer be attributed solely to natural climate variability.

Passage B
Over the past two decades, an extreme view of global warming has developed. While it contains
(30) some facts, this view also contains exaggerations and misstatements, and has sometimes resulted in unreasonable environmental policies.
According to this view, global warming will cause the polar ice to melt, raising global sea levels,
(35) flooding entire regions, destroying crops, and displacing millions of people. However, there is still a great deal of uncertainty regarding a potential rise in sea levels. Certainly, if the earth warms, sea levels will rise as the water heats up and expands. If the
(40) polar ice caps melt, more water will be added to the oceans, raising sea levels even further. There is some evidence that melting has occurred; however, there is also evidence that the Antarctic ice sheets are growing. In fact, it is possible that a warmer sea-
(45) surface temperature will cause more water to evaporate, and when wind carries the moisture-laden air over the land, it will precipitate out as snow, causing the ice sheets to grow. Certainly, we need to have better knowledge about the hydrological cycle
(50) before predicting dire consequences as a result of recent increases in global temperatures.
This view also exaggerates the impact that human activity has on the planet. While human activity may be a factor in global warming, natural events appear
(55) to be far more important. The 1991 eruption of Mount Pinatubo in the Philippines, for example, caused a decrease in the average global temperature, while El Niño, a periodic perturbation in the ocean's temperature and circulation, causes extreme global
(60) climatic events, including droughts and major flooding. Of even greater importance to the earth's climate are variations in the sun's radiation and in the earth's orbit. Climate variability has always existed and will continue to do so, regardless of human
(65) intervention.

Question 8

Which one of the following questions is central to both passages?

(A) How has an increase in the burning of fossil fuels raised the earth's temperature?
(B) To what extent can global warming be attributed to human activity?
(C) What steps should be taken to reduce the rate of global warming?
(D) What kinds of human activities increase the amount of carbon dioxide in the atmosphere?
(E) To what extent is global warming caused by variations in the sun's radiation and the earth's orbit?

Explanation for Question 8

Most traditional reading comprehension sets start with a question that asks about the passage's main point or central topic, or the author's main purpose in writing. The same is true of most comparative reading sets, but in comparative reading the questions might ask about the main point, primary purpose, or central issue of both passages, as is the case here.

The correct response is (B), "To what extent can global warming be attributed to human activity?" Both passages are concerned with the current warming trend in the earth's climate, which is generally referred to as "global warming." Both passages agree that the earth's climate is indeed getting warmer, but it is clear that the two authors differ in their views on the issue. In the third paragraph of each passage, the author raises the question of the causes of global warming. Passage A cites a report by the Intergovernmental Panel on

Climate Change (IPCC) that attributes warming "directly to the increasing quantities of carbon dioxide released by our burning of fossil fuels" (lines 20–22). The author concludes, "The IPCC report thus clearly identifies a pattern of climatic response to human activities in the climatological record, thereby establishing without doubt that global warming can no longer be attributed solely to natural climate variability" (lines 22–27). In contrast, the author of passage B argues, "While human activity may be a factor in global warming, natural events appear to be far more important" (lines 53–55). In other words, a central concern in each passage is the cause of global warming, and more specifically, the extent to which the phenomenon can be attributed to human activity or to natural climate variability. Thus, response (B) expresses a question that is central to both passages.

Response (A) is incorrect because passage B does not address the issue of fossil fuels. While passage A states that the IPCC scientists attributed global warming "directly to the increasing quantities of carbon dioxide released by our burning of fossil fuels" (lines 20–22), passage B makes no mention of fossil fuels or carbon dioxide.

Response (C) is incorrect because neither passage discusses steps that should be taken to reduce global warming. The author of passage A believes that global warming is a serious problem for which human activity bears significant responsibility, so he or she presumably believes that some steps should indeed be taken. But he or she does not actually discuss any such steps. Meanwhile, the author of passage B is not even convinced that human activity bears much responsibility for global warming; accordingly, passage B is not concerned at all with the question of what steps should be taken to address the problem.

Response (D) is incorrect because, as mentioned in the explanation of response (A) above, passage B makes no mention of carbon dioxide or any human activities that increase carbon dioxide in the atmosphere.

Response (E) is incorrect because passage A does not mention variations in the sun's radiation and the earth's orbit as possible causes of global warming. The author of passage B mentions variations in the sun's radiation and the earth's orbit as natural contributors to climate variation, but does so in order to illustrate a more general point, namely, that natural climate variability may very well explain global warming. The sun's radiation and the earth's orbit are not the central concern of passage B.

Question 9

Which one of the following is mentioned in passage B but not in passage A as a possible consequence of global warming?

(A) an increase in the size of the Antarctic ice sheet
(B) a decrease in the amount of snowfall
(C) a falling of ocean sea levels
(D) an increase in the severity of heat waves
(E) an increase in the frequency of major flooding

Explanation for Question 9

This question is designed to test the ability to recognize a significant difference in the content of the two passages.

The correct response is (A), "an increase in the size of the Antarctic ice sheet." In lines 42–48, passage B explicitly cites the possibility that the Antarctic ice sheet will grow as a result of warmer sea temperatures brought about by global warming. On the other hand, passage A does not mention any possibility that the Antarctic ice sheet might grow. In fact, on the topic of the Antarctic ice sheet, passage A alludes only to the breaking off of part of the Larsen ice shelf (lines 1–2), which suggests that, if anything, the author of passage A believes that the Antarctic ice sheet is shrinking because of global warming. Thus response (A) describes something that is mentioned in passage B, but not passage A, as a possible consequence of global warming.

Response (B) is incorrect because passage B mentions only *increased* snowfall as a possible consequence of global warming. The correct response must be something mentioned in passage B but not in passage A.

Response (C) is incorrect because passage B mentions only *rising* sea levels as a possible consequence of global warming. The author's reference to the possibility that the Antarctic ice sheet might grow suggests that, in the author's eyes, the rise in sea level might be slowed. But nowhere does the author say that sea levels might drop as a consequence of global warming.

Response (D) is incorrect because, while passage A mentions extended heat waves as a consequence of global warming, passage B does not mention heat waves in any connection.

Response (E) is incorrect because passage A discusses major flooding as a consequence of global warming in the first two paragraphs.

Question 10

The authors of the two passages would be most likely to disagree over

(A) whether or not any melting of the polar ice caps has occurred
(B) whether natural events can cause changes in global climate conditions
(C) whether warmer air temperatures will be likely to raise oceanic water temperatures
(D) the extent to which natural climate variability is responsible for global warming
(E) the extent to which global temperatures have risen in recent decades

Explanation for Question 10

A significant number of questions for comparative reading passages require an ability to infer what the authors' views are and how they compare. Some questions ask about points of agreement between the authors. Others, such as this one, ask about points on which the authors disagree.

As you read the response choices for a question of this sort, it is a good idea to recall what you may have already concluded about points of agreement and disagreement between the authors. For example, it was noted above that the authors of these two passages disagree on at least one key issue (see the explanation of question 8)—the causes of global warming. The correct response to this question is related to this point of contention: the correct response is (D), "the extent to which natural climate variability is responsible for global warming." Passage A states, "The IPCC report thus clearly identifies a pattern of climatic response to human activities in the climatological record, thereby establishing without doubt that global warming can no longer be attributed solely to natural climate variability" (lines 22-27). In contrast, passage B states, "While human activity may be a factor in global warming, natural events appear to be far more important" (lines 53-55). In short, while the author of passage A holds that human activity is substantially responsible for global warming, the author of passage B holds that natural events may exert far more influence on the earth's climate.

Response (A) is incorrect because it is not clear that the authors would disagree over this issue. The author of passage A describes the breaking off of part of the Larsen ice shelf in Antarctica as "the direct result of a regional warming trend that began in the 1940s" (lines 3-4). The author does not use the precise words "the melting of the polar ice caps," but the implication of what the author does say is that such melting is obviously taking place. On the other hand, it is not clear that the author of passage B would disagree with this claim, since the author concedes that there is evidence supporting the position: "There is some evidence that melting has occurred…" (lines 41-42).

Response (B) is incorrect because both authors would agree that natural events can cause changes in global climate conditions. Since the author of passage B argues that natural events appear to be a more important factor in global warming than human activity, he or she must agree that natural events can affect global climate. And indeed, the author cites the eruption of Mt. Pinatubo, El Niño, and variations in the sun's radiation and the earth's orbit as examples of natural events that are known to have done so (lines 55-63). On the other hand, the concluding sentence of passage A—which ends with the claim that the IPCC report has established "that global warming can no longer be attributed *solely* to natural climate variability" (lines 25-27, emphasis added)—indirectly acknowledges that natural events do play a role in changes in the earth's climate. Thus the authors would agree with respect to response (B).

Response (C) is incorrect because the passages provide no evidence for concluding that the authors would disagree over the effect of warmer air temperatures on oceanic water temperatures. The author of passage B holds that warmer air temperatures would heat up the oceans. Passage B states, "Certainly, if the earth warms, sea levels will rise as the water heats up and expands" (lines 38-39). However, the author of passage A says nothing at all about a causal relationship between air temperature and oceanic water temperatures, and this lack of evidence does not allow us to conclude that the author would disagree with the view expressed by the author of passage B.

Response (E) is incorrect because the passages do not provide any specific indications regarding either author's views on *the extent* to which global temperatures have risen in recent decades. Both authors presume that global temperatures have risen, but they say nothing that would allow us to draw any clear inferences regarding their views on how much.

Question 11

Which one of the phenomena cited in passage A is an instance of the kind of "evidence" referred to in the second paragraph of passage B (line 42)?

(A) the breaking off of part of the Larsen ice shelf in 1995
(B) higher regional temperatures since the 1940s
(C) increases in storm intensities over the past several years
(D) the increased duration of droughts in recent years
(E) the increased duration of heat waves over the past decade

Explanation for Question 11

This question concerns the use of the word "evidence" in line 42 in passage B. The author acknowledges that there is "some evidence" that melting of the polar ice caps has occurred. This question asks the examinee to identify which of the phenomena cited in passage A could be seen as an example of that kind of evidence.

The correct response is (A), "the breaking off of part of the Larsen ice shelf in 1995." The author of passage A cites this event (lines 1-2), and it is evidence of melting of the polar ice caps.

Response (B) is incorrect because, while the higher temperatures in the Antarctic region since the 1940s might well be the cause of any melting of the polar ice that has taken place, it cannot be used as evidence of that melting.

Responses (C), (D), and (E) are incorrect because the phenomena they refer to—increased storm intensities, longer droughts, and longer heat waves—are all different possible consequences of global warming, like the melting of the polar ice caps. None of these phenomena can be taken as evidence of the melting of the polar ice caps.

Question 12

The author of passage B would be most likely to make which one of the following criticisms about the predictions cited in passage A concerning a rise in sea level?

(A) These predictions incorrectly posit a causal relationship between the warming of the earth and rising sea levels.
(B) These predictions are supported only by inconclusive evidence that some melting of the polar ice caps has occurred.
(C) These predictions exaggerate the degree to which global temperatures have increased in recent decades.
(D) These predictions rely on an inadequate understanding of the hydrological cycle.
(E) These predictions assume a continuing increase in global temperatures that may not occur.

Explanation for Question 12

This question requires the examinee to infer what the opinion of one of the authors would be regarding a view expressed in the other passage. Specifically, the question asks which criticism the author of passage B would be most likely to offer in response to the predictions made in passage A concerning rising sea levels. The predictions in question are found in the second paragraph of passage A. There the author cites scientific estimates that global warming will result in a sea-level rise of 3 feet (1 meter) within the next century. The author adds, "Such a rise could submerge vast coastal areas, with potentially irreversible consequences" (lines 13–15).

The correct response is (D). The author of passage B addresses the effects of global warming on sea levels in the second paragraph. The author concedes that warming water would expand, causing sea levels to rise, and that the problem would be compounded if the polar ice caps melt (lines 38–41). But the author of passage B goes on to argue that warmer water temperatures might also result in more evaporation, which in turn could produce more snowfall on the polar ice caps, causing the ice caps to grow (lines 44–48). The author concludes the discussion of sea levels by stating, "Certainly, we need to have better knowledge about the hydrological cycle before predicting dire consequences as a result of recent increases in global temperatures" (lines 48–51). Since the author of passage A does in fact cite predictions of dire consequences, which are evidently made without taking into account the possible mitigating factors discussed in passage B, the author of passage B would be likely to regard those predictions as relying on an inadequate understanding of the hydrological cycle.

Response (A) is incorrect because the author of passage B agrees that there is a causal relationship between the warming of the earth and rising sea levels (lines 38–39). The author of passage B holds, however, that the relationship between global temperatures and sea levels is more complex than acknowledged by those who make dire predictions. But the author does not object to merely positing that there is such a causal relationship.

Response (B) is incorrect because the author of passage B is aware that at least one factor other than the melting of the ice caps—namely the expansion of water as it warms—can cause sea levels to rise (lines 38–39). There is no indication that the author of passage B believes that those who make the predictions cited in passage A are unaware of this additional factor, or that that the melting of the polar ice caps is the only causal mechanism they rely on in making their predictions.

Response (C) is incorrect. The author of passage B does dispute the conclusions drawn by some people, such as the author of passage A, regarding the causes and consequences of the warming trend. But, as noted in the explanation for question 10, there is no evidence that the author of passage B disputes any claims made about the extent of the warming that has taken place so far.

Response (E) is incorrect because the author of passage B says nothing about any assumptions concerning future temperature increases underlying the dire predictions cited in passage A. There is therefore no evidence that the author of passage B is likely to view such assumptions as grounds for criticism.

Question 13

The relationship between passage A and passage B is most analogous to the relationship between the documents described in which one of the following?

(A) a research report that raises estimates of damage done by above-ground nuclear testing; an article that describes practical applications for nuclear power in the energy production and medical fields
(B) an article arguing that corporate patronage biases scientific studies about the impact of pollution on the ozone layer; a study suggesting that aerosols in the atmosphere may counteract damaging effects of atmospheric carbon dioxide on the ozone layer
(C) an article citing evidence that the spread of human development into pristine natural areas is causing catastrophic increases in species extinction; an article arguing that naturally occurring cycles of extinction are the most important factor in species loss
(D) an article describing the effect of prolonged drought on crop production in the developing world; an article detailing the impact of innovative irrigation techniques in water-scarce agricultural areas
(E) a research report on crime and the decline of various neighborhoods from 1960 to 1985; an article describing psychological research on the most important predictors of criminal behavior

Explanation for Question 13

The response choices in this question describe pairs of hypothetical documents. Based on the descriptions of those documents, you are asked to identify the pair of documents that stand in a relationship to each other that is most analogous to the relationship between passage A and passage B. In order to answer this question, you need to determine, at least in a general way, what the relationship between passage A and passage B is.

As already discussed, the authors of passage A and passage B agree that global warming is occurring, but they disagree as to its cause. Passage A holds that human activity is substantially responsible, and the author quotes the IPCC claim that warming is due "directly to the increasing quantities of carbon dioxide released by our burning of fossil fuels" (lines 20-22). Passage B, on the other hand, states, "While human activity may be a factor in global warming, natural events appear to be far more important" (lines 53-55).

The closest analogy to this relationship is found in response (C):

> an article citing evidence that the spread of human development into pristine natural areas is causing catastrophic increases in species extinction; an article arguing that naturally occurring cycles of extinction are the most important factor in species loss

Like passage A and passage B, these two documents both agree that a trend—loss of species—is occurring. And also like passage A and passage B, these two documents differ in their assignment of responsibility for the trend. The first document identifies human activity as the salient cause, while the second document identifies natural cycles as the salient cause. Most importantly, both articles discuss the same phenomenon, and they propose conflicting explanations of the phenomenon, as is the case with passage A and B.

Response (A) is incorrect because the two documents discuss related topics—damage done by above-ground nuclear testing and practical applications of nuclear power—rather than the same topic, as in passage A and passage B. They are not attempting to explain the same phenomenon.

Response (B) is incorrect because while, at a general level, both documents engage the same topic—the effect of pollution on the ozone layer—they do not appear to agree that there is a phenomenon that needs to be explained, much less offer competing or conflicting explanations. The first document argues that at least some studies of the problem are beset with bias, without apparently making any claims about how pollution affects the ozone layer. Meanwhile, the second document seems to argue that the effects of different types of pollution may cancel each other out.

Response (D) is incorrect because the second document describes what appears to be a potential way to address the problem identified in the first document. Neither passage A nor passage B discusses a method for addressing the problem of global warming.

Response (E) is incorrect because the two documents discuss related problems, rather than the same problem. The first document discusses the relationship between crime and the decline of various neighborhoods over 25 years, while the second document addresses a different question: factors that might predict criminal behavior in individuals.

Question 14

Which one of the following most accurately describes the relationship between the argument made in passage A and the argument made in passage B?

(A) Passage A draws conclusions that are not based on hard evidence, while passage B confines itself to proven fact.
(B) Passage A relies on evidence that dates back to the 1940s, while passage B relies on much more recent evidence.
(C) Passage A warns about the effects of certain recent phenomena, while passage B argues that some inferences based on those phenomena are unfounded.
(D) Passage A makes a number of assertions that passage B demonstrates to be false.
(E) Passage A and passage B use the same evidence to draw diametrically opposed conclusions.

Explanation for Question 14

This question tests for the ability to understand how the arguments in the two passages unfold and how they are related.

The correct response is (C). The author of passage A begins by describing some of the recent phenomena attributed to atmospheric heating. Some of the author's particular choices of words—such as "the most spectacular manifestation *yet*" (lines 4-5, italics added) and "have been emerging around the world for several years" (lines 9-10)—clearly imply that such "spectacular" phenomena are likely to continue to emerge in the coming years. And in the second paragraph, the author describes the effects of a predicted sea-level rise due to global warming as "potentially irreversible." In contrast, the author of passage B argues that an "extreme view" of global warming has developed, containing "exaggerations and misstatements" (lines 28-31). For example, the author of passage B argues, "Certainly, we need to have better knowledge about the hydrological cycle before predicting dire consequences as a result of recent increases in global temperatures" (lines 48-51). Thus, unlike the author of passage A, the author of passage B argues that some of the conclusions based on the phenomena surrounding global warming lack foundation.

Response (A) is incorrect because the author of passage A does in fact rely on hard evidence in drawing his or her conclusions. Though the author of Passage B obviously questions *inferences* like those drawn in passage A, the evidence used in passage A (the breaking off of the Larsen ice shelf, more intense storms, etc.) is not in dispute. Nor does the argument in passage B confine itself exclusively to proven fact: in lines 44-48, the author speculates about possible implications of the "hydrological cycle" for the Antarctic ice sheet.

Response (B) is incorrect because both passages rely on recent evidence—for example, see the beginning and end of the first paragraph of passage A and the reference to Mount Pinatubo in passage B (lines 55-57).

Response (D) is incorrect because passage B does not *demonstrate* that any of the assertions made in passage A are false. For example, the author of passage B concludes the discussion of sea level in the second paragraph by stating, "Certainly, we need to have better knowledge about the hydrological cycle before predicting dire consequences as a result of recent increases in global temperatures" (lines 48-51). This does not amount to a demonstration of the falsity of the predictions.

Response (E) is incorrect because, while both passages refer to some of the same phenomena—such as melting of polar ice—each also cites evidence that the other passage does not mention. In reaching its conclusion, passage A cites intense storms and extended heat waves in the first paragraph, and the release of carbon dioxide from burning fossil fuels in the third paragraph; passage B mentions none of these things. In reaching its quite different conclusion, passage B cites the eruption of Mount Pinatubo, El Niño, and variations in the sun's radiation and in the earth's orbit, as well as evidence that the Antarctic ice sheets might be growing. None of this evidence is mentioned in passage A.

■ Analytical Reasoning Questions

Analytical reasoning items are designed to measure your ability to understand a structure of relationships and to draw logical conclusions about the structure. You are asked to make deductions from a set of statements, rules, or conditions that describe relationships among entities such as persons, places, things, or events. They simulate the kinds of detailed analyses of relationships that a law student must perform in solving legal problems. For example, a passage might describe four diplomats sitting around a table, following certain rules of protocol as to who can sit where. You must answer questions about the implications of the given information, for example, who is sitting between diplomats X and Y.

The passage used for each group of questions describes a common relationship such as the following:

- Assignment: Two parents, P and O, and their children, R and S, must go to the dentist on four consecutive days, designated 1, 2, 3, and 4;

- Ordering: X arrived before Y but after Z;

- Grouping: A manager is trying to form a project team from seven staff members—R,S,T,U,V,W, and X. Each staff member has a particular strength—writing, planning, or facilitating;

- Spatial: A certain country contains six cities and each city is connected to at least one other city by a system of roads, some of which are one-way.

Careful reading and analysis are necessary to determine the exact nature of the relationships involved. Some relationships are fixed (e.g., P and R always sit at the same table). Other relationships are variable (e.g., Q must be assigned to either table 1 or table 3). Some relationships that are not stated in the conditions are implied by and can be deduced from those that are stated. (e.g., If one condition about books on a shelf specifies that Book L is to the left of Book Y, and another specifies that Book P is to the left of Book L, then it can be deduced that Book P is to the left of Book Y.)

No formal training in logic is required to answer these questions correctly. Analytical reasoning questions are intended to be answered using knowledge, skills, and reasoning ability generally expected of college students and graduates.

Suggested Approach

Some people may prefer to answer first those questions about a passage that seem less difficult and then those that seem more difficult. In general, it is best not to start another passage before finishing one begun earlier, because much time can be lost in returning to a passage and reestablishing familiarity with its relationships. Do not assume that because the conditions for a set of questions look long or complicated, the questions based on those conditions will necessarily be especially difficult.

Reading the passage. In reading the conditions, do not introduce unwarranted assumptions. For instance, in a set establishing relationships of height and weight among the members of a team, do not assume that a person who is taller than another person must weigh more than that person. All the information needed to answer each question is provided in the passage and the question itself.

The conditions are designed to be as clear as possible; do not interpret them as if they were intended to trick you. For example, if a question asks how many people could be eligible to serve on a committee, consider only those people named in the passage unless directed otherwise. When in doubt, read the conditions in their most obvious sense. Remember, however, that the language in the conditions is intended to be read for precise meaning. It is essential to pay particular attention to words that describe or limit relationships, such as "only," "exactly," "never," "always," "must be," "cannot be," and the like.

The result of this careful reading will be a clear picture of the structure of the relationships involved, including the kinds of relationships permitted, the participants in the relationships, and the range of actions or attributes allowed by the relationships for these participants.

Questions are independent. Each question should be considered separately from the other questions in its set; no information, except what is given in the original conditions, should be carried over from one question to another.

In some cases a question will simply ask for conclusions to be drawn from the conditions as originally given. Some questions may, however, add information to the original conditions or temporarily suspend one of the original conditions for the purpose of that question only. For example, if Question 1 adds the information "if P is sitting at table 2 ...," this information should NOT be carried over to any other question in the group.

Highlighting the text; using diagrams. Many people find it useful to underline key points in the passage and in each question. In addition, it may prove very helpful to draw a diagram to assist you in finding the solution to the problem.

In preparing for the test, you may wish to experiment with different types of diagrams. For a scheduling problem, a calendar-like diagram may be helpful. For a spatial relationship problem, a simple map can be a useful device.

Even though some people find diagrams to be very helpful, other people seldom use them. And among those who do regularly use diagrams in solving these problems, there is by no means universal agreement on which kind of diagram is best for which problem or in which cases a diagram is most useful. Do not be concerned if a particular problem in the test seems to be best approached without the use of a diagram.

Nine Sample Analytical Reasoning Questions and Explanations

The sample questions that follow are typical of the analytical reasoning problems you will find on the LSAT. A brief passage presents a set of conditions, followed by questions about the relationships defined by the conditions. While each passage here is followed by only one or two sample questions, each passage in the Analytical Reasoning section of the actual LSAT is followed by five to seven questions.

Directions: Each group of questions in this section is based on a set of conditions. In answering some of the questions, it may be useful to draw a rough diagram. Choose the response that most accurately and completely answers the question and blacken the corresponding space on your answer sheet.

Passage for Question 1

An island has exactly seven villages—S,T,U,V,X,Y, and Z—and three roads—Routes 1, 2, and 3. The following is a complete listing of the road connections on the island:
  Route 1 has its ends at S and U, and passes through T only.
  Route 2 has its ends at T and U, and passes through V only.
  Route 3 has its ends at X and Z, and passes through Y only.
Directly connected villages are those villages between which there is a road connection that passes through no other village on the way from one to the other.

Question 1

Which one of the following villages is directly connected to the most other villages?

(A) T
(B) U
(C) V
(D) X
(E) Y

Explanation for Question 1

As with most problems involving spatial relationships, this question can be answered with the aid of a simple map.

Route 1 can be sketched out as follows, based on the information that it "*has its ends at S and U, and passes through T only*":

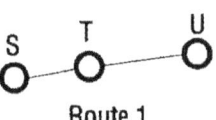

Route 2 is defined by the information that it "*has its ends at T and U, and passes through V only*":

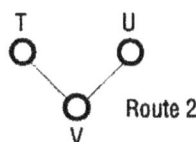

Route 3 can be drawn from the condition that it "*has its ends at X and Z, and passes through Y only*":

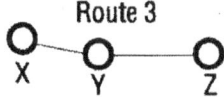

Combining the sketches of the three roads, a completed map of the island might look like this:

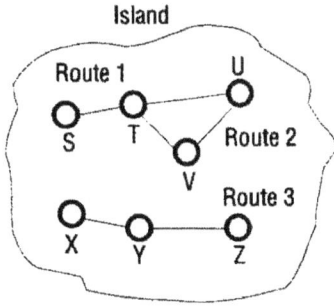

Looking at the map, we can see that village T is directly connected to three other villages, the most of any village, and that (A) is therefore the correct response. U, V, and Y are each directly connected to two other villages, and S, X, and Z are each directly connected to only one other village.

This is a "middle difficulty" problem. It was answered correctly by 61 percent of the persons who took the LSAT on which it appeared. Twenty-one percent chose response (B) while 12 percent chose response (C).

Passage for Question 2

A medical clinic has a staff of five doctors—Drs. Albert, Burns, Calogero, Defeo, and Evans. The national medical society sponsors exactly five conferences, which the clinic's doctors attend, subject to the following constraints:
  If Dr. Albert attends a conference, then Dr. Defeo does not attend it.
  If Dr. Burns attends a conference, then either Dr. Calogero or Dr. Defeo, but not both, attends it.
  If Dr. Calogero attends a conference, then Dr. Evans does not attend it.
  If Dr. Evans attends a conference, then either Dr. Albert or Dr. Burns, but not both, attends it.

Question 2

If Dr. Burns attends one of the conferences, then which one of the following could be a complete and accurate list of the other members of the clinic who also attend that conference?

(A)   Drs. Albert and Defeo
(B)   Drs. Albert and Evans
(C)   Drs. Calogero and Defeo
(D)   Dr. Defeo
(E)   Dr. Evans

Explanation for Question 2

This question requires you to determine, from the conditions given, which doctors can attend the same conferences. The question tells us that "Doctor Burns attends one of the conferences," and we are asked to choose the response that could be a list of all and only those doctors who attend the conference with Dr. Burns. Since we are asked what *could* be a *"complete and accurate list"* [emphasis added] of those doctors who attend the conference with Dr. Burns, we can eliminate as incorrect those responses which either are inaccurate (that is, cannot be true), or incomplete (that is, do not include everyone who must accompany one or more of the doctors going to the conference). This can be determined easily without the use of a diagram.

Response (A) states that, along with Dr. Burns, Drs. Albert and Defeo also attend the conference. But the first condition tells us that "*if Dr. Albert attends a conference, then Dr. Defeo does not attend it.*" So, Drs. Burns, Albert, and Defeo cannot all attend the same conference. Response (A), then, is incorrect.

Response (B) is incorrect for a similar reason. The fourth condition tells us what must be true if Dr. Evans attends a conference, namely, that "*either Dr. Albert or Dr. Burns, but not both, attends it.*" Since we know that Dr. Burns attends the conference, we know that it cannot be true that *both* Drs. Albert and Evans also attend that conference.

Response (C) is also incorrect. The second condition tells us what must be true if Dr. Burns attends a conference. Since we know that Dr. Burns *does* attend the conference, we also know that "*either Dr. Calogero or Dr. Defeo, but not both, attends it.*"

Responses (D) and (E) must be evaluated slightly differently. No condition rules out Dr. Burns's and Dr. Defeo's going to the same conference—response (D)—and no condition forbids Dr. Evans's going with Dr. Burns to a conference—response (E). But recall that the question asks for what could be a "complete and accurate list" of the doctors who attend the conference with Dr. Burns. We know from the second condition that at least one other person must accompany Dr. Burns, and that among those who accompany Dr. Burns are either Dr. Calogero or else Dr. Defeo. Since the conditions do not require anyone to accompany Dr. Defeo, it is possible that Dr. Defeo is the only person to accompany Dr. Burns. Thus, response (D) is an accurate response, in that it is possible that Drs. Burns and Defeo attend the same conference, and it is a complete response, in that Drs. Burns and Defeo could be the only doctors of the five to attend the conference. So response (D) is correct.

Response (E) is incorrect because we know that if Dr. Burns goes, someone other than Dr. Evans must also go. Response (E) then is incomplete. It fails to list at least one doctor whom we know must also accompany Dr. Burns.

This is a question of "moderate difficulty"; 60 percent of those who took the LSAT on which it appeared answered it correctly. The most common error was selecting response (B) (chosen by 17 percent).

Passage for Questions 3 and 4

Seven piano students—T, U, V, W, X, Y, and Z—are to give a recital, and their instructor is deciding the order in which they will perform. Each student will play exactly one piece, a piano solo. In deciding the order of performance, the instructor must observe the following restrictions:
  X cannot play first or second.
  W cannot play until X has played.
  Neither T nor Y can play seventh.
  Either Y or Z must play immediately after W plays.
  V must play either immediately after or immediately before U plays.

Question 3

If V plays first, which one of the following must be true?

(A) T plays sixth.
(B) X plays third.
(C) Z plays seventh.
(D) T plays immediately after Y.
(E) W plays immediately after X.

Explanation for Question 3

This question deals with an ordering relationship defined by a set of conditions as to when the seven piano students will perform. As an aid in visualizing this problem we can draw a simple diagram that shows the seven recital slots arranged in order from left to right. Student V is shown in the first slot, as specified by the condition that "V plays first":

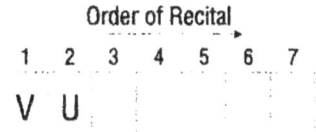

We can immediately fill in one of the empty slots in the diagram. The condition that *"V must play either immediately after or immediately before U plays"* tells us that U must occupy the second slot in the recital schedule. This is shown below:

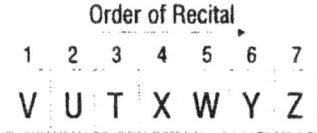

Since the question asks us what *must be true*, we can eliminate incorrect responses by showing that they could be *false* without violating the conditions. Response (A) is incorrect because the statement that "T plays sixth" is not necessarily true—we can place T in one of the slots other than sixth and still meet all the conditions of the problem. One such recital schedule, with T playing third, is shown in the diagram below:

Order of Recital

1 2 3 4 5 6 7
V U T X W Y Z

We can develop this schedule as follows. With V, U, and T in the first three positions, there are four positions left for W, X, Y, and Z.

- W must come after X—because of the condition that *"W cannot play until X has played"*—so if we put X fourth and W fifth, this condition will be met.

- This leaves two possible slots for Y and Z. Y cannot play seventh because of the condition that *"Neither T nor Y can play seventh,"* so we will place Y sixth and Z seventh.

A check will verify that this schedule meets the given conditions of the problem, including the one that *"Either Y or Z must play immediately after W plays."*

The schedule shown in the diagram also demonstrates that response (B) is incorrect. In it, *X plays fourth*, so it is not correct that the statement, "X plays third," *must* be true.

Response (C), "Z plays seventh," is the credited response. We can show this by demonstrating that:

- all the conditions can be met with Z in the *seventh* slot, and

- some of the conditions would be violated with Z in any slot *other* than seventh.

To demonstrate that Z *can* play seventh, we can refer to the schedule that was developed for the discussion of response (A), above. In it, Z *plays seventh*, and all the conditions in the problem are met.

To demonstrate that Z *cannot* play in a slot *other* than seventh, we can attempt to find another student to play seventh. We already know that neither U nor V can play seventh. Hence, there are four remaining players: T, W, X, and Y. However, a review of the given conditions shows that none of those players can play seventh:

- The third condition states that *"Neither T nor Y can play seventh."*

- W can't play seventh, because there must be a slot following W's in order to meet the condition, *"Either Y or Z must play immediately after W plays."* If W plays seventh, then there is no such slot left for Y or Z.

- For a similar reason X can't play seventh, because there must be a slot following X's in order to meet the condition, *"W cannot play until X has played."*

Since Z can play seventh and no other player can, then the statement that Z *must play seventh* is correct and (C) is the credited response.

Response (D) is incorrect because it is not necessarily true that "T plays immediately after Y." In our discussion of response (A), we developed a schedule in which T plays third and Y plays sixth, yet all conditions are satisfied.

Response (E) is incorrect because, as shown in the diagram below, it is not necessarily true that "W plays immediately after X." This schedule is obtained by simply reversing the order of players W and Y in the schedule we developed in the analysis of response (A). A review will show that all of the given conditions are met by this schedule.

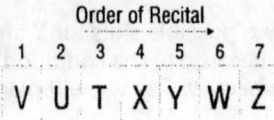

This is a "difficult" problem; only 39 percent of the persons who took the LSAT on which it appeared answered it correctly. Twenty-six percent chose response (B), and another 19 percent chose response (E). This problem is difficult because it requires the test taker to go beyond simply matching each response with the given conditions. In solving this problem, one must use the given conditions to infer relationships such as the one that W cannot perform seventh.

Question 4

If U plays third, what is the latest position in which Y can play?

(A) first
(B) second
(C) fifth
(D) sixth
(E) seventh

Explanation for Question 4

This question involves the same original conditions as the previous problem, but it begins with a different assumption: "U plays third." The test taker must determine what effect this assumption would have on the possible positions in which Y can appear in the recital schedule.

The correct response is (D), because student Y can play as late as *sixth* under the given constraint that "U plays third." The diagram below shows a recital order that meets all the given conditions and has Y performing in the sixth position.

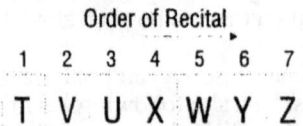

One strategy for arriving at this solution is to work backward to see which position is the latest in which we can place Y and at the same time produce a recital schedule that meets all the given conditions.

Using that approach, we immediately see that Y cannot play as late as seventh, because of the condition that *"Neither T nor Y can play seventh."* Backing up and placing Y sixth, we can begin to fill in the schedule, as follows:

Order of Recital
1 2 3 4 5 6 7
      U   Y

This schedule has five empty slots, into which we must fit players T, V, W, X, and Z. The following is a series of reasoning steps that can be used:

- From our analysis of the previous question, we know that players T, W, and X cannot play seventh, but that Z can, so we can tentatively place Z in the *seventh* slot.

- We also know that *"Either Y or Z must play immediately after W plays."* If we place W in the *fifth* slot, this condition will be met.

- By placing V in the *second* slot, we can meet the condition that *"V must play either immediately after or immediately before U plays."*

- We must place the remaining two players, T and X, in the two remaining slots, the first and the fourth. Because the first condition states that *"X cannot play first . . . ."* we will place X in the *fourth* slot and T in the *first*. These positions will meet the conditions that apply to T and X: T will avoid playing seventh and X will play before W.

Since Y can play as late as *sixth*, response (D) is the correct solution.

This problem is classified as a "middle difficulty" problem. Sixty-three percent of those who took the LSAT on which it appeared answered it correctly. Sixteen percent chose response (C).

Passage for Question 5

Seven computers—A, B, C, D, E, F, and G—are connected in a network. Each computer belongs to only one of three classes—Class I, Class II, and Class III. Class I computers can receive data only from other Class I computers. Class II computers can receive data only from other Class II computers and from Class III computers. Class III computers can receive data only from other Class III computers and from Class I computers. The computers are distributed as follows:
   A and B are the same class computer.
   E and G are the same class computer.
   There are exactly twice as many Class II
      computers as Class III computers.
   F is a Class III computer.
   There is at least one computer of each class.

Question 5

If C is a Class II computer, then all of the following must be true EXCEPT:

(A) A can receive data from G.
(B) C can receive data from E.
(C) D can receive data from F.
(D) E can receive data from B.
(E) F can receive data from A.

Explanation for Question 5

This item involves two tasks: grouping the computers into classes and determining which computers can receive data from other computers. To begin, we first need to determine what are the possible groupings of computers into classes. We know that there are seven computers, that there is at least one computer in each class, and that there are twice as many Class II computers as there are Class III computers. From this information alone we can determine that there can be *at most two* Class III computers. If there were more than two Class III computers, then there would be at least six Class II computers, and at least one Class I computer, giving us a total of at least ten computers. Since there are only seven computers, this cannot be. Thus, the number of computers in each class is limited to the following two possibilities:

Class I	Class II	Class III	Total Computers
4	2	1	7
1	4	2	7

Now, we are told that F is a Class III computer, and we know from the above that there can be at most two Class III computers. We are also told that A and B are both the same class of computer, and that E and G are both the same class of computer (that is, A and B can be both Class I or both Class II, and E and G can be both Class I or both Class II). So only C or D could be a Class III computer together with F.

If F is the *only* Class III computer, then from the above there must be two Class II computers and four Class I computers. There are, then, three possibilities:

Scenario 1: If C and D are in Class II, then the four others (A, B, E, and G) must be in Class I.
Scenario 2: If E and G are in Class II, then the four others (A, B, C, and D) must be in Class I.
Scenario 3: If A and B are in Class II, then the four others (C, D, E, and G) must be in Class I.

If there are *two* Class III computers, then as we said above, along with F, either C or D must also be in Class III:

Scenario 4: If F and C are in Class III, then D must be in Class I and the remaining four (A, B, E, and G) must be in Class II.

Scenario 5: If F and D are in Class III, then C must be in Class I and the remaining four (A, B, E, and G) must be in Class II.

All five possible scenarios are shown below.

Scenarios	Class I	Class II	Class III
1	A,B,E,G	C,D	F
2	A,B,C,D	E,G	F
3	C,D,E,G	A,B	F
4	D	A,B,E,G	F,C
5	C	A,B,E,G	F,D

We now have all the possible scenarios. In the question we are given the information that C is a Class II computer. Only one of the five scenarios places C into Class II, namely, Scenario 1. The remaining information in the passage can now be used to find the answer.

Class I computers can receive data only from other Class I computers.

Class II computers can receive data only from Class III computers and other Class II computers.

Class III computers can receive data only from Class I computers and other Class III computers.

According to Scenario 1, computers A and G are in the same class. Since we know from the above that any computers in the same class can receive information from each other, we know that responses (A) and (D) must be true, and so incorrect. Since Class II computers can receive data from Class III computers, response (C) must also be incorrect. Further, given that Class III computers can receive data from Class I computers, response (E) is also incorrect. So we are left only with response (B) as an option. Response (B) claims that computer C, a member of Class II, can receive data from computer E, a member of Class I. By the rules above, this is false. So response (B) is the correct answer.

This is classified as a "difficult" question; 40 percent of test takers answered it correctly when it appeared on the LSAT. The most common error was selecting response (C) (chosen by 20 percent).

Passage for Questions 6 and 7

From a group of seven people—J, K, L, M, N, P, and Q—exactly four will be selected to attend a diplomat's retirement dinner. Selection conforms to the following conditions:

> Either J or K must be selected, but J and K cannot both be selected.
> Either N or P must be selected, but N and P cannot both be selected.
> N cannot be selected unless L is selected.
> Q cannot be selected unless K is selected.

Question 6

If P is not selected to attend the retirement dinner, then exactly how many different groups of four are there each of which would be an acceptable selection?

(A) one
(B) two
(C) three
(D) four
(E) five

Explanation for Question 6

This question essentially adds a new assumption to the original set of conditions—"P is not selected to attend the retirement dinner." The test taker is supposed to determine all of the different possible selections that are compatible with this new assumption. A compatible solution is one that violates neither the new assumption nor the original conditions.

Since the second condition states "[e]ither N or P must be selected ... ," we can infer from the new assumption and the second condition that N is selected. And since N is selected, we know from the third condition that L is selected. In other words every acceptable selection must include both L and N. We are now in a good position to enumerate the groups of four which would be acceptable selections. Notice that K may or may not be selected. We need to examine what happens in either case. First, assume that K is not selected. In this case, J is selected (since the first condition indicates that one of J or K must be selected) and Q is not selected (since the fourth condition implies that if K is not selected, then Q cannot be selected either). Since exactly four people must be selected, and since P, K, and Q are not selected, M, the only remaining person, must be selected. Since M's selection does not violate any of the conditions or the new assumption, N, L, J, and M is an acceptable selection; in fact, it is the only acceptable selection when K is not selected. So far we have one acceptable selection, but we must now examine what holds in the case where K is selected.

Suppose that K is selected. In this case J is not selected (as one can see by the first condition), but Q may or may not be selected. Again we look at both possibilities. If Q is selected, it is part of an acceptable selection—N, L, K, and Q. If Q is not selected, remembering that J and P are also not selected, M must be selected. This gives us our final acceptable selection—N, L, K, and M.

Thus there are exactly three different groups of four which make up acceptable selections, and (C) is the correct response.

This is considered a "difficult" question; only 37 percent of test takers answered it correctly when it appeared on the LSAT.

Question 7

There is only one acceptable group of four that can be selected to attend the retirement dinner if which one of the following pairs of people is selected?

(A) J and L
(B) K and M
(C) L and N
(D) L and Q
(E) M and Q

Explanation for Question 7

The way in which this question is phrased is rather complex, and so it is important to get very clear what exactly is being asked. Unlike other questions which give the test taker a new assumption to consider in conjunction with the original conditions, this question asks the test taker to determine what assumption is needed, in addition to the original conditions, to guarantee that only one group of four is acceptable.

There is probably no better way to approach this question than to consider each option individually, and determine for each option whether only one acceptable group of four can be selected when the pair indicated in the option is selected. The test taker may wish to vary the order in which the options are considered according to personal preferences. We will consider the options in order from (A) through to (E).

Option (A): When both J and L are selected, K cannot be selected (first condition). Consequently Q cannot be selected (fourth condition). More than one group of four is acceptable under these circumstances however. J, L, M, and N may be selected, and J, L, M, and P may be selected.

Option (B): When K and M are both selected, J cannot be selected (first condition). Other than that, anyone else could be selected. This leaves more than one acceptable group of four. K, L, M, and N may be selected; K, L, M, and P may be selected; and K, M, P, and Q may be selected.

Option (C): When L and N are both selected, P cannot be selected (second condition), but, as in the case of option (B), anyone else can be selected. This leaves more than one acceptable group of four. J, L, M, and N may be selected; K, L, M, and N may be selected; and K, L, N, and Q may be selected.

Option (D): When L and Q are both selected, K must be selected (fourth condition). Consequently J cannot be selected (first condition). More than one group of four is acceptable under these circumstances however. K, L, N, and Q may be selected, and K, L, P, and Q may be selected.

Option (E): When M and Q are both selected, K must be selected (fourth condition), and hence J cannot be selected (first condition). Furthermore, N cannot be selected: if N were selected, then L would also have to be selected (third condition), and this would violate the restriction that exactly four people are to be selected. And since N cannot be selected, P must be selected (second condition). Thus when M and Q are both selected, both K and P must be selected as well, and only one group of four—K, M, P, and Q—is acceptable. (E) is therefore the correct response.

This is considered a "very difficult" question; only 18 percent of test takers answered it correctly when it appeared on the LSAT.

Passage for Question 8

A law firm has exactly nine partners: Fox, Glassen, Hae, Inman, Jacoby, Kohn, Lopez, Malloy, and Nassar. Their salary structure must meet the following conditions:
  Kohn's salary is greater than both Inman's and Lopez's.
  Lopez's salary is greater than Nassar's.
  Inman's salary is greater than Fox's.
  Fox's salary is greater than Malloy's.
  Malloy's salary is greater than Glassen's.
  Glassen's salary is greater than Jacoby's.
  Jacoby's salary is greater than Hae's.

Question 8

If Malloy and Nassar earn the same salary, what is the minimum number of partners that must have lower salaries than Lopez?

(A) 3
(B) 4
(C) 5
(D) 6
(E) 7

Explanation for Question 8

As with many problems involving relative rank or order, the test taker should attempt to diagram the various relationships given in the stimulus.

In what follows, each partner's name is abbreviated by the first letter of that partner's name, and the symbol ">" indicates that the person whose initial appears to the left of the sign has a greater salary than that of the person whose initial is to the right of the sign. So, for instance, "K > L" means "Kohn's salary is greater than Lopez's."

The conditions indicate the following eight relative orderings of salary:

(1) K > I
(2) K > L
(3) L > N
(4) I > F
(5) F > M
(6) M > G
(7) G > J
(8) J > H

It should be obvious that if person A's salary is greater than person B's and if person B's salary is greater than person C's, then person A's salary is also greater than person C's. Using this principle, we may combine and condense several of the above orderings into two separate "chains" of relative order:

(9) K > I > F > M > G > J > H
    (This combines [1], and [4] through [8].)
(10) K > L > N
    (This combines [2] and [3].)

We are now in a position to determine the correct response for question 8. The test taker is asked to determine the minimum number of partners whose salaries must be lower than that of Lopez, if Malloy and Nassar earn the same salary. Assuming that Malloy's and Nassar's salary are equal allows us to infer from chains (9) and (10) the following chain of relative ordering:

(11) K > L > (N,M) > G > J > H

(11) shows that since M and N have the same salary, anyone whose salary is less than M's is also less than N's, and therefore also less than L's. So, at least Malloy, Nassar, Glassen, Jacoby, and Hae must have lower salaries than Lopez. This shows that response options (A) and (B) are both incorrect. If we can now show that no partner other than these five must have lower salaries than Lopez, then we will have shown that (C) is the correct response.

To see that there could be fewer than six partners with lower salaries than Lopez, one need merely look at (9) and (10) above to see that as long as Inman and Fox have lower salaries than Kohn, they could have salaries equal to or higher than Lopez's. This allows us to construct the following possible complete chain of relative order:

(12) K > I > F > L > (N,M) > G > J > H

In this possible case no more than five partners have lower salaries than Lopez, and since there must be at least five such partners, five is the minimum number of such partners. (C) is therefore the correct response.

This is considered an item of "middle difficulty."

Passage for Question 9

The organisms W, X, Y, and Z respond to the antibiotics ferromycin, ganocyclene, and heptocillin in a manner consistent with the following:

    Each of the organisms responds to at least one of the antibiotics.
    No organism responds to all three antibiotics.
    At least two but not all four of the organisms respond to ferromycin.
    If W responds to any antibiotic, then X responds to that antibiotic.
    If an organism responds to ferromycin, then it responds to ganocyclene.
    Y responds to ferromycin.

Question 9

If none of the organisms responds to heptocillin, then which one of the following must be true?
(A) W responds to ferromycin.
(B) X responds to ferromycin.
(C) Z responds to ferromycin.
(D) Exactly three of the organisms respond to ganocyclene.
(E) Exactly four of the organisms respond to ganocyclene.

Explanation for Question 9

This question requires the test taker to determine which of the response options must be true if in addition to the given conditions it is also assumed that none of the organisms responds to heptocillin.

As with many questions that ask the test taker to determine what must be true, a good way to approach answering this question is by trying to falsify each of the response options. If one can show that it is possible for an option to be false given the conditions and the additional assumption, then one knows that it need not be true, and so is not the correct answer.

Let us consider options (A) through (C) first, since they are more similar to each other than they are to options (D) and (E). We need to see if it is possible for W not to respond to ferromycin, if it is possible for X not to respond to ferromycin, and if it is possible for Y not to respond to ferromycin. Using a table that lists each antibiotic, and, underneath each, the organisms that respond to the antibiotic, we can show the different possibilities allowed by the original conditions and the added assumption.

Y, we are told, responds to ferromycin and so, by the fifth condition, must also respond to ganocyclene. We represent this as follows:

ferromycin	ganocyclene	heptocillin
Y	Y	

Since we are trying to show that W does not have to respond to ferromycin, we place it under ganocyclene (remember, nothing is to be placed under heptocillin). Nothing in the conditions prevents this. But we are told that whatever W responds to X responds to, so we must also place X under ganocyclene. The chart should be updated as follows:

ferromycin	ganocyclene	heptocillin
Y	W, X, Y	

Knowing that all the organisms must respond to at least one of the antibiotics, and that we are assuming that none of them respond to heptocillin, we must find a place on our chart for Z under either ferromycin (and therefore also ganocyclene) or ganocyclene alone. The third condition requires us to place one other organism under ferromycin, so we should place Z underneath both ferromycin and ganocyclene, completing our chart as follows:

ferromycin	ganocyclene	heptocillin
Y, Z	W, X, Y, Z	

The above shows that neither W nor X must respond to ferromycin. Therefore, we can eliminate response options (A) and (B). Indeed, since there are four organisms that respond to ganocyclene in this possible state of affairs—showing that it need not be true that exactly three organisms respond to ferromycin—we can also eliminate option (D).

Response option (C) is also incorrect, as the following table shows:

ferromycin	ganocyclene	heptocillin
Y, X	W, X, Y, Z	

This leaves option (E), and, under timed conditions, it would be reasonable at this point to select this option as your answer.

To prove, however, that (E) is indeed the correct response, we need to show that it is impossible to have fewer than four of the organisms responding to ganocyclene. Given that none of the organisms responds to heptocillin, each must respond to either ganocyclene, or to ferromycin. Of course, if any organism responds to ferromycin, it must also respond to ganocyclene. This latter fact makes it impossible to have fewer than four organisms respond to ganocyclene. Any organism that did not respond to ganocyclene would have to respond to only ferromycin. And since no organism can respond to only ferromycin, all four must respond to ganocyclene. (E) is therefore the credited response.

Only 34 percent of test takers answered this item correctly, making it a "very difficult" problem.

Logical Reasoning Questions

Logical reasoning questions evaluate your ability to understand, analyze, criticize, and complete a variety of arguments. The arguments are contained in short passages taken from a variety of sources, including letters to the editor, speeches, advertisements, newspaper articles and editorials, informal discussions and conversations, as well as articles in the humanities, the social sciences, and the natural sciences.

Each logical reasoning question requires you to read and comprehend a short passage, then answer one or two questions about it. The questions test a variety of abilities involved in reasoning logically and thinking critically. These include:

- recognizing the point or issue of an argument or dispute;
- detecting the assumptions involved in an argumentation or chain of reasoning;
- drawing reasonable conclusions from given evidence or premises;
- identifying and applying principles;
- identifying the method or structure of an argument or chain of reasoning;
- determining how additional evidence or argumentation affects an argument or conclusion; and
- identifying explanations and recognizing resolutions of conflicting facts or arguments.

The questions do not presuppose knowledge of the terminology of formal logic. For example, you will not be expected to know the meaning of specialized terms such as "ad hominem" or "syllogism." On the other hand, you will be expected to understand and critique the reasoning contained in arguments. This requires that you possess, at a minimum, a college-level understanding of widely used concepts such as argument, premise, assumption, and conclusion.

Suggested Approach

Read each question carefully. Make sure that you understand the meaning of each part of the question. Make sure that you understand the meaning of each answer choice and the ways in which it may or may not relate to the question posed.

Do not pick a response simply because it is a true statement. Although true, it may not answer the question posed.

Answer each question on the basis of the information that is given, even if you do not agree with it. Work within the context provided by the passage. LSAT questions do not involve any tricks or hidden meanings.

Nine Sample Logical Reasoning Questions and Explanations

The sample questions on the following pages are typical of the logical reasoning questions you will find on the LSAT. However, each passage here is accompanied by one question, whereas some passages in the actual LSAT will be accompanied by two questions.

Directions: The questions in this section are based on the reasoning contained in brief statements or passages. For some questions, more than one of the choices could conceivably answer the question. However, you are to choose the best answer; that is, the response that most accurately and completely answers the question. You should not make assumptions that are by commonsense standards implausible, superfluous, or incompatible with the passage. After you have chosen the best answer, blacken the corresponding space on your answer sheet.

Question 1

A study has shown that there are still millions of people who are unaware that they endanger their health by smoking cigarettes. This is so despite government campaigns to warn people of the dangers of smoking. Reluctantly, one has to draw the conclusion that the mandatory warnings that tobacco companies are required to print have had no effect.

Which one of the following, if true, would refute the argument in the passage?

(A) Many people who continue to smoke are aware of the dangers of smoking.
(B) Some people smoke cigarettes for legitimate reasons.
(C) Government has had to force companies to warn potential customers of the dangers of their products.
(D) Some people who are aware of the dangers of smoking were made aware of them by the mandatory warnings.
(E) Smoking is clearly responsible for a substantial proportion of preventable illness in the country.

Explanation for Question 1

This question requires the test taker to read the argument presented in the passage, and then to evaluate the effect of additional evidence on the argument.

The argument concludes that "*the mandatory warnings that tobacco companies are required to print have had no effect*" [emphasis added]. It holds that the warnings have had no effect because "*there are still millions of people who are unaware*" that their smoking endangers their health. In order to refute the argument it is sufficient to present evidence of two things: (1) that there are some people who are aware of the dangers of smoking and (2) that these people are aware because of the mandatory warnings. Since response (D) presents this evidence, it is the credited response.

Response (A) is incorrect because it includes only the first part of the refutation described above. An attempt to refute the author's argument by showing that some smokers are indeed "aware of the dangers of smoking" must also show that the smokers' awareness was produced by the warnings. Had it been produced through some other means, the author's argument about the ineffectiveness of the warnings would not be undermined.

Response (B) is incorrect because the author's argument does not deal with the reasons people smoke. It maintains that warnings have had no effect because many smokers are still unaware of the dangers; why those smokers smoke is irrelevant to the awareness issue.

Response (C) is incorrect because the fact that "government has had to force companies to warn ... of the dangers" is irrelevant to the issue of warnings and awareness. Moreover, the author already describes the warnings as *mandatory warnings*; therefore, this response adds little or nothing new to the discussion.

Response (E) is incorrect because it merely elaborates a minor detail in the passage (that smokers "*endanger their health by smoking cigarettes*"), and it supports rather than refutes the author's argument.

This question is classified as "difficult"; only 44 percent of test takers answered it correctly. Almost as many— 40 percent—chose response (A), overlooking its failure to address the issue of how the smokers who are aware of the dangers became aware.

Question 2

Electrons orbit around the nucleus of an atom in the same way that the Earth orbits around the Sun. It is well known that gravity is the major force that determines the orbit of the Earth. We may, therefore, expect that gravity is the main force that determines the orbit of an electron.

The argument above attempts to prove its case by

(A) applying well-known general laws to a specific case
(B) appealing to well-known specific cases to prove a general law about them
(C) testing its conclusion by a definite experiment
(D) appealing to an apparently similar case
(E) stating its conclusion without giving any kind of reason to think it might be true

Explanation for Question 2

This question requires the examinee to identify the method exhibited in an argument. The passage draws a parallel between two cases that share a similar trait: (1) the orbit of electrons around an atom's nucleus and (2) the orbit of the Earth around the Sun in our solar system. It uses knowledge about the second case (the fact that "*gravity is the major force that determines the orbit of the Earth*") to draw an inference about the first (that "*gravity is the main force that determines the orbit of an electron*"). The passage is "appealing to an apparently similar case" (the role of gravity in determining the Earth's orbit) to establish a conclusion about the role of gravity in determining an electron's orbit. Therefore, (D) is the credited response.

Response (A) is incorrect because it mistakes the argument made in the passage, based on an analogy, for an argument that applies "well-known general laws to a specific case." For the facts in this passage, such an argument from general laws to a specific case would go as follows:

1. General law: For all bodies in orbit, gravity is the main force that determines the body's orbit.
2. Specific case: An electron is a body in orbit.
3. Conclusion: Gravity is the main force that determines an electron's orbit.

Comparing this with the passage makes it clear that the argument in the passage builds its case on an apparently analogous situation, not on a general law. That the law of gravity, a well-known general law, applies to the specific case of the orbit of electrons is the *conclusion* the argument is drawing, not the *method* by which the argument attempts to prove its case.

Response (B) is incorrect because the argument is not trying to prove a general law about both electrons and planets. Its conclusion is only about electrons and their nuclei based on information about a comparable case.

Response (C) is incorrect because there is no evidence in the passage that the argument is using data from an *experiment* to make its point.

Response (E) is incorrect because the argument clearly does provide a reason for its conclusion, which can be stated as follows: since an electron orbits around its nucleus in the same way as the Earth orbits around the Sun, it is logical to conclude that there are other similarities between the two phenomena.

This test question is a "middle difficulty" item— approximately 60 percent of test takers answered it correctly. Approximately 25 percent incorrectly chose response (A).

Question 3

During the construction of the Quebec Bridge in 1907, the bridge's designer, Theodore Cooper, received word that the suspended span being built out from the Bridge's cantilever was deflecting downward by a fraction of an inch [2.56 centimeters]. Before he could telegraph to freeze the project, the whole cantilever arm broke off and plunged, along with seven dozen workers, into the St. Lawrence River. It was the worst bridge construction disaster in history. As a direct result of the inquiry that followed, the engineering "rules of thumb" by which thousands of bridges had been built around the world went down with the Quebec Bridge. Twentieth-century bridge engineers would thereafter depend on far more rigorous applications of mathematical analysis.

Which one of the following statements can be properly inferred from the passage?

(A) Bridges built before about 1907 were built without thorough mathematical analysis and, therefore, were unsafe for the public to use.
(B) Cooper's absence from the Quebec Bridge construction site resulted in the breaking off of the cantilever.
(C) Nineteenth-century bridge engineers relied on their rules of thumb because analytical methods were inadequate to solve their design problems.
(D) Only a more rigorous application of mathematical analysis to the design of the Quebec Bridge could have prevented its collapse.
(E) Prior to 1907 the mathematical analysis incorporated in engineering rules of thumb was insufficient to completely assure the safety of bridges under construction.

Explanation for Question 3

The question requires the examinee to identify the response that can be properly inferred from the passage. The passage indicates that the Quebec Bridge disaster in 1907 and the inquiry that followed caused the engineering "rules of thumb" used in construction of thousands of bridges to be abandoned. Since the Quebec Bridge disaster in 1907 prompted this abandonment, it can be inferred that these were the rules of thumb under which the Quebec Bridge was being built when it collapsed and that these were the rules of thumb used in bridge building before 1907. Further, since the Quebec Bridge collapsed while under construction and the rules of thumb being used were abandoned as a result, it can be inferred that the rules of thumb used in building the Quebec Bridge and bridges prior to 1907 were insufficient to completely assure the safety of bridges under construction. Finally, since the alternative to the old engineering rules of thumb that was adopted was to "depend on far more rigorous applications of mathematical analysis," it can be inferred that it was the mathematical analysis incorporated in the engineering rules of thumb used prior to 1907 that made them insufficient to completely assure the safety of bridges under construction. Thus, (E) is the credited response.

Response (A) is incorrect. (A) asserts that the lack of thorough mathematical analysis in construction of bridges before about 1907 was sufficient to establish that those bridges were *unsafe* for the public to use. But, the rules of thumb used in bridge construction before 1907 were abandoned because they were not sufficient to establish that the bridges being constructed using them were *safe* when under construction. It does not follow that the lack of more rigorous or thorough mathematical analysis in the rules of thumb was sufficient to establish that the bridges built before about 1907 using them were *unsafe* even while under construction, let alone for the public. In fact, some, or even all, may have been quite safe. In addition, the passage gives evidence only about the safety of bridges built before 1907 while they were *under construction*. It is silent on whether bridges built before about 1907 were safe when open for use *by the public*.

Response (B) is incorrect in claiming that Cooper's absence from the construction site *caused* the breaking off of the cantilever.

The passage does not establish that, had Cooper been at the site, he could have successfully intervened to prevent the cantilever from breaking off. By freezing the project, he might have spared lives by stopping work, but there is nothing in the passage to indicate that he necessarily would have prevented the collapse.

Response (C) is incorrect; there is no evidence in the passage about why nineteenth-century engineers relied on their rules of thumb.

Response (D) is also incorrect. While the passage suggests that a more rigorous application of mathematical analysis would have prevented the collapse of the bridge, it offers no evidence that it is the only way the collapse could have been prevented. For example, it might have been prevented had corrective measures been taken in time.

The question is "moderately difficult"; 48 percent of the test takers answered it correctly; 22 percent incorrectly chose (D).

Question 4

No one who has a sore throat need consult a doctor, because sore throats will recover without medical intervention. In recent years several cases of epiglottitis have occurred. Epiglottitis is a condition that begins with a sore throat and deteriorates rapidly in such a way that the throat becomes quite swollen, thus restricting breathing. Sometimes the only way to save a patient's life in these circumstances is to insert a plastic tube into the throat below the blockage so that the patient can breathe. It is highly advisable in such cases that sufferers seek medical attention when the first symptoms occur, that is, before the condition deteriorates.

Which one of the following is the best statement of the flaw in the argument?

(A) The author draws a general conclusion on the basis of evidence of a particular instance.
(B) The author assumes that similar effects must have similar causes.
(C) The author uses a medical term, "epiglottitis," and does not clarify its meaning.
(D) The author makes two claims that contradict each other.
(E) The author bases her conclusion at the end of the passage on inadequate evidence.

Explanation for Question 4

This question requires the test taker to identify the reasoning error in the argument.

The argument states initially that "*no one who has a sore throat need consult a doctor.*" However, it is then pointed out that "*several cases of epiglottitis have occurred*" and argued that for this condition, which begins with a sore throat and then deteriorates, it is "*highly advisable*" for sufferers to seek medical attention *before* the condition deteriorates, that is, *when* the symptom is a sore throat. So the author claims both that no one with a sore throat need seek medical attention and that some people with a sore throat do need to seek medical attention, and these claims contradict each other. Therefore, (D) is the credited response.

Response (A) is incorrect because the author does not clearly draw "a general conclusion on the basis of evidence of a particular instance" of anything. Even though a specific disease (epiglottitis) is discussed, no conclusion about diseases in general is drawn. And having this disease is discussed in terms of "*several cases*" and "*sometimes,*" not in terms of a "particular instance."

Response (B) is incorrect because the author is not concerned with the causes of sore throats and epiglottitis.

Response (C) is incorrect because the meaning of the medical term "epiglottitis" is specified in the third and fourth sentences of the passage in sufficient detail for purposes of the argument.

Response (E) is incorrect because the evidence given in the third and fourth sentences of the passage is adequate for the conclusion that "*it is highly advisable*" in cases of epiglottitis "*that sufferers seek medical attention when the first symptoms first occur.*"

This test question is a "very easy" item; 91 percent of examinees answered it correctly when it appeared on the LSAT.

Question 5

Photovoltaic power plants produce electricity from sunlight. As a result of astonishing recent technological advances, the cost of producing electric power at photovoltaic power plants, allowing for both construction and operating costs, is one-tenth of what it was 20 years ago, whereas the corresponding cost for traditional plants, which burn fossil fuels, has increased. Thus, photovoltaic power plants offer a less expensive approach to meeting demand for electricity than do traditional power plants.

The conclusion of the argument is properly drawn if which one of the following is assumed?

(A) The cost of producing electric power at traditional plants has increased over the past 20 years.
(B) Twenty years ago, traditional power plants were producing 10 times more electric power than were photovoltaic plants.
(C) None of the recent technological advances in producing electric power at photovoltaic plants can be applied to producing power at traditional plants.
(D) Twenty years ago, the cost of producing electric power at photovoltaic plants was less than 10 times the cost of producing power at traditional plants.
(E) The cost of producing electric power at photovoltaic plants is expected to decrease further, while the cost of producing power at traditional plants is not expected to decrease.

Explanation for Question 5

This question requires the test taker to identify an assumption that would allow the argument's conclusion to be properly drawn. As the argument is stated, there is a logical gap between the information given in the premises and the claim made in the conclusion:

Premise 1: The cost of producing electric power at photovoltaic power plants is one-tenth of what it was 20 years ago.

Premise 2: The corresponding cost for traditional plants has increased.

Conclusion: Photovoltaic power plants offer a less expensive approach to meeting demand for electricity than do traditional power plants.

From the fact that one cost has gone down while another has risen, it does not necessarily follow that the first is now lower than the second. In particular, if the cost of producing electric power at photovoltaic power plants twenty years ago was *more* than ten times the corresponding cost for traditional plants, then the fact that it is now one-tenth what it was is not sufficient to show that it is now lower than the corresponding cost for traditional plants, even though we are told in Premise 2 that the cost for traditional plants has increased. To conclude from the premises given in the argument that photovoltaic power plants now offer a *less expensive* approach than do traditional power plants, we need to know how the costs of the two methods of production were related 20 years ago—specifically that the cost of producing power at photovoltaic plants was less than 10 times the cost of producing it at traditional plants. (D) gives this information and is, thus, the credited response.

Response (A) is incorrect because it tells us about only one of the two costs, not about how the two were related 20 years ago. It in effect restates premise 2, and premises 1 and 2 together are not sufficient for drawing the conclusion.

Response (B) is incorrect. The amount of electricity produced by the different kinds of plants is not at issue.

Response (C) is incorrect. While it is relevant to the discussion, (C) does not provide the information about the *comparative* costs of the two kinds of plants 20 years ago that allows the conclusion to be properly drawn.

Response (E) is incorrect because the conclusion in the argument is about the present only. Whether or not the change described in (E) is expected to take place has no bearing on the claim in the conclusion that the one kind of plant offers a less expensive approach at present.

This question is classified as "difficult." Approximately 35 percent of test takers answered it correctly. Most of those who answered incorrectly chose response (E).

Question 6

Some legislators refuse to commit public funds for new scientific research if they cannot be assured that the research will contribute to the public welfare. Such a position ignores the lessons of experience. Many important contributions to the public welfare that resulted from scientific research were never predicted as potential outcomes of that research. Suppose that a scientist in the early twentieth century had applied for public funds to study molds: who would have predicted that such research would lead to the discovery of antibiotics— one of the greatest contributions ever made to the public welfare?

Which one of the following most accurately expresses the main point of the argument?

(A) The committal of public funds for new scientific research will ensure that the public welfare will be enhanced.
(B) If it were possible to predict the general outcome of a new scientific research effort, then legislators would not refuse to commit public funds for that effort.
(C) Scientific discoveries that have contributed to the public welfare would have occurred sooner if public funds had been committed to the research that generated those discoveries.
(D) In order to ensure that scientific research is directed toward contributing to the public welfare, legislators must commit public funds to new scientific research.
(E) Lack of guarantees that new scientific research will contribute to the public welfare is not sufficient reason for legislators to refuse to commit public funds to new scientific research.

Explanation for Question 6

This question requires the test taker to determine the most accurate expression of the main point of the argument in the passage. The main point of an argument is not only a salient point, but one which draws on the rest of the argument for support. The primary purpose of an argument such as that in the passage on which this question is based is to convince the reader to accept the main point.

The passage begins by stating the position that some legislators hold. These legislators "refuse to commit public funds for new scientific research if they cannot be assured that the research will contribute to the public welfare." Then a reason is given for rejecting this position. Many important contributions to the public welfare come from scientific research for which no assurance could be given of a contribution to public welfare. These contributions "that resulted from scientific research were never predicted as potential outcomes of that research." Finally, this reason is emphasized by giving an example.

Clearly the purpose of this argument is to refute the position of the legislators mentioned. The main point is the denial of that position. Since response (E) most accurately expresses the denial of the legislators' position, it is the correct answer.

Response (A) is incorrect because it expresses a point that the argument does not make. Nothing is expressed or implied about whether committing public funds for new scientific research ensures that public welfare will be enhanced. All that is said is that legislators ought not insist on assurances of enhanced public welfare before committing public funds for new scientific research.

Response (B) is incorrect because it is a prediction of what legislators *would* do in cases where it is possible to predict the outcome of scientific research. The argument states what the legislators would *not* do if they *cannot* be assured that the research will contribute to the public welfare. Moreover, nothing is stated or implied about what legislators would do, the issue is rather what legislators *should* do. (B) implies that if it is possible to predict a *negative* outcome of a new scientific research effort, then legislators would not refuse to commit public funds for that effort. Nothing in the argument suggests anything close to this.

Response (C) is incorrect because it speculates that scientific discoveries that have contributed to the public welfare would have occurred sooner if public funds had been committed to the underlying research. Response (C) takes the argument much further than it has committed itself—the issue of whether any discoveries may have occurred sooner is never addressed within the argument.

Response (D) is incorrect because it addresses an issue that is not discussed in the argument. The argument does not say that the existence of research contributing to the public's welfare is conditional upon legislators committing public funds to that research.

This test question is an "easy" item. Eighty-two percent of examinees answered it correctly when it appeared on the LSAT.

Question 7

Situation: In the island nation of Bezun, the government taxes gasoline heavily in order to induce people not to drive. It uses the revenue from the gasoline tax to subsidize electricity in order to reduce prices charged for electricity.

Analysis: The greater the success achieved in meeting the first of these objectives, the less will be the success achieved in meeting the second.

The analysis provided for the situation above would be most appropriate in which one of the following situations?

(A) A library charges a late fee in order to induce borrowers to return books promptly. The library uses revenue from the late fee to send reminders to tardy borrowers in order to reduce the incidence of overdue books.

(B) A mail-order store imposes a stiff surcharge for overnight delivery in order to limit use of this option. The store uses revenue from the surcharge to pay the extra expenses it incurs for providing the overnight delivery service.

(C) The park management charges an admission fee so that a park's users will contribute to the park's upkeep. In order to keep admission fees low, the management does not finance any new projects from them.

(D) A restaurant adds a service charge in order to spare customers the trouble of individual tips. The service charge is then shared among the restaurant's workers in order to augment their low hourly wages.

(E) The highway administration charges a toll for crossing a bridge in order to get motorists to use other routes. It uses the revenue from that toll to generate a reserve fund in order to be able one day to build a new bridge.

Explanation for Question 7

This question requires the test taker to select from among the options the situation that most appropriately illustrates the principle expressed by the analysis of the situation in the passage. The analysis states that the two objectives described in the situation are related in such a way that more success in the first objective, the reduction of driving, will result in less success in the second, a reduction in the price of electricity. To see this, suppose that the gasoline taxes mentioned in the passage prove successful in inducing people not to drive. This would mean that people would have a diminished need to purchase gasoline, since they do not drive as much. Since less gasoline is being purchased, there is less revenue from taxes on gasoline purchases. There is therefore less revenue from the gasoline tax with which to subsidize electricity. With less of a subsidy, it will be more difficult to reduce prices charged for electricity. Among the options, (E) most closely presents exactly such a situation. The more motorists there are who begin to use other routes, thus reducing bridge traffic, the less toll money there will be for the new bridge fund. (E) is the credited response.

Response (A) is incorrect. Two devices are named, late fees and reminders, but they share the one objective stated, which is described in two ways: to get "borrowers to return books promptly" and to "reduce the incidence of overdue books." Success in one *is* success in the "other."

Response (B) is incorrect. This situation has two objectives, to limit the use of overnight delivery service, and to offset the extra expense of the overnight delivery still requested. However, these objectives are related in such a way that success in the first, a reduction in overnight delivery, would contribute to success in the second by lowering the extra expenses incurred by the service.

Response (C) is also incorrect. We cannot infer that more success in achieving the first objective, getting park users to help keep up the park, will cause less success in the second objective, keeping the fees low. It is conceivable that success in the former would enable the fees to be lowered; after all, if there were enough park users paying the fees (i.e., contributing to the park's upkeep), then the park management would not have to charge a high fee—fifteen park users paying $1.00 generates more revenue than one park user paying $10.00. Furthermore, there is nothing in the passage that functions like the last clause of (C). This makes the situation expressed in (C) even less similar to the passage than that expressed in (E), the credited response.

Response (D) is incorrect. The two objectives in this situation, sparing customers an inconvenience and augmenting restaurant workers' wages, are not necessarily related so more success in the former would cause less success in the latter. The quantitative relation between the restaurant's service charge and the average amount of individual tips is information needed to determine what effect satisfying the first objective would have on the second. A successful service charge could very well gather enough money that the employees' wages would be augmented even more by sharing this service charge than their salaries would be augmented by individual tips.

This was classified as a "difficult" item, with 33 percent of examinees correctly answering it when it appeared on the LSAT.

Question 8

The ancient Romans understood the principles of water power very well, and in some outlying parts of their empire they made extensive and excellent use of water as an energy source. This makes it all the more striking that the Romans made do without water power in regions dominated by large cities.

Which one of the following, if true, contributes most to an explanation of the difference described above in the Romans' use of water power?

(A) The ancient Romans were adept at constructing and maintaining aqueducts that could carry quantities of water sufficient to supply large cities over considerable distances.
(B) In the areas in which water power was not used, water flow in rivers and streams was substantial throughout the year but nevertheless exhibited some seasonal variation.
(C) Water power was relatively vulnerable to sabotage, but any damage could be quickly and inexpensively repaired.
(D) In most areas to which the use of water power was not extended, other, more traditional sources of energy continued to be used.
(E) In heavily populated areas the introduction of water power would have been certain to cause social unrest by depriving large numbers of people of their livelihood.

Explanation for Question 8

This question requires the test taker to identify the response that does most to explain an apparent discrepancy presented in the passage. The first step, then, is to determine clearly what this discrepancy is. The passage notes the Romans' extensive use of water power in some outlying parts of their empire, but in regions dominated by large cities, it says, they did without water power. Given the efficiency of water power, an adequate response must help answer the question why ancient Romans did not use water power in regions near their cities when they had a demonstrated ability to do so.

Response (A) is incorrect. Rather than explaining the puzzle, it merely describes their ability to supply water over distances. Response (B) is also incorrect. While it speaks of the region near cities, it indicates the natural water supply there was substantial although seasonally variable. Both (A) and (B) give reasons to expect water power to be used, not reasons the Romans did without it near cities. (C) is incorrect for a similar reason. It notes that even sabotage of water power could be overcome easily—a reason to use it, not to do without it near cities.

Response (D) reports what was used in place of water power in areas near cities, viz., "more traditional" energy sources. This may help explain how cities got along without water power: the use of traditional sources prevented them from being entirely without energy. This response appealed to many test takers, in fact it was the most popular option. However, merely saying that one can do without something, does not entail that one should do without something. Response (D) does help explain how cities and their immediately surrounding areas did without the demonstrated facility with water power that was extensively and excellently applied elsewhere, but it does not explicitly say why this facility was not applied in and around cities. While (D) may appear to explain the discrepancy more than either (A), (B), or (C), which give no explanation at all, it really does not give a reason against using water power in cities. Recall that the search is for the statement that contributes *most* to an explanation. Response (E) must therefore be examined.

(E) presents an undesirable consequence that would have followed from the use of water power in regions near cities: social unrest due to significant loss of livelihood. So while the other candidate for an explanation, response (D), notes a diminished need for water power in these regions, response (E) identifies a negative aspect of water power use in heavily populated areas, and that gives a reason not to use it near cities. Thus, (E) is the credited response.

This was a "very difficult" item. Approximately one third of test takers answered it correctly when it appeared on the test.

Question 9

All intelligent people are nearsighted. I am very nearsighted. So I must be a genius.

Which one of the following exhibits both of the logical flaws exhibited in the argument above?

(A) I must be stupid because all intelligent people are nearsighted and I have perfect eyesight.
(B) All chickens have beaks. This bird has a beak. So this bird must be a chicken.
(C) All pigs have four legs, but this spider has eight legs. So this spider must be twice as big as any pig.
(D) John is extremely happy, so he must be extremely tall because all tall people are happy.
(E) All geniuses are very nearsighted. I must be very nearsighted since I am a genius.

Explanation for Question 9

Note carefully that this question refers to two logical flaws that are in the argument. It requires the test taker to select the option that exhibits both of those flaws. It is worth a bit of time to make clear what the two flaws are. The first sentence identifies a group, intelligent people, and says all its members have a particular characteristic, nearsightedness. In the second sentence, the speaker admits to being nearsighted then concludes, in the third sentence, that he or she must be a member of the group of intelligent people (a genius). The justification for this inference, presumably, is that since the speaker has one characteristic that belongs to all members of a certain group, then the speaker also belongs to that group. This is one flaw. The error can be seen by noting that the first sentence speaks of all intelligent people but not of all nearsighted people. So we cannot legitimately infer from this statement that any particular nearsighted person, here the speaker, is (or is not) intelligent.

The second flaw also arises from attributing something to the first sentence that is not legitimate. The speaker acknowledges being *very* nearsighted, and concludes that he or she is *very* intelligent, i.e., a genius. The presumed justification here is that the *degree* of one characteristic is associated with the *degree* of the other characteristic. Again the error can be seen by noticing that the first sentence speaks of groups and characteristics but says nothing about quantities or degrees. The intensification of one characteristic does not justify inferring that the other is intensified as well. This error could have been committed without committing the first error. For example, after the first sentence, the speaker might have said "I am very intelligent, therefore I must be very nearsighted."

With the two flaws identified, the options may be examined in search of one that exhibits both flaws.

Response (A) shares the following premise with the passage: all intelligent people are nearsighted. Here, the speaker denies having the characteristic of nearsightedness, and instead claims perfect eyesight, then concludes that he or she must not belong to the group of intelligent people. This inference is legitimate because the effect of the shared premise is to rule out any intelligent person's being without nearsightedness. This response does, however, commit the intensification flaw seen above. It makes the illegitimate inference from being intensely "not nearsighted," i.e., having perfect vision, to being intensely "not intelligent," i.e., stupid. So (A) is an incorrect response.

Response (B)'s first premise is similar to the premise shared by the passage and (A); all members of the class "chickens" are said to have a beak. A particular bird is said to have a beak; then it is concluded that this particular bird is a chicken. This is the first mentioned flaw in the original argument: taking a characteristic that belongs to all members of a group as sufficient indication that an individual having that characteristic is also a member of that group. (B), however, does not commit the intensification flaw seen in the original. So, responses (A) and (B) each exhibit *one* of the flaws in the original argument, but neither of them exhibits both.

Response (C) illicitly presumes that size is directly proportional to the number of legs a creature has, and so concludes that the spider with eight legs is twice as big as a pig which has four legs. This is an interesting mistake, but not the two errors committed by the original argument.

(D) is the correct response. Even though the order of presentation is different than the original argument, the structure of the reasoning is the same, and exhibits both of the flaws. (D) makes an inference from "all tall people are happy" and "John is extremely happy" to "he must be extremely tall." This is to take a characteristic belonging to all members of a class as sufficient indication that an individual having that characteristic is also a member of that class. It also infers from the intensification of that characteristic to the possession of an intense degree of the defining characteristic of the class. (D) thus exhibits both flaws seen in the original argument; it is the credited response.

Response (E) exhibits neither of the flaws. Indeed, it is a valid argument. Note that the intensification appears in the main premise: all geniuses, i.e., very intelligent people, are said to be very nearsighted. And the conclusion states of one particular genius, the speaker, that he or she is very nearsighted. This of course must be true if the first premise is true. So (E) is incorrect.

This was classified as a "very difficult" question. Twenty-seven percent of examinees answered this question correctly. Most of those who answered incorrectly chose response (B), indicating, perhaps, that test takers were less apt to recognize the intensification flaw than they were to identify the other flaw.

The Writing Sample

On the day of the test, you will be asked to write one sample essay. LSAC does not score the writing sample, but copies are sent to all law schools to which you apply. According to a 2006 LSAC survey of 157 United States and Canadian law schools, almost all utilize the writing sample in evaluating some applications for admission. Frivolous responses or no responses to writing sample prompts have been used by law schools as grounds for rejection of applications for admission.

In developing and implementing the writing sample portion of the LSAT, LSAC has operated on the following premises: First, law schools and the legal profession value highly the ability to communicate effectively in writing. Second, it is important to encourage potential law students to develop effective writing skills. Third, a sample of an applicant's writing, produced under controlled conditions, is a potentially useful indication of that person's writing ability. Fourth, the writing sample can serve as an independent check on other writing submitted by applicants as part of the admission process. Finally, writing samples may be useful for diagnostic purposes.

You will have 35 minutes in which to plan and write an essay on the topic you receive. Read the topic and the accompanying directions carefully. You will probably find it best to spend a few minutes considering the topic and organizing your thoughts before you begin writing. In your essay, be sure to develop your ideas fully, leaving time, if possible, to review what you have written. Do not write on a topic other than the one specified. Writing on a topic of your own choice is not acceptable.

No special knowledge is required or expected for this writing exercise. Law schools are interested in the reasoning, clarity, organization, language usage, and writing mechanics displayed in your essay. How well you write is more important than how much you write. Confine your essay to the blocked, lined area on the front and back of the separate Writing Sample Response Sheet. Only that area will be reproduced for law schools. Be sure that your writing is legible.

The writing prompt presents a decision problem. You are asked to make a choice between two positions or courses of action. Both of the choices are defensible, and you are given criteria and facts on which to base your decision. There is no "right" or "wrong" position to take on the topic, so the quality of each test taker's response is a function not of which choice is made, but of how well or poorly the choice is supported and how well or poorly the other choice is criticized. The two example topics below are typical of decision prompts that have been administered with the LSAT in the past.

Directions:
The scenario presented below describes two choices, either one of which can be supported on the basis of the information given. Your essay should consider both choices and argue for one over the other, based on the two specified criteria and the facts provided. There is no "right" or "wrong" choice: a reasonable argument can be made for either.

Example 1

Denyse Barnes, a young country music singer who has just released her debut CD, is planning a concert tour to promote it. Her agent has presented her with two options: she can tour as the opening act for Downhome, a famous country band that is mounting a national tour this year, or she can be the solo act in a tour in her home region. Using the facts below, write an essay in which you argue for one option over the other based on the following two criteria:

- Barnes wants to build a large and loyal fan base.

- Barnes wants to begin writing new songs for her next CD.

Downhome is scheduled to perform in over 100 far-flung cities in 8 months, playing in large arenas, including sports stadiums. This ambitious schedule would take Barnes far away from her home recording studio, where she prefers to compose. Downhome's last concert tour was sold out, and the band's latest release is a top seller. Many concertgoers at large arenas skip the opening act. But it is possible that Barnes would be invited by Downhome to play a song or two with them.

The solo tour in her home region would book Barnes in 30 cities over a 4-month period, including community theaters and country-and-blues music clubs, a few of which have reputations for launching new talent. These venues have loyal patrons; most shows are inexpensive and are well-attended, even for new talent. Barnes would have a promotion budget for her solo tour, but it would be far smaller than that for Downhome's tour.

Example 2

The City of Ridleyville must decide whether a decommissioned military base now owned by Ridleyville and located on its downtown riverfront should be developed as a business complex or converted to park and open space. Using the facts below, write an essay in which you argue for one option over the other based on the following two criteria:

- Ridleyville wants to address a growing budget deficit.

- Ridleyville wants to increase the amount of parkland and open space in the city, especially in the downtown riverfront area.

Ridleyville is considering selling the property for development as a business complex. Through tax incentives, the city could potentially preserve a small portion of the property as open space. The business complex would generate substantial tax revenue from the new businesses that would locate there. Before it realizes any of these revenues, Ridleyville would need to pay for a variety of costly infrastructure improvements, and these revenues would be partly offset by ongoing costs for increased municipal services. The city would likely incur greater environmental cleanup costs converting the base to a business complex than converting it to a park.

Ridleyville has no parks on its extensive river frontage, which is otherwise developed, and no parks in its downtown area. Several corporate sponsors are willing to underwrite the cost of converting the property into parkland. These corporations are also willing to contribute towards ongoing operating costs. The park could host revenue-generating events like concerts and the popular "Taste of Ridleyville," an annual food festival. Fees could be charged for boat launching. These combined revenues could enable the park to pay for itself.

HOW TO TAKE A TEST

You have studied long, hard and conscientiously.

With your official admission card in hand, and your heart pounding, you have been admitted to the examination room.

You note that there are several hundred other applicants in the examination room waiting to take the same test.

They all appear to be equally well prepared.

You know that nothing but your best effort will suffice. The "moment of truth" is at hand: you now have to demonstrate objectively, in writing, your knowledge of content and your understanding of subject matter.

You are fighting the most important battle of your life—to pass and/or score high on an examination which will determine your career and provide the economic basis for your livelihood.

What extra, special things should you know and should you do in taking the examination?

I. YOU MUST PASS AN EXAMINATION

A. WHAT EVERY CANDIDATE SHOULD KNOW
Examination applicants often ask us for help in preparing for the written test. What can I study in advance? What kinds of questions will be asked? How will the test be given? How will the papers be graded?

B. HOW ARE EXAMS DEVELOPED?
Examinations are carefully written by trained technicians who are specialists in the field known as "psychological measurement," in consultation with recognized authorities in the field of work that the test will cover. These experts recommend the subject matter areas or skills to be tested; only those knowledges or skills important to your success on the job are included. The most reliable books and source materials available are used as references. Together, the experts and technicians judge the difficulty level of the questions.
Test technicians know how to phrase questions so that the problem is clearly stated. Their ethics do not permit "trick" or "catch" questions. Questions may have been tried out on sample groups, or subjected to statistical analysis, to determine their usefulness.
Written tests are often used in combination with performance tests, ratings of training and experience, and oral interviews. All of these measures combine to form the best-known means of finding the right person for the right job.

II. HOW TO PASS THE WRITTEN TEST

A. BASIC STEPS

1) Study the announcement

How, then, can you know what subjects to study? Our best answer is: "Learn as much as possible about the class of positions for which you've applied." The exam will test the knowledge, skills and abilities needed to do the work.

Your most valuable source of information about the position you want is the official exam announcement. This announcement lists the training and experience qualifications. Check these standards and apply only if you come reasonably close to meeting them. Many jurisdictions preview the written test in the exam announcement by including a section called "Knowledge and Abilities Required," "Scope of the Examination," or some similar heading. Here you will find out specifically what fields will be tested.

2) Choose appropriate study materials

If the position for which you are applying is technical or advanced, you will read more advanced, specialized material. If you are already familiar with the basic principles of your field, elementary textbooks would waste your time. Concentrate on advanced textbooks and technical periodicals. Think through the concepts and review difficult problems in your field.

These are all general sources. You can get more ideas on your own initiative, following these leads. For example, training manuals and publications of the government agency which employs workers in your field can be useful, particularly for technical and professional positions. A letter or visit to the government department involved may result in more specific study suggestions, and certainly will provide you with a more definite idea of the exact nature of the position you are seeking.

3) Study this book!

III. KINDS OF TESTS

Tests are used for purposes other than measuring knowledge and ability to perform specified duties. For some positions, it is equally important to test ability to make adjustments to new situations or to profit from training. In others, basic mental abilities not dependent on information are essential. Questions which test these things may not appear as pertinent to the duties of the position as those which test for knowledge and information. Yet they are often highly important parts of a fair examination. For very general questions, it is almost impossible to help you direct your study efforts. What we can do is to point out some of the more common of these general abilities needed in public service positions and describe some typical questions.

1) General information

Broad, general information has been found useful for predicting job success in some kinds of work. This is tested in a variety of ways, from vocabulary lists to questions about current events. Basic background in some field of work, such as sociology or economics, may be sampled in a group of questions. Often these are principles which have become familiar to most persons through exposure rather than through formal training. It is difficult to advise you how to study for these questions; being alert to the world around you is our best suggestion.

2) Verbal ability

An example of an ability needed in many positions is verbal or language ability. Verbal ability is, in brief, the ability to use and understand words. Vocabulary and grammar tests are typical measures of this ability. Reading comprehension or paragraph interpretation questions are common in many kinds of civil service tests. You are given a paragraph of written material and asked to find its central meaning.

IV. KINDS OF QUESTIONS

1. Multiple-choice Questions

Most popular of the short-answer questions is the "multiple choice" or "best answer" question. It can be used, for example, to test for factual knowledge, ability to solve problems or judgment in meeting situations found at work.

A multiple-choice question is normally one of three types:
- It can begin with an incomplete statement followed by several possible endings. You are to find the one ending which best completes the statement, although some of the others may not be entirely wrong.
- It can also be a complete statement in the form of a question which is answered by choosing one of the statements listed.
- It can be in the form of a problem – again you select the best answer.

Here is an example of a multiple-choice question with a discussion which should give you some clues as to the method for choosing the right answer:

When an employee has a complaint about his assignment, the action which will best help him overcome his difficulty is to
- A. discuss his difficulty with his coworkers
- B. take the problem to the head of the organization
- C. take the problem to the person who gave him the assignment
- D. say nothing to anyone about his complaint

In answering this question, you should study each of the choices to find which is best. Consider choice "A" – Certainly an employee may discuss his complaint with fellow employees, but no change or improvement can result, and the complaint remains unresolved. Choice "B" is a poor choice since the head of the organization probably does not know what assignment you have been given, and taking your problem to him is known as "going over the head" of the supervisor. The supervisor, or person who made the assignment, is the person who can clarify it or correct any injustice. Choice "C" is, therefore, correct. To say nothing, as in choice "D," is unwise. Supervisors have and interest in knowing the problems employees are facing, and the employee is seeking a solution to his problem.

2. True/False

3. Matching Questions

Matching an answer from a column of choices within another column.

V. RECORDING YOUR ANSWERS

Computer terminals are used more and more today for many different kinds of exams.

For an examination with very few applicants, you may be told to record your answers in the test booklet itself. Separate answer sheets are much more common. If this separate answer sheet is to be scored by machine – and this is often the case – it is highly important that you mark your answers correctly in order to get credit.

VI. BEFORE THE TEST

YOUR PHYSICAL CONDITION IS IMPORTANT

If you are not well, you can't do your best work on tests. If you are half asleep, you can't do your best either. Here are some tips:

1) Get about the same amount of sleep you usually get. Don't stay up all night before the test, either partying or worrying—DON'T DO IT!
2) If you wear glasses, be sure to wear them when you go to take the test. This goes for hearing aids, too.
3) If you have any physical problems that may keep you from doing your best, be sure to tell the person giving the test. If you are sick or in poor health, you relay cannot do your best on any test. You can always come back and take the test some other time.

Common sense will help you find procedures to follow to get ready for an examination. Too many of us, however, overlook these sensible measures. Indeed, nervousness and fatigue have been found to be the most serious reasons why applicants fail to do their best on civil service tests. Here is a list of reminders:

- Begin your preparation early – Don't wait until the last minute to go scurrying around for books and materials or to find out what the position is all about.
- Prepare continuously – An hour a night for a week is better than an all-night cram session. This has been definitely established. What is more, a night a week for a month will return better dividends than crowding your study into a shorter period of time.
- Locate the place of the exam – You have been sent a notice telling you when and where to report for the examination. If the location is in a different town or otherwise unfamiliar to you, it would be well to inquire the best route and learn something about the building.
- Relax the night before the test – Allow your mind to rest. Do not study at all that night. Plan some mild recreation or diversion; then go to bed early and get a good night's sleep.
- Get up early enough to make a leisurely trip to the place for the test – This way unforeseen events, traffic snarls, unfamiliar buildings, etc. will not upset you.
- Dress comfortably – A written test is not a fashion show. You will be known by number and not by name, so wear something comfortable.
- Leave excess paraphernalia at home – Shopping bags and odd bundles will get in your way. You need bring only the items mentioned in the official notice you received; usually everything you need is provided. Do not bring reference books to the exam. They will only confuse those last minutes and be taken away from you when in the test room.

- Arrive somewhat ahead of time – If because of transportation schedules you must get there very early, bring a newspaper or magazine to take your mind off yourself while waiting.
- Locate the examination room – When you have found the proper room, you will be directed to the seat or part of the room where you will sit. Sometimes you are given a sheet of instructions to read while you are waiting. Do not fill out any forms until you are told to do so; just read them and be prepared.
- Relax and prepare to listen to the instructions
- If you have any physical problem that may keep you from doing your best, be sure to tell the test administrator. If you are sick or in poor health, you really cannot do your best on the exam. You can come back and take the test some other time.

VII. AT THE TEST

The day of the test is here and you have the test booklet in your hand. The temptation to get going is very strong. Caution! There is more to success than knowing the right answers. You must know how to identify your papers and understand variations in the type of short-answer question used in this particular examination. Follow these suggestions for maximum results from your efforts:

1) Cooperate with the monitor

The test administrator has a duty to create a situation in which you can be as much at ease as possible. He will give instructions, tell you when to begin, check to see that you are marking your answer sheet correctly, and so on. He is not there to guard you, although he will see that your competitors do not take unfair advantage. He wants to help you do your best.

2) Listen to all instructions

Don't jump the gun! Wait until you understand all directions. In most civil service tests you get more time than you need to answer the questions. So don't be in a hurry. Read each word of instructions until you clearly understand the meaning. Study the examples, listen to all announcements and follow directions. Ask questions if you do not understand what to do.

3) Identify your papers

Civil service exams are usually identified by number only. You will be assigned a number; you must not put your name on your test papers. Be sure to copy your number correctly. Since more than one exam may be given, copy your exact examination title.

4) Plan your time

Unless you are told that a test is a "speed" or "rate of work" test, speed itself is usually not important. Time enough to answer all the questions will be provided, but this does not mean that you have all day. An overall time limit has been set. Divide the total time (in minutes) by the number of questions to determine the approximate time you have for each question.

5) Do not linger over difficult questions

If you come across a difficult question, mark it with a paper clip (useful to have along) and come back to it when you have been through the booklet. One caution if you do this – be sure to skip a number on your answer sheet as well. Check often to be sure that you have not lost your place and that you are marking in the row numbered the same as the question you are answering.

6) Read the questions

Be sure you know what the question asks! Many capable people are unsuccessful because they failed to read the questions correctly.

7) Answer all questions

Unless you have been instructed that a penalty will be deducted for incorrect answers, it is better to guess than to omit a question.

8) Speed tests

It is often better NOT to guess on speed tests. It has been found that on timed tests people are tempted to spend the last few seconds before time is called in marking answers at random – without even reading them – in the hope of picking up a few extra points. To discourage this practice, the instructions may warn you that your score will be "corrected" for guessing. That is, a penalty will be applied. The incorrect answers will be deducted from the correct ones, or some other penalty formula will be used.

9) Review your answers

If you finish before time is called, go back to the questions you guessed or omitted to give them further thought. Review other answers if you have time.

10) Return your test materials

If you are ready to leave before others have finished or time is called, take ALL your materials to the monitor and leave quietly. Never take any test material with you. The monitor can discover whose papers are not complete, and taking a test booklet may be grounds for disqualification.

VIII. EXAMINATION TECHNIQUES

1) Read the general instructions carefully. These are usually printed on the first page of the exam booklet. As a rule, these instructions refer to the timing of the examination; the fact that you should not start work until the signal and must stop work at a signal, etc. If there are any special instructions, such as a choice of questions to be answered, make sure that you note this instruction carefully.

2) When you are ready to start work on the examination, that is as soon as the signal has been given, read the instructions to each question booklet, underline any key words or phrases, such as least, best, outline, describe and the like. In this way you will tend to answer as requested rather than discover on reviewing your paper that you listed without describing, that you selected the worst choice rather than the best choice, etc.

3) If the examination is of the objective or multiple-choice type – that is, each question will also give a series of possible answers: A, B, C or D, and you are called upon to select the best answer and write the letter next to that answer on your answer paper – it is advisable to start answering each question in turn. There may be anywhere from 50 to 100 such questions in the three or four hours allotted and you can see how much time would be taken if you read through all the questions before beginning to answer any. Furthermore, if you

come across a question or group of questions which you know would be difficult to answer, it would undoubtedly affect your handling of all the other questions.

4) If the examination is of the essay type and contains but a few questions, it is a moot point as to whether you should read all the questions before starting to answer any one. Of course, if you are given a choice – say five out of seven and the like – then it is essential to read all the questions so you can eliminate the two that are most difficult. If, however, you are asked to answer all the questions, there may be danger in trying to answer the easiest one first because you may find that you will spend too much time on it. The best technique is to answer the first question, then proceed to the second, etc.

5) Time your answers. Before the exam begins, write down the time it started, then add the time allowed for the examination and write down the time it must be completed, then divide the time available somewhat as follows:
    - If 3-1/2 hours are allowed, that would be 210 minutes. If you have 80 objective-type questions, that would be an average of 2-1/2 minutes per question. Allow yourself no more than 2 minutes per question, or a total of 160 minutes, which will permit about 50 minutes to review.
    - If for the time allotment of 210 minutes there are 7 essay questions to answer, that would average about 30 minutes a question. Give yourself only 25 minutes per question so that you have about 35 minutes to review.

6) The most important instruction is to read each question and make sure you know what is wanted. The second most important instruction is to time yourself properly so that you answer every question. The third most important instruction is to answer every question. Guess if you have to but include something for each question. Remember that you will receive no credit for a blank and will probably receive some credit if you write something in answer to an essay question. If you guess a letter – say "B" for a multiple-choice question – you may have guessed right. If you leave a blank as an answer to a multiple-choice question, the examiners may respect your feelings but it will not add a point to your score. Some exams may penalize you for wrong answers, so in such cases only, you may not want to guess unless you have some basis for your answer.

7) Suggestions
    a. Objective-type questions
        1. Examine the question booklet for proper sequence of pages and questions
        2. Read all instructions carefully
        3. Skip any question which seems too difficult; return to it after all other questions have been answered
        4. Apportion your time properly; do not spend too much time on any single question or group of questions
        5. Note and underline key words – all, most, fewest, least, best, worst, same, opposite, etc.
        6. Pay particular attention to negatives
        7. Note unusual option, e.g., unduly long, short, complex, different or similar in content to the body of the question
        8. Observe the use of "hedging" words – probably, may, most likely, etc.

9. Make sure that your answer is put next to the same number as the question
10. Do not second-guess unless you have good reason to believe the second answer is definitely more correct
11. Cross out original answer if you decide another answer is more accurate; do not erase until you are ready to hand your paper in
12. Answer all questions; guess unless instructed otherwise
13. Leave time for review

b. Essay questions
1. Read each question carefully
2. Determine exactly what is wanted. Underline key words or phrases.
3. Decide on outline or paragraph answer
4. Include many different points and elements unless asked to develop any one or two points or elements
5. Show impartiality by giving pros and cons unless directed to select one side only
6. Make and write down any assumptions you find necessary to answer the questions
7. Watch your English, grammar, punctuation and choice of words
8. Time your answers; don't crowd material

8) Answering the essay question

Most essay questions can be answered by framing the specific response around several key words or ideas. Here are a few such key words or ideas:

M's: manpower, materials, methods, money, management
P's: purpose, program, policy, plan, procedure, practice, problems, pitfalls, personnel, public relations

a. Six basic steps in handling problems:
1. Preliminary plan and background development
2. Collect information, data and facts
3. Analyze and interpret information, data and facts
4. Analyze and develop solutions as well as make recommendations
5. Prepare report and sell recommendations
6. Install recommendations and follow up effectiveness

b. Pitfalls to avoid
1. Taking things for granted – A statement of the situation does not necessarily imply that each of the elements is necessarily true; for example, a complaint may be invalid and biased so that all that can be taken for granted is that a complaint has been registered
2. Considering only one side of a situation – Wherever possible, indicate several alternatives and then point out the reasons you selected the best one
3. Failing to indicate follow up – Whenever your answer indicates action on your part, make certain that you will take proper follow-up action to see how successful your recommendations, procedures or actions turn out to be
4. Taking too long in answering any single question – Remember to time your answers properly

EXAMINATION SECTION

READING COMPREHENSION
UNDERSTANDING AND INTERPRETING WRITTEN MATERIAL
EXAMINATION SECTION
TEST 1

DIRECTIONS: Each question or incomplete statement is followed by several suggested answers or completions. Select the one that *BEST* answers the question or completes the statement. *PRINT THE LETTER OF THE CORRECT ANSWER IN THE SPACE AT THE RIGHT.*

PASSAGE

It is a common belief that a thing is desirable because it is scarce and thereby has ostentation value. The notion that such a standard of value is an inescapable condition of settled social existence rests on one of two implicit assumptions. The first is that the attempt to educate the human race so that the desire to display one's possessions is not a significant feature of man's social behavior, is an infringement against personal freedom. The greatest obstacle to lucid discourse in these matters is the psychological anti-vaccinationist who uses the word freedom to signify the natural right of men and women to be unhappy and unhealthy through scientific ignorance instead of being healthy and happy through the knowledge which science confers. Haunted by a perpetual fear of the dark, the last lesson which man learns in the difficult process of growing up is "ye shall know the truth, and the truth shall make you free." The professional economist who is too sophisticated to retreat Into the obscurities of this curious conception of liberty may prefer to adopt the second assumption, that the truth does not and cannot make us free because the need for ostentation is a universal species characteristic, and all attempts to eradicate the unconscionable nuisance and discord which arise from overdeveloped craving for personal distinction artificially fostered by advertisement propaganda and so-called good breeding are therefore destined to failure. It may be earnestly, hoped that those who entertain this view have divine guidance. No rational basis for it will be found in textbooks of economics. Whatever can be said with any plausibility in the existing state of knowledge rests on the laboratory materials supplied by anthropology and social history.

1. According to the writer, the second assumption

    A. Is fostered by propaganda and so-called good breeding
    B. is basically opposite to the view of the psychological anti-vaccinationist
    C. is not so curious a conception of liberty as Is the first assumption
    D. is unsubstantiated
    E. is a religious explanation of an economic phenomenon

2. The author's purpose in writing this paragraph is MOST probably to

    A. denounce the psychological anti-vaccinationists
    B. demonstrate that the question under discussion is an economic rather than a psychological problem
    C. prove the maxim "ye shall know the truth, and the truth shall make you free"
    D. prove that ostentation is not an inescapable pheonomenon of settled social existence
    E. prove the inability of economics to account for ostentation

3. The writer implies that

   A. neither the psychological anti-vaccinationist nor the professional economist recognizes the undesirability of ostentation
   B. our cultural standards are at fault in enhancing ostentation value
   C. scarcity as a criterion of value Is an inexplicable concept
   D. his main objection Is to the inescapable standard of values
   E. the results of studies of ostentation in anthropology and social history are Irrational

4. The writer believes that both assumptions

   A. are invalid because they ignore the lesson "ye shall know the truth, and the truth shall make you free"
   B. are fallacious because they agree that a thing is desirable because it is scarce
   C. arise from overdeveloped craving for personal distinction
   D. are implicit in the conception of ostentation value
   E. dispute the efficacy of education in eliminating ostentation

5. In his reference to divine guidance, the writer is

   A. being ironic
   B. implying that only divine guidance can solve the problem
   C. showing how the professional economist is opposing divine laws
   D. referring to opposition which exists between religion and science
   E. indicating that the problem is not a matter for divine guidance

6. The writer believes that personal freedom is

   A. less important than is scientific knowledge
   B. a requisite for the attainment of truth
   C. attained by eradicating false beliefs
   D. no concern of the professional economist
   E. an unsophisticated concept

7. We may infer that this writer does NOT believe that

   A. education can solve the problem
   B. people have any "natural rights"
   C. science can solve the problem
   D. the psychological anti-vaccinationist is more than a lipservant of the cause of freedom
   E. people can be happy under the present value system

8. The writer would consider as MOST comparable to the effect of a vaccination on the body, the effect of

   A. fear upon personality
   B. science upon the supposed need for ostentation
   C. truth upon the mind
   D. knowledge upon ignorance
   E. knowledge upon happiness

KEY (CORRECT ANSWERS)

1. D
2. D
3. B
4. D
5. A
6. C
7. E
8. C

TEST 2

DIRECTIONS: Each question or incomplete statement is followed by several suggested answers or completions. Select the one that *BEST* answers the question or completes the statement. *PRINT THE LETTER OF THE CORRECT ANSWER IN THE SPACE AT THE RIGHT.*

PASSAGE

In any country the wages commanded by laborers who have comparable skills but who work in various industries are determined by the productivity of the least productive unit of labor, i.e., that unit of labor which works in the industry which has the greatest economic disadvantage. We will represent the various opportunities of employment in a country like the United States by symbols: A, standing for a group of industries in which we have exceptional economic advantages over foreign countries; B, for a group in which our advantages are less; C, one in which they are still less; D, the group of industries in which they are least of all.

When our population is so small that all our labor can be engaged in the group represented by A, productivity of labor (and therefore wages) will be at their maximum. When our population increases so that some of the labor will have to be set to work in group B, the wages of all labor must decline to the level of the productivity in that group. But no employer, without government aid, will yet be able to afford to hire labor to exploit the opportunities represented by C and D, unless there is a further increase in population.

But suppose that the political party in power holds the belief that we should produce everything that we consume, that the opportunities represented by C and D should be exploited. The commodities that the industries composing C and D will produce have been hitherto obtained from abroad in exchange for commodities produced by A and B. The government now renders this difficult by placing high duties upon the former class of commodities. This means that workers in A and B must pay higher prices for what they buy, but do not receive higher prices for what they sell.

After the duty has gone into effect and the prices of commodities that can be produced by C and D have risen sufficiently, enterprisers will be able to hire labor at the wages prevailing in A and B, and establish industries in C and D. So far as the remaining laborers in A and B buy the products of C and D, the difference between the price which they pay for those products and the price that they would pay if they were permitted to import those products duty-free is a tax paid not to the government, but to the producers in C and D, to enable the latter to remain in business. It is an uncompensated deduction from the natural earnings of the laborers in A and B. Nor are the workers in C and D paid as much, estimated in purchasing power, as they would have received if they had been allowed to remain in A and B under the earlier conditions.

1. When C and D are established, workers in these industries

    A. receive higher wages than do the workers in A and B
    B. receive lower wages than do the workers in A and B
    C. must be paid by government funds collected from the duties on imports
    D. are not affected so adversely by the levying of duties as are workers in A and B
    E. receive wages equal to those workers in A and B

2. We cannot exploit C and D unless

   A. the productivity of labor in all industries is increased
   B. the prices of commodities produced by A and B are raised
   C. we export large quantities of commodities produced by A and B
   D. the producers in C and D are compensated for the disadvantages under which they operate
   E. we allow duties to be paid to the producers in C and D rather than to the government

2.____

3. "No employer; without government aid, will yet be able to afford to hire labor to exploit the opportunities represented by C and D" because

   A. productivity of labor is not at the maximum
   B. we cannot produce everything we consume
   C. the population has increased
   D. enterprisers would have to pay wages equivalent to those obtained by workers in A and B, while producing under greater economic disadvantages
   E. productivity would drop correspondingly with the wages of labor

3.____

4. The government, when it places high duties on imported commodities of classes C and D,

   A. raises the price of commodities produced by A and B
   B. is, in effect, taxing the workers in A and B
   C. raises the wages of workers in C and D at the expense of the workers in A and B
   D. does not affect the productivity of the workers in A and B, although the wages of these workers are reduced
   E. is adopting a policy made necessary by the stability of the population

4.____

5. The author's MAIN point is that

   A. it is impossible to attain national self-sufficiency
   B. the varying productivity of the various industries leads to the inequalities in wages of workers in these industries
   C. a policy that draws labor from the fields of greater natural productiveness to fields of lower natural productiveness tends to reduce purchasing power
   D. wages ought to be independent of international trade
   E. the government ought to subsidize C and D.

5.____

6. The author's arguments in this passage could BEST be used to

   A. refute the belief that it is theoretically possible for us to produce everything that we consume
   B. disprove the theory that national self-sufficiency can be obtained by means of protective tariffs
   C. advocate the levying of duties on imported goods
   D. advocate equal wages for workers who have comparable skills but who work in various industries
   E. advocate free trade

6.____

7. When could C and D, as here defined, be exploited without the assistance of an artificially boosted price and without resultant lowering of wage levels?

    A. When a duty is placed on competing products from other countries
    B. When the products of C and D are exchanged in trade for other commodities
    C. When the country becomes economically self-sufficient
    D. When there is a favorable balance of trade
    E. At no time

7.___

8. In the last sentence in the selection, the statement is made: "Nor are the workers in C and D paid as much, estimated in purchasing power, as they would have received if they had been allowed to remain in A and B under the earlier conditions." This is because

    A. they must pay higher prices for commodities produced by C and D
    B. C and D cannot pay so high wages as can A and B
    C. products of C and D do not command sufficiently high prices
    D. there has not been an increase in population
    E. wages in all groups have declined

8.___

KEY (CORRECT ANSWERS)

1. E   5. C
2. D   6. E
3. D   7. B
4. B   8. E

TEST 3

DIRECTIONS: Each question or incomplete statement is followed by several suggested answers or completions. Select the one that BEST answers the question or completes the statement. PRINT THE LETTER OF THE CORRECT ANSWER IN THE SPACE AT THE RIGHT.

PASSAGE

In the Federal Convention of 1787, the members were fairly well agreed as to the desirability of some check on state laws; but there was sharp difference of opinion whether this check should be political in character as in the form of a congressional veto, or whether the principle of judicial review should be adopted.

Madison was one of the most persistent advocates of the congressional veto and in his discussion of the subject he referred several times to the former imperial prerogative of disallowing provincial statutes. In March, 1787, he wrote to Jefferson, urging the necessity of a federal negative upon state laws. He referred to previous colonial experience in the suggestion that there should be "some emanation" of the federal prerogative "within the several states, so far as to enable them to give a temporary sanction to laws of immediate necessity." This had been provided for in the imperial system through the action of the royal governor in giving immediate effect to statutes, which nevertheless remained subject to royal disallowance. In a letter to Randolph a few weeks later, Madison referred more explicitly to the British practice, urging that the national government be given "a negative, in all cases whatsoever, on the Legislative acts of the States, as the King of Great Britain heretofore had." Jefferson did not agree with Madison; on practical grounds rather than as a matter of principle, he expressed his preference for some form of judicial control.

On July 17, Madison came forward with a speech in support of the congressional veto, again supporting his contention by reference to the royal disallowance of colonial laws: "Its utility is sufficiently displayed in the British System. Nothing could maintain the harmony and subordination of the various parts of the empire, but the prerogative by which the Crown stifles in the birth every Act of every part tending to discord or encroachment. It is true the prerogative is sometimes misapplied thro' ignorance or a partiality to one particular part of the empire: but we have not the same reason to fear such misapplications in our System." This is almost precisely Jefferson's theory of the legitimate function of an imperial veto.

This whole issue shows that the leaders who wrestled with confederation problems during and after the war understood, in some measure at least, the attitude of British administrators when confronted with the stubborn localism of a provincial assembly.

1. Madison was advocating   1._____

    A. royal disallowance of state legislation
    B. a political check on state laws
    C. the supremacy of the states over the federal government
    D. the maintenance of a royal governor to give immediate effect to statutes
    E. discord and encroachment among the states

2. From this passage there is no indication

    A. of what the British System entailed
    B. of Jefferson's stand on the question of a check on state laws
    C. that the royal negative had been misapplied in the past
    D. that Jefferson understood the attitude of British administrators
    E. of what judicial review would entail

3. According to this passage, Madison believed that the federal government

    A. ought to legislate for the states
    B. should recognize the sovereignty of the several states
    C. ought to exercise judicial control over state legislation
    D. should assume the king's veto power
    E. was equivalent to a provincial assembly

4. Madison's conception of a congressional veto

    A. was opposed to Jefferson's conception of a congressional veto
    B. developed from fear that the imperial negative might be misused
    C. was that the federal prerogative should be exercised in disallowing state laws
    D. was that its primary function was to give temporary sanction to laws of immediate necessity
    E. was that its primary function was to prevent such injustices as "taxation without representation"

5. Madison believed that

    A. the congressional veto would not be abused
    B. the royal prerogative ought to have some form of check to correct misapplications
    C. the review of state legislation by the federal government ought to remain subject to a higher veto
    D. the imperial veto had not been misused
    E. utility rather than freedom is the criterion for governmental institutions

6. Jefferson believed that

    A. the congressional veto would interfere with states' rights
    B. Madison's proposal smacked of imperialism
    C. the veto of state legislation was outside the limits of the federal prerogative
    D. the British System would be harmful if applied in the United States
    E. an imperial veto should include the disallowance of all legislation leading to discord

7. Madison's MAIN principle was that

    A. the national interest is more important than the interests of any one state
    B. the national government should have compulsive power over the states
    C. the king can do no wrong
    D. the United States should follow the English pattern of government
    E. the veto power of the royal governor should be included in the federal prerogative

8. Madison thought of the states as 8.____
    A. emanations of the federal government
    B. comparable to provinces of a colonial empire
    C. incapable of creating sound legislation
    D. having no rights specifically delegated to them
    E. incapable of applying judicial review of their legislation

9. Which of the following is the BEST argument which could be made against Madison's 9.____
proposition?
    A. The United States has no king.
    B. The federal government is an entity outside the jurisdiction of the states.
    C. Each state has local problems concerning which representatives from other states are not equipped to pass judgment.
    D. The federal prerogative had been misused in the past.
    E. It provides no means of dealing with stubborn localism.

KEY (CORRECT ANSWERS)

1. B   5. A
2. E   6. D
3. D   7. B
4. C   8. B
        9. C

TEST 4

DIRECTIONS: Each question or incomplete statement is followed by several suggested answers or completions. Select the one that BEST answers the question or completes the statement. PRINT THE LETTER OF THE CORRECT ANSWER IN THE SPACE AT THE RIGHT.

PASSAGE

The nucleus of its population is the local businessmen, whose interests constitute the municipal policy and control its municipal administration. These local businessmen are such as the local bankers, merchants of many kinds and degrees, real estate promoters, local lawyers, local clergymen...The businessmen, who take up the local traffic in merchandising, litigation, church enterprise and the like, commonly begin with some share in the real estate speculation. This affords a common bond and a common ground of pecuniary interest, which commonly masquerades under the name of local patriotism, public spirit, civic pride, and the like. This pretense of public spirit is so consistently maintained that most of these men come presently to believe in their own professions on that head. Pecuniary interest in local land values involves an interest in the continued growth of the town. Hence any creditable misrepresentation of the town's volume of business traffic, population, tributary farming community, or natural resources, is rated as serviceable to the common good. And any member of this business-like community will be rated as a meritorious citizen in proportion as he is serviceable to this joint pecuniary interest of these "influential citizens."

1. The tone of the paragraph is

    A. bitter
    B. didactic
    C. complaining
    D. satirical
    E. informative

2. The foundation for the "influential citizens" interest in their community is

    A. their control of the municipal administration
    B. their interests in trade and merchandising
    C. their natural feeling of civic pride
    D. a pretense of public spirit
    E. ownership of land for speculation

3. The "influential citizens" type of civic pride may be compared with the patriotism of believers in

    A. a balance of power in international diplomacy
    B. racial superiority
    C. laissez faire
    D. a high tariff
    E. dollar diplomacy

4. The IMPORTANT men in the town

    A. are consciously insincere in their local patriotism
    B. are drawn together for political reasons
    C. do not scruple to give their community a false boost
    D. regard strict economy as a necessary virtue
    E. are extremely jealous of their prestige

5. The writer considers that the influential men of the town 5.____

   A. are entirely hypocritical in their conception of their motives
   B. are blinded to facts by their patriotic spirit
   C. have deceived themselves into thinking they are altruistic
   D. look upon the welfare of their community as of paramount importance
   E. form a closed corporation devoted to the interests of the town

6. PROBABLY the author's own view of patriotism is that it 6.____

   A. should be a disinterested passion untinged by commercial motives
   B. is found only among the poorer classes
   C. is usually found in urban society
   D. grows out of a combination of the motives of selfinterest and altruism
   E. consists in the main of a feeling of local pride

KEY (CORRECT ANSWERS)

1.	B	4.	C
2.	E	5.	C
3.	E	6.	A

TEST 5

DIRECTIONS: Each question or incomplete statement is followed by several suggested answers or completions. Select the one that *BEST* answers the question or completes the statement. *PRINT THE LETTER OF THE CORRECT ANSWER IN THE SPACE AT THE RIGHT.*

PASSAGE

Negative thinking and lack of confidence in oneself or in the pupils are probably the greatest hindrances to inspirational teaching. Confronted with a new idea, one teacher will exclaim: "Oh, my children couldn't do that! They're too young." Another will mutter, "If I tried that stunt, the whole class would be in an uproar." Such are the self-justifications for mediocrity.

Here and there it is good to see a teacher take a bold step away from the humdrum approach. For example, Natalie Robinson Cole was given a class of fourth-year pupils who could hardly speak English. Yet in her book, THE ARTS IN THE CLASSROOM, she describes how she tried clay work, creative writing, interpretive dancing and many other exciting activities with them. Did her control of the class suffer? Were the results poor? Was morale adversely affected? The answer is *NO* on all three counts.

But someone may point out that what Mrs. Cole could do on the fourth-grade could not be done in the primary grades. Wrong again! The young child is more malleable than his older brother. Furthermore, his radiant heritage of originality has not been enveloped in clouds of self-consciousness. Given the proper encouragement, he will paint an interesting design on the easel, contribute a sparkling expression to the "class poem" as it takes shape on the blackboard, make a puppet speak his innermost thoughts, and react with sensitivity in scores of other ways.

All teachers on all grade levels need to think positively and act confidently. Of course, any departure from the commonplace must be buttressed by careful preparation, firm handling of the situation, and consistent attention to routines. Since these assets are within the reach of all teachers there should be no excuse for not putting some imagination into their work.

1. The central idea of the above passage is BEST conveyed by the

   A. first sentence in the first paragraph
   B. last sentence in the first paragraph
   C. first sentence in the second paragraph
   D. last sentence in the passage
   E. third sentence in the third paragraph

   1.___

2. If the concepts of this passage were to be expanded into a book, the one of the following titles which would be MOST suitable is

   A. THE ARTS IN THE CLASSROOM
   B. THE POWER OF POSITIVE THINKING
   C. THE HIDDEN PERSUADERS
   D. KIDS SAY THE DARNDEST THINGS
   E. ARMS AND THE MAN

   2.___

3. Of the following reasons for uninspired teaching, the one which is *NOT* given explicitly in the passage is

   A. negative thinking
   B. teachers' underestimation of pupils' ability or stability
   C. teachers' failure to broaden themselves culturally
   D. teachers' lack of self-assurance
   E. teachers' rationalizations

4. From reading the passage one can gather that Natalie R. Cole

   A. teaches in New York City
   B. has been married
   C. is an expert in art
   D. teaches in the primary grades
   E. is a specialist in child psychology

5. An activity for children in the primary grades which is NOT mentioned in the passage is

   A. creative expression
   B. art work
   C. puppetry
   D. constructing with blocks
   E. work on the blackboard

6. A basic asset of the inspirational teacher NOT mentioned in the passage is

   A. a pleasant, outgoing personality
   B. a firm hand
   C. a thorough, careful plan
   D. consistent attention to routines
   E. acting confidently

KEY (CORRECT ANSWERS)

1. A   4. B
2. B   5. D
3. C   6. A

TEST 6

DIRECTIONS: Each question or incomplete statement is followed by several suggested answers or completions. Select the one that *BEST* answers the question or completes the statement. *PRINT THE LETTER OF THE CORRECT ANSWER IN THE SPACE AT THE RIGHT.*

PASSAGE

Of all the areas of learning the most important is the development of attitudes. Emotional reactions as well as logical thought processes affect the behavior of most people. "The burnt child fears the fire" is one instance; another is the rise of despots like Hitler. Both these examples also point up the fact that attitudes stem from experience. In the one case the experience was direct and impressive; in the other it was indirect and cumulative. The Nazis were indoctrinated largely by the speeches they heard and the books they read.

The classroom teacher in the elementary school is in a strategic position to influence attitudes. This is true partly because children acquire attitudes from these adults whose word they respect. Another reason it is true is that pupils often delve somewhat deeply into a subject in school that has only been touched upon at home or has possibly never occurred to them before. To a child who had previously acquired little knowledge of Mexico, his teacher's method of handling such a unit would greatly affect his attitude toward Mexicans.

The media through which the teacher can develop wholesome attitudes are innumerable. Social studies (with special reference to races, creeds and nationalities), science, matters of health and safety, the very atmosphere of the classroom... these are a few of the fertile fields for the inculcation of proper emotional reactions.

However, when children come to school with undesirable attitudes, it is unwise for the teacher to attempt to change their feelings by cajoling or scolding them. She can achieve the proper effect by helping them obtain constructive experiences. To illustrate, firstgrade pupils afraid of policemen will probably alter their attitudes after a classroom chat with the neighborhood officer in which he explains how he protects them. In the same way, a class of older children can develop attitudes through discussion, research, outside reading and all-day trips.

Finally, a teacher must constantly evaluate her own attitude because her influence can be deleterious if she has personal prejudices. This is especially true in respect to controversial issues and questions on which children should be encouraged to reach their own decisions as a result of objective analysis of all the facts.

1. The central idea conveyed in the above passage is that

   A. attitudes affect our actions
   B. teachers play a significant role in developing or changing pupils' attitudes
   C. by their attitudes, teachers inadvertently affect pupils' attitudes
   D. attitudes can be changed by some classroom experiences
   E. attitudes are affected by experience

1.___

2. The author implies that

   A. children's attitudes often come from those of other children
   B. in some aspects of social studies a greater variety of methods can be used in the upper grades than in the lower grades
   C. the teacher should guide all discussions by revealing her own attitude
   D. people usually act on the basis of reasoning rather than on emotion
   E. parents' and teachers' attitudes are more often in harmony than in conflict

3. A statement NOT made or implied in the passage is that

   A. attitudes cannot easily be changed by rewards and lectures
   B. a child can develop in the classroom an attitude about the importance of brushing his teeth
   C. attitudes can be based on the learning of falsehoods
   D. the attitudes of children are influenced by all the adults in their environment
   E. the children should accept the teacher's judgment in controversial matters

4. The passage SPECIFICALLY states that

   A. teachers should always conceal their own attitudes
   B. whatever attitudes a child learns in school have already been introduced at home
   C. direct experiences are more valuable than indirect ones
   D. teachers can sometimes have an unwholesome influence on children
   E. it is unwise for the teacher to attempt to change children's attitudes

5. The first and fourth paragraphs have all the following points in common EXCEPT

   A. how reading affects attitudes
   B. the importance of experience in building attitudes
   C. how attitudes can be changed in the classroom
   D. how fear sometimes governs attitudes
   E. how differences in approach change attitudes

KEY (CORRECT ANSWERS)

1. B
2. B
3. D
4. D
5. C

TEST 7

DIRECTIONS: Each question or incomplete statement is followed by several suggested answers or completions. Select the one that BEST answers the question or completes the statement. PRINT THE LETTER OF THE CORRECT ANSWER IN THE SPACE AT THE RIGHT.

PASSAGE

The word geology refers to the study of the composition, structure, and history of the earth. The term is derived from the Latin, geologia. coined by Bishop Richard de Bury in 1473 to distinguish lawyers who study "earthy things" from theologians. It was first consistently used in its present sense in the latter part of the 17th century. The great mass of detail that constitutes geology is classified under a number of subdivisions which, in turn, depend upon the fundamental sciences, physics, chemistry and biology.

The principal subdivisions of geology are: mineralogy, petrology, structural geology, physiography (geomorphology), usually grouped under physical or dynamical geology; and paleontology, stratigraphy and paleogeography, grouped under historical geology. The term economic geology usually refers to the study of valuable mineral "ore" deposits, including coal and oil. The economic aspects of geology are, however, much more embracive, including many subjects associated with civil engineering, economic geography, and conservation. Some of the more important of these subjects are: meteorology, hydrology, agriculture, and seismology. Subjects which are also distinctly allied to geology are geophysics, geochemistry, and cosmogony.

1. The statement that geology treats of the history of the earth and its life, especially as recorded in the rocks, is

    A. contrary to the paragraph
    B. made in the paragraph
    C. neither made nor implied in the paragraph
    D. not made, but implied in the paragraph
    E. unclear from the passage

2. The statement that the principal branches or phases of geology are dynamical geology and historical geology are

    A. contrary to the paragraph
    B. made in the paragraph
    C. neither made nor implied in the paragraph
    D. not made, but implied in the paragraph
    E. unclear from the passage

3. The statement that mining geology is a subdivision of geophysics is

    A. contrary to the paragraph
    B. made in the paragraph
    C. neither made nor implied in the paragraph
    D. not made, but implied in the paragraph
    E. unclear from the passage

2 (#7)

4. The statement that the study of both the exterior of the earth and its inner constitution constitutes the fundamental subject matter of geology is

4.____

   A. contrary to the paragraph
   B. made in the paragraph
   C. neither made nor implied in the paragraph
   D. not made, but implied in the paragraph
   E. unclear from the passage

5. The statement that geology utilizes the principles of astronomy, zoology, and botany is

5.____

   A. contrary to the paragraph
   B. made in the paragraph
   C. neither made nor implied in the paragraph
   D. not made, but implied in the paragraph
   E. unclear from the passage

6. The statement that geology is synonymous with the study of the attributes of rocks, rock formation, or rock attributes is

6.____

   A. contrary to the paragraph
   B. made in the paragraph
   C. neither made nor implied in the paragraph
   D. not made, but implied in the paragraph
   E. unclear from the passage

KEY (CORRECT ANSWERS)

1.	D	4.	D
2.	B	5.	D
3.	C	6.	A

TEST 8

DIRECTIONS: Each question or incomplete statement is followed by several suggested answers or completions. Select the one that *BEST* answers the question or completes the statement. *PRINT THE LETTER OF THE CORRECT ANSWER IN THE SPACE AT THE RIGHT.*

PASSAGE

1   Schiller was the first to ring a change on this state of things
2   by addressing himself courageously to the entire population of his
3   country in all its social strata at one time. He was the great popularizer of our
4   theatre, and remained for almost a century the guiding
5   spirit of the German drama of which Schiller's matchless tragedies
6   are still by many people regarded as the surpassing manifestoes.
7   Schiller's position, while it demonstrates a whole people's gratitude
8   to those who respond to its desires, does not however furnish a
9   weapon of self-defense to the "popularizers" of drama, or rather its
10   diluters. Schiller's case rather proves that the power of popular
11   influence wrought upon a poet may be vastly inferior to the strength
12   that radiates from his own personality. Indeed, whereas the secret
13   of ephemeral power is only too often found in paltriness or mediocrity,
14   an influence of enduring force such as Schiller exerts on the Germans
15   can only emanate from a strong and self-assertive character. No poet
16   lives beyond his day who does not exceed the average in mental stature
17   or who, through a selfish sense of fear of the general, allows
18   himself to be ground down to the conventional size and shape.
19   Schiller, no less than Ibsen, forced his moral demands tyrannically
20   upon his contemporaries. And in the long run your moral despot, pro-
21   vided he be high-minded, vigorous, and able, has a better chance of
22   fame than the pliant time-server. However, there is a great difference
23   between the two cases. For quite apart from the striking dissimilarities
24   between the poets themselves, the public, through the
25   gradual growth of social organization, has become greatly altered.

1. Schiller's lasting popularity may be attributed to

    A. his meeting the desires of a whole people, not just a segment of the people
    B. his abiding by his inmost convictions
    C. his mediocrity and paltriness
    D. his courageous facing up to the problems of his day
    E. his ability to popularize the unknown

2. In the first line, "on this state of things" refers to

    A. romantic drama
    B. the French play of contrived construction
    C. drama directed to the rich and well-born
    D. the popularizers of the theatre of today
    E. the ruling class

3. In the second sentence from the last, "the two cases" refer to

    A. pliant time-server and moral despot
    B. the one who exceeds the average In mental stature and the one who allows himself to be ground down to conventional size
    C. the popularizer and the poet of enduring fame
    D. Ibsen and Schiller
    E. the man of character and the man of wealth

4. We may assume that the author

    A. is no believer in the democratic processes
    B. has no high opinions of the "compact majority"
    C. regards popularity with the people as a measure of enduring success
    D. is opposed to the aristocracy
    E. has no fixed opinions

5. A word used in an ambiguous sense (having two or more possible meanings) in this passage is

    A. "poet" (lines 11,15, 24)
    B. "power" (lines 10, 13)
    C. "people" (lines 6, 7)
    D. "popularizer" (lines 3, 9)
    E. "moral" (lines 19, 20)

KEY (CORRECT ANSWERS)

1. B
2. C
3. D
4. B
5. D

TEST 9

DIRECTIONS: Each question or incomplete statement is followed by several suggested answers or completions. Select the one that BEST answers the question or completes the statement. PRINT THE LETTER OF THE CORRECT ANSWER IN THE SPACE AT THE RIGHT.

PASSAGE

In one sense, of course, this is not a new insight: all our great social and philosophical thinkers have been keenly aware of the fact of individual differences. It has remained, however, for psychologists to give the insight scientific precision.

What all this adds up to is more than just a working body of information about this and that skill. It adds up to a basic recognition of one important factor in the maturing of the individual. If each individual has a certain uniqueness of power, his maturing will best be accomplished along the line of that power. To try to develop him along lines that go in directions contrary to that of his major strength is to condition him to defeat. Thus, the non-mechanical person who is arbitrarily thrust into a mechanical occupation cannot help but do his work poorly and reluctantly, with some deep part of himself in conscious or unconscious rebellion.

He may blame himself for the low level of his accomplishment or for his persistent discontent; but not all his self-berating, nor even all his efforts to become more competent by further training, can make up for the original aptitude-lack. Unless he discovers his aptitude-lack, he may be doomed to a lifetime of self-blame, with a consequent loss of self-confidence and a halting of his psychological growth.

Or he may take refuge in self-pity – finding reason to believe that his failure is due to one or another bad break, to the jealousy of a superior, to lack of sympathy and help at home, to an initial bad start, to a lack of appreciation of what he does. If he thus goes the way of self-pity, he is doomed to a lifetime of self-commiseration that makes sound growth impossible.

The characteristic of the mature person is that he affirms life. To affirm life he must be involved, heart and soul, in the process of living. Neither the person who feels himself a failure nor the person who consciously or unconsciously resents what life has done to him can feel his heart and soul engaged in the process of living. That experience is reserved for the person whose full powers are enlisted. This, then, is what this fourth insight signifies: to mature, the individual must know what his powers are and must make them competent for life.

1. It is the author's view that

   A. "all men are created equal"
   B. "each man in his life plays many parts"
   C. "all comes to him who waits"
   D. "no kernel of nourishing corn can come to one but through his toil bestowed on that plot of ground given to him to till...."
   E. "that is what it is not to be alive. To move about in a cloud of ignorance... to live with envy... in quiet despair... to feel oneself sunk into a common grey mass..."

1.___

2. Ignorance of this fourth insight

   A. may very likely cause one to take refuge in self pity or conscious or unconscious rebellion
   B. constitutes a failure to understand that each individual is different and must cultivate his special powers in socially rewarding ways
   C. is a major deterrent to a growth to maturity
   D. means unawareness of the fact that each must use all his energy and powers to the best of his ability to make him competent for life
   E. may becloud the use of scientific precision

3. Two possible maladjustments of a man thrust into a position he is unfitted for may be summed up in the phrase,

   A. conscious and unconscious rebellion
   B. guilt-feelings and scapegoating
   C. halting of psychological growth and blaming the "breaks"
   D. "Peccavi – I have sinned" and "all the world is made except thee and me and I am not so sure of thee"
   E. light and darkness

4. We will expect a person placed in a job he is unequal to, to

   A. strike out for himself as an entrepreneur
   B. display quick angers and fixed prejudices
   C. show a great love of life outside of his work
   D. engage in labor union activities
   E. join political and social movements

KEY (CORRECT ANSWERS)

1. D   3. B
2. B   4. B

TEST 10

DIRECTIONS: Each question or incomplete statement is followed by several suggested answers or completions. Select the one that *BEST* answers the question or completes the statement. *PRINT THE LETTER OF THE CORRECT ANSWER IN THE SPACE AT THE RIGHT.*

PASSAGE

1   "For the ease and pleasure of treading the old road, accepting
2   the fashions, the education, the religion of society, he takes the
3   cross of making his own, and, of course, the self-accusation, the
4   faint heart, the frequent uncertainty and loss of time, which are the
5   nettles and tangling vines in the way of the self-relying and self-
6   directed; and the state of virtual hositility in which he seems to
7   stand to society, and especially to educated society. For all this
8   loss and scorn, what offset? He is to find consolation in exercising
9   the highest functions of human nature. He is one who raises himself
10 from private consideration and breathes and lives on public and
11 illustrious thoughts. He is the world's eye. He is the world's
12 heart. He is to resist the vulgar prosperity that retrogrades ever
13 to barbarism, by preserving and communicating heroic sentiments,
14 noble biographies, melodious verse, and the conclusions of history.
15 Whatsoever oracles the human heart, in all emergencies, in all solemn
16 hours, has uttered as its commentary on the world of actions – these
17 he shall receive and impart. And whatsoever new verdict Reason from
18 her inviolable seat pronounces on the passing men and events of
19 today – this he shall hear and promulgate.
20   "These being his functions, it becomes him to feel all confidence
21 in himself, and to defer never to the popular cry. He and he only
22 knows the world. The world of any moment is the merest appearance.
23 Some great decorum, some fetish of a government, some ephemeral
24 trade, or war, or man, is cried up by half mankind and cried down by
25 the other half, as if all depended on this particular up or down.
26 The odds are that the whole question is not worth the poorest thought
27 which the scholar has lost in listening to the controversy. Let him
28 not quit his belief that a popgun is a popgun, though the ancient and
29 honorable of the earth affirm it to be the crack of doom. In silence,
30 in steadiness, in severe abstraction, let him hold by himself; add
31 observation to observation, patient of neglect, patient of reproach,
32 and bide his own time – happy enough if he can satisfy himself alone
33 that this day he has seen something truly. Success treads on every
34 right step. For the instinct is sure, that prompts him to tell his
35 brother what he thinks. He then learns that in going down into the
36 secrets of his own mind he has descended into the secrets of all
37 minds. He learns that he who has mastered any law in his private
38 thoughts, is master to the extent of all translated. The poet, in
39 utter solitude remembering his spontaneous thoughts and recording
40 them, is found to have recorded that which men in crowded cities
41 find true for them also. The orator distrusts at first the fitness

```
42  of his frank confessions, his want of knowledge of the persons he
43  addresses, until he finds that he is the complement of his hearers—
44  that they drink his words because he fulfills for them their own
45  nature; the deeper he delves into his privatest, secretest presentiment,
46  to his wonder he finds this is the most acceptable, most public, and
47  universally true. The people delight in it; the better part of every
48  man feels. This is my music; this is myself."
```

1. It is a frequent criticism of the scholar that he lives by himself, in an "ivory tower," remote from the problems and business of the world. Which of these below constitutes the *BEST* refutation by the writer of the passage to the criticism here noted?

    A. The world's concern being ephemeral, the scholar does well to renounce them and the world.
    B. The scholar lives in the past to interpret the present.
    C. The scholar at his truest is the spokesman of the people.
    D. The scholar is not concerned with the world's doing because he is not selfish and therefore not engrossed in matters of importance to himself and neighbors.
    E. The scholar's academic researches of today are the businessman's practical products of tomorrow.

2. The scholar's road is rough, according to the passage. Which of these is his GREATEST difficulty?

    A. He must renounce religion.
    B. He must pioneer new approaches.
    C. He must express scorn for, and hostility to, society.
    D. He is uncertain of his course.
    E. There is a pleasure in the main-traveled roads in education, religion, and all social fashions.

3. When the writer speaks of the "world's eye" and the "world's heart" he means

    A. the same thing
    B. culture and conscience
    C. culture and wisdom
    D. a scanning of all the world's geography and a deep sympathy for every living thing
    E. mind and love

4. By the phrase, "nettles and tangling vines," the author PROBABLY refers to

    A. "self-accusation" and "loss of time"
    B. "faint heart" and "self accusation"
    C. "the slings and arrows of outrageous fortune"
    D. a general term for the difficulties of a scholar's life
    E. "self-accusation" and "uncertainty"

3 (#10)

5. The various ideas in the passage are BEST summarized in which of these groups?   5.___
    1. (a) truth versus society
       (b) the scholar and books
       (c) the world and the scholar
    2. (a) the ease of living traditionally
       (b) the glory of a scholar's life
       (c) true knowledge versus trivia
    3. (a) the hardships of the scholar
       (b) the scholar's function
       (c) the scholar's justifications for disregarding the world's business

    A. 1 and 3 together
    B. 3 only
    C. 1 and 2 together
    D. 1 only
    E. 1, 2, and 3 together

6. "seems to stand" (lines 6 and 7) means   6.___

    A. is
    B. gives the false impression of being
    C. ends probably in becoming
    D. is seen to be
    E. the quicksands of time

7. "public and illustrious thoughts" (lines 10 and 11) means   7.___

    A. what the people think
    B. thoughts for the good of mankind
    C. thoughts in the open
    D. thoughts transmitted by the people
    E. the conclusions of history

KEY (CORRECT ANSWERS)

1. C   5. B
2. B   6. B
3. C   7. B
4. E

READING COMPREHENSION
UNDERSTANDING AND INTERPRETING
WRITTEN MATERIAL

EXAMINATION SECTION

TEST 1

DIRECTIONS: Each question or incomplete statement is followed by several suggested answers or completions. Select the one that BEST answers the question or completes the statement. *PRINT THE LETTER OF THE CORRECT ANSWER IN THE SPACE AT THE RIGHT.*

    In its current application to art, the term *"primitive"* is as vague and unspecific as the term "heathen" is in its application to religion. A heathen sect is simply one which is not affiliated with one or another of three or four organized systems of theology. Similarly, a primitive art is one which flourishes outside the small number of cultures which we have chosen to designate as civilizations. Such arts differ vastly and it is correspondingly difficult to generalize about them. Any statements which will hold true for such diverse aesthetic experiences as the pictographs of the Australians, the woven designs of the Peruvians, and the abstract sculptures of the African tribes must be of the broadest and simplest sort. Moreover, the problem is complicated by the meaning attached to the term "primitive" in its other uses. It stands for something simple, undeveloped, and, by implication, ancestral to more evolved forms. Its application to arts and cultures other than our own is an unfortunate heritage from the nineteenth-century scientists who laid the foundations of anthropology. Elated by the newly enunciated doctrines of evolution, these students saw all cultures as stages in a single line of development and assigned them to places in this series on the simple basis of the degree to which they differed from European culture, which was blandly assumed to be the final and perfect flower of the evolutionary process. This idea has long since been abandoned by anthropologists, but before its demise it diffused to other social sciences and became a part of the general body of popular misinformation. It still tinges a great deal of the thought and writing about the arts of non-European peoples and has been responsible for many misunderstandings.

1. The MAIN purpose of the passage is to
    A. explain the various definitions of the term "primitive"
    B. show that the term "primitive" can be applied validly to art
    C. compare the use of the term "primitive" to the use of the term "heathen"
    D. deprecate the use of the term "primitive" as applied to art
    E. show that "primitive" arts vary greatly among themselves

2. The nineteenth-century scientists believed that the theory of evolution
    A. could be applied to the development of culture
    B. was demonstrated in all social sciences
    C. was substantiated by the diversity of "primitive" art
    D. could be applied only to European culture
    E. disproved the idea that some arts are more "primitive" than others

1.____

2.____

3. With which of the following would the author agree?
   A. The term "primitive" is used only by the misinformed.
   B. "Primitive" arts may be as highly developed as "civilized" arts.
   C. The arts of a culture often indicated how advanced that culture was.
   D. Australian, Peruvian, and African tribal arts are much like the ancestral forms from which European art evolved.
   E. A simple culture is likely to have a simple art.

4. According to the author, many misunderstandings have been caused by the belief that
   A. most cultures are fundamentally different
   B. inferior works of art in any culture are "primitive" art
   C. "primitive" arts are diverse
   D. non-European arts are diverse
   E. European civilization is the final product of the evolutionary process

KEY (CORRECT ANSWERS)

1. D
2. A
3. B
4. E

TEST 2

DIRECTIONS: Each question or incomplete statement is followed by several suggested answers or completions. Select the one that BEST answers the question or completes the statement. *PRINT THE LETTER OF THE CORRECT ANSWER IN THE SPACE AT THE RIGHT.*

    One of the ways the intellectual *avant-garde* affects the technical intelligentsia is through the medium of art, and art is, if only implicitly, a critique of experience. The turning upon itself of modern culture in the forms of the new visual art, the utilization of the detritus of daily experience to mock that experience, constitutes a mode of social criticism. Pop art, it is true, does not go beyond the surface of the visual and tactile experience of an industrial (and a commercialized) culture. Dwelling on the surface, it allows its consumers to mock the elements of their daily life, without abandoning it. Indeed, the consumption of art in the organized market for leisure serves at times to encapsulate the social criticism of the *avant-garde*. However, the recent engagement of writers, artists, and theater people in contemporary issues suggests that this sort of containment may have begun to reach its limits.
    In an atmosphere in which the intellectually dominant group insists on the contradictions inherent in daily experience, the technical intelligentsia will find it difficult to remain unconscious of those contradictions. The technical intelligentsia have until now avoided contradictions by accepting large rewards for their expertise. As expertise becomes increasingly difficult to distinguish from ordinary service on the one hand, and merges on the other with the change of the social environment, the technical intelligentsia's psychic security may be jeopardized. Rendering of labor services casts it back into spiritual proletarianization; a challenge to the social control exercised by elites, who use the technical intelligentsia's labor power, pushes it forward to social criticism and revolutionary politics. That these are matters, for the moment, of primarily spiritual import does not diminish their ultimate political significance. A psychological precondition for radical action is usually far more important than an "objectively" revolutionary situation—whatever that may be.
    The chances for a radicalization of the technical intelligentsia, thus extending the student revolt cannot be even approximated. I believe I have shown there is a chance.

1. It may be *inferred* that the technical intelligentsia are
   I. The executives and employers in society
   II. Critics of *avant-garde* art
   III. Highly skilled technical workers
   The CORRECT answer is:
   A. I only   B. I and III   C. I, II, and III
   D. III only   E. I and II

2. The engagement of the intellectual *avant-garde* in contemporary issues
   A. indicates that people tire of questioning the contradictions inherent in day-to-day living
   B. indicates that the technical intelligentsia are close to the point where they will rebel against the *avant-garde*
   C. could cause a challenge to the social control of the elites
   D. could cause the public to become more leisure-oriented
   E. could cause an increase in the consumption of art in the organized market for leisure services

3. The *possible* effect of the intellectual *avant-garde* on the technical intelligentsia is that
   A. the intellectual *avant-garde* makes the technical intelligentsia conscious of society's contradictions
   B. rapid curtailment of large rewards for expertise will result
   C. it may cause a strong likelihood of a radicalization of the technical intelligentsia
   D. the *avant-garde* will replace the employment of the technical intelligentsia in contemporary issues
   E. the rendering of labor services will be eliminated

4. If it is assumed that the technical intelligentsia becomes fully aware of the contradictions of modern life, it is the author's position that
   A. revolution will result
   B. the technical intelligentsia may refuse to perform manual labor
   C. the technical intelligentsia will be pushed forward to social criticism and revolutionary politics
   D. the technical intelligentsia will experience some psychic dislocation
   E. ordinary service will replace technical expertise

5. According to the author,
   A. the state of mind of a particular group may have more influence on its action than the effect of environmental factors
   B. the influence of art will often cause social upheaval
   C. matters of primarily spiritual import necessarily lack political significance
   D. the detritus of day-to-day living should be mocked by the intellectual *avant-garde*
   E. the technical intelligentsia can only protect their psychic security by self-expression through art

6. With which of the following would the author agree?
   I. As contradictions are less contained, the psychic security of all members of the working class would be jeopardized.
   II. The expertise of the technical intelligentsia evolved from the ownership and management of property.
   III. The technical intelligentsia is not accustomed to rendering labor services.
   The CORRECT answer is:
   A. I only   B. III only   C. I and III
   D. II only   E. None of the above

7. The MAIN purpose of the passage is to
   A. discuss the influence of the *avant-garde* art form on the expertise of the technical intelligentsia
   B. discuss the effect of the intellectual *avant-garde* on the working classes
   C. discuss the social significance of the technical intelligentsia
   D. discuss the possible effects of the de-encapsulation of *avant-garde* social criticism
   E. point out that before a change psychological preconditions are first established

KEY (CORRECT ANSWERS)

1. D
2. C
3. A
4. D
5. A
6. B
7. D

TEST 3

DIRECTIONS: Each question or incomplete statement is followed by several suggested answers or completions. Select the one that BEST answers the question or completes the statement. *PRINT THE LETTER OF THE CORRECT ANSWER IN THE SPACE AT THE RIGHT.*

Turbulent flow over a boundary is a complex phenomenon for which there is no really complete theory even in simple laboratory cases. Nevertheless, a great deal of experimental data has been collected on flows over solid surfaces, both in the laboratory and in nature, so that, from an engineering point of view at least, the situation is fairly well understood. The force exerted on a surface varies with the roughness of that surface and approximately with the square of the wind speed at some fixed height above it. A wind of 10 meters per second (about 20 knots, or 22 miles per hour) measured at a height of 10 meters will produce a force of some 30 tons per square kilometer on a field of mown grass or of about 70 tons per square kilometer on a ripe wheat field. On a really smooth surface, such as glass, the force is only about 10 tons per square kilometer.

When the wind blows over water, the whole thing is much more complicated. The roughness of the water is not a given characteristic of the surface but depends on the wind itself. Not only that, the elements that constitute the roughness—the waves—themselves move more or less in the direction of the wind. Recent evidence indicates that a large portion of the momentum transferred from the air into the water goes into waves rather than directly into making currents in the water; only as the waves break, or otherwise lose energy, does their momentum become available to generate currents, or produce Ekman layers. Waves carry a substantial amount of both energy and momentum (typically about as much as is carried by the wind in a layer about one wavelength thick), and so the wave-generation process is far from negligible. A violently wavy surface belies its appearance by acting, as far as the wind is concerned, as though it were very smooth. At 10 meters per second, recent measurements seem to agree, the force on the surface is quite a lot less than the force over mown grass and scarcely more than it is over glass; some observations in light winds of two or three meters per second indicate that the force on the wavy surface is less than it is on a surface as smooth as glass. In some way the motion of the waves seems to modify the airflow so that air slips over the surface even more freely than it would without the waves. This seems not to be the case at higher wind speeds, above about five meters per second, but the force remains strikingly low compared with that over other natural surfaces.

One serious deficiency is the fact that there are no direct observations at all in those important cases in which the wind speed is greater than about 12 meters per second and has had time and fetch (the distance over water) enough to raise substantial waves. The few indirect studies indicate that the apparent roughness of the surface increases somewhat under high-wind conditions, so that the force on the surface increases rather more rapidly than as the square of the wind speed.

Assuming that the force increases at least as the square of the wind speed, it is evident that high-wind conditions produce effects far more important than their frequency of occurrence would suggest. Five hours of 60-knot storm winds will put more momentum into the water than a week of 10-knot breezes. If it should be shown that, for high winds, the force on the surface increases appreciably more rapidly than as the square of the wind speed, then the transfer of momentum to the ocean will turn out to be dominated by what happens during the occasional storm rather than by the long-term average winds.

1. According to the passage, several hours of storm winds (60 miles per hour) over the ocean would
   A. be similar to the force exerted by light winds for several hours over glass
   B. create an ocean roughness which reduces the force exerted by the high winds
   C. have proved to be more significant in creating ocean momentum than light winds
   D. create a force not greater than 6 times the force of a 10-mile-per-hour wind
   E. eventually affect ocean current

2. According to the passage, a rough-like ocean surface
   A. is independent of the force of the wind
   B. has the same force exerted against it by high and light winds
   C. is more likely to have been caused by a storm than by continuous light winds
   D. nearly always allows airflow to be modified so as to cause the force of the wind to be less than on glass
   E. is a condition under which the approximate square of wind speed can never be an accurate figure in measuring the wind force

3. The author indicates that, where a hurricane is followed by light winds of 10 meters per second or less,
   I. ocean current will be unaffected by the light winds
   II. ocean current will be more affected by the hurricane winds than the following light winds
   III. the force of the light winds on the ocean would be less than that exerted on a wheat field.
   The CORRECT combination is:
   A. I only   B. III only   C. II and III   D. I and III   E. II only

4. The MAIN purpose of the passage is to discuss
   A. oceanic momentum and current
   B. turbulent flow of wind over water
   C. wind blowing over water as related to causing tidal flow
   D. the significance of high wind conditions on ocean momentum
   E. experiments in wind force

5. The author would be incorrect in concluding that the transfer of momentum to the ocean is dominated by the occasional storm if
   A. air momentum went directly into making ocean current
   B. high speed winds slipped over waves as easily as low speed winds
   C. waves did not move in the direction of wind
   D. the force exerted on a wheat field was the same as on mown grass
   E. the force of wind under normal conditions increased as the square of wind speed

6. A wind of 10 meters per second measured at a height of 10 meters will produce   6.____
   a force close to 30 tons per square mile on which of the following?
   A. Unmown grass
   B. Mown grass
   C. Glass
   D. Water
   E. A football field

KEY (CORRECT ANSWERS)

1. E
2. C
3. C
4. B
5. B
6. A

TEST 4

DIRECTIONS: Each question or incomplete statement is followed by several suggested answers or completions. Select the one that BEST answers the question or completes the statement. *PRINT THE LETTER OF THE CORRECT ANSWER IN THE SPACE AT THE RIGHT.*

Political scientists, as practitioners of a negligibly formalized discipline, tend to be accommodating to formulations and suggested techniques developed in related behavioral sciences. They even tend, on occasion, to speak of psychology, sociology, and anthropology as "hard core sciences." Such a characterization seems hardly justified. The disposition to uncritically adopt into political science non-indigenous sociological and general systems concepts tends, at times, to involve little more than the adoption of a specific, and sometimes barbarous, academic vocabulary which is used to redescribe reasonably well-confirmed or intuitively-grasped low-order empirical generalizations.

At its worst, what results in such instances is a runic explanation, a redescription in a singular language style, i.e., no explanation at all. At their best, functional accounts as they are found in the contemporary literature provide explanation sketches, the type of elliptical explanation characteristic of historical and psychoanalytic accounts. For each such account there is an indeterminate number of equally plausible ones, the consequence of either the complexity of the subject matter, differing perspectives, conceptual vagueness, the variety of sometimes mutually exclusive empirical or quasi-empirical generalizations employed, or syntactical obscurity, or all of them together.

Functional explanations have been most reliable in biology and physiology (where they originated) and in the analysis of servo mechanical and cybernetic systems (to which they have been effectively extended). In these areas we possess a well-standardized body of lawlike generalizations. Neither sociology nor political science has as yet the same resource of well-confirmed lawlike statements. Certainly sociology has few more than political science. What passes for functional explanation in sociology is all too frequently parasitic upon suggestive analogy and metaphor, trafficking on our familiarity with goal-directed systems.

What is advanced as "theory" in sociology is frequently a non-theoretic effort at classification or "codification," the search for an analytic conceptual schema which provides a typology or a classificatory system serviceable for convenient storage and ready retrieval of independently established empirical regularities. That such a schema takes on a hierarchic and deductive character, imparting to the collection of propositions a *prima facie* theoretical appearance, may mean no more than that the terms employed in the high-order propositions are so vague that they can accommodate almost any inference and consequently can be made to any conceivable state of affairs.

1. The author *implies* that, when the political scientist is at his best, his explanations   1.____
   A. are essentially a retelling of events
   B. only then form the basis of an organized discipline
   C. plausibly account for past occurrences
   D. are prophetic of future events
   E. are confirmed principles forming part of the political scientist's theory

2. With which of the following would the author probably agree?
   I. Because of an abundance of reasonable explanations for past conduct, there is the possibility of contending schools within the field of political science developing.
   II. Political science is largely devoid of predictive power.
   III. Political science has very few verified axioms.
   The CORRECT answer is:
   A. III only   B. I and III   C. I and II   D. I, II, III   E. I only

3. The passage *implies* that many sociological theories
   A. are capable of being widely applied to various situations
   B. do not even appear to be superficially theoretical in appearance
   C. contrast with those of political science in that there are many more confirmed lawlike statements
   D. are derived from deep analysis and exhaustive research
   E. appear theoretical but are really very well proved

4. The author's thesis would be UNSUPPORTABLE if
   A. the theories of the political scientist possessed predictive power
   B. political science did not consist of redescription
   C. political scientists were not restricted to "hard core sciences"
   D. political science consisted of a body of theories capable of application to any situation
   E. none of the above

5. The author believe that sociology as a "hard core science," contains reliable and functional explanations
   A. is never more than a compilation of conceptual schema
   B. is in nearly every respect unlike political science
   C. is a discipline which allows for varied inferences to be drawn from its general propositions
   D. is a science indigenous *prima facie* theoretical appearance containing very little codification posing as theory

KEY (CORRECT ANSWERS)

1. C
2. D
3. A
4. A
5. D

TEST 5

DIRECTIONS: Each question or incomplete statement is followed by several suggested answers or completions. Select the one that BEST answers the question or completes the statement. *PRINT THE LETTER OF THE CORRECT ANSWER IN THE SPACE AT THE RIGHT.*

James' own prefaces to his works were devoted to structural composition and analytics and his approach in those prefaces has only recently begun to be understood. One of his contemporary critics, with the purest intention to blame, wrote what might be recognized today as sophisticated praise when he spoke of the later James as "an impassioned geometer" and remarked that "what interested him was not the figures but their relations, the relations which alone make pawns significant." James's explanations of his works often are so bereft of interpretation as to make some of our own austere defenses against interpretation seem almost embarrassingly rich with psychological meanings. They offer, with a kind of brazen unselfconsciousness, an astonishingly artificial, even mechanical view of novelistic invention. It's not merely that James asserts the importance of technique; more radically, he tends to discuss character and situation almost entirely as functions of technical ingenuities. The very elements in a Jamesian story which may strike us as requiring the most explanation are presented by James either as a *solution* to a problem of compositional harmony or else as the *donnee* about which it would be irrelevant to ask any questions at all.

James should constantly be referred to as a model of structuralist criticism. He consistently redirects our attention from the referential aspect of a work of art (its extensions into "reality") to its own structural coherence as the principal source of inspiration.

What is most interesting about James's structurally functional view of character is that a certain devaluation of what we ordinarily think of as psychological interest is perfectly consistent with an attempt to portray reality. It's as if he came to feel that a kind of autonomous geometric pattern, in which the parts appeal for their value to nothing but their contributive place in the essentially abstract pattern, is the artist's most successful representation of life. Thus, he could perhaps even think that verisimilitude—a word he liked—has less to do with the probability of the events the novelist describes than with those processes, deeply characteristic of life, by which he creates sense and coherence from any event. The only faithful picture of life in art is not in the choice of a significant subject (James always argues against the pseudo realistic prejudice), but rather in the illustration of sense- or design-making processes. James proves the novel's connection with life by deprecating its derivation from life; and it's when he is most abstractly articulating the growth of a structure that James is almost most successfully defending the mimetic function of art (and of criticism). His deceptively banal position that only execution matters means most profoundly that verisimilitude, properly considered, is the grace and the truth of a formal unity.

1. The author suggests that James, in explanations of his own art,   1.____
   A. was not bound by formalistic strictures but concentrated on verisimilitude
   B. was deeply psychological and concentrated on personal insight
   C. felt that his art had a one-to-one connection with reality
   D. was basically mechanical and concentrated on geometrical form
   E. was event-and-character-oriented rather than technique-oriented

2. The passage indicates that James's method of approaching reality was
   A. that objective reality did not exist and was patterned only by the mind
   B. that formalism and pattern were excellent means of approaching reality
   C. not to concentrate on specific events but rather on character development
   D. that the only objective reality is the psychological processes of the mind
   E. that in reality events occur which are not structured but rather as random occurrences

3. The MAIN purpose of the paragraph is to
   A. indicate that James's own approach to his work is only now beginning to be understood
   B. deprecate the geometrical approach towards the novel
   C. question whether James's novels were related to reality
   D. indicate that James felt that society itself could be seen as a geometric structure
   E. discuss James's explanation of his works

4. In discussing his own works, James
   I. talks of people and events as a function of technique to the exclusion of all else
   II. is quick to emphasize the referential aspect of the work
   III. felt that verisimilitude could be derived not from character but rather from the ordering of event
   The CORRECT answer is:
   A. I only   B. II only   C. III only   D. I and III   E. I and II

5. The author
   A. *approves* of James's explanations of his work but *disapproves* his lack of discussion into the psychological makings of his characters
   B. *disapproves* of James's explanation of his own work and his lack of discussion into the psychological makings of his characters
   C. *approves* of James's explanations of his works in terms of structure as being well-rated to life
   D. *disapproves* of James's explanation of his works in terms of structure as lacking verisimilitude
   E. *approves* of James's explanation of his works because of the significance of the subjects chosen

6. The following is NOT true of James's explanation of his own works: He
   A. did not explain intriguing elements of a story except as part of a geometric whole
   B. felt the artist could represent life by its patterns rather than its events
   C. defended the imitative function of art by detailing the growth of a structure
   D. attempted to give the reader insight into the psychology of his characters by insuring that his explanation followed a strict geometrical pattern
   E. was able to devalue psychological interest and yet be consistent with an attempt to truly represent life

7. James believed it to be *essential* to
   A. carefully choose a subject which would lend itself to processes by which sense and cohesion is achieved
   B. defend the mimetic function of art by emphasizing verisimilitude
   C. emphasize the manner in which different facets of a story could fit together
   D. explain character in order to achieve literary harmony
   E. be artificial and unconcerned with representing life

7.____

KEY (CORRECT ANSWERS)

1.	D	5.	C
2.	B	6.	D
3.	E	7.	C
4.	C		

TEST 6

DIRECTIONS: Each question or incomplete statement is followed by several suggested answers or completions. Select the one that BEST answers the question or completes the statement. *PRINT THE LETTER OF THE CORRECT ANSWER IN THE SPACE AT THE RIGHT.*

    The popular image of the city as it is now is a place of decay, crime, of fouled streets, and of people who are poor or foreign or odd. But what is the image of the city of the future? In the plans for the huge redevelopment projects to come, we are being shown a new image of the city. Gone are the dirt and the noise—and the variety and the excitement and the spirit. That it is an ideal makes it all the worse; these bleak new utopias are not bleak because they have to be; they are the concrete manifestation—and how literally—of a deep, and at times arrogant, misunderstanding of the function of the city.
    Being made up of human beings, the city is, of course, a wonderfully resilient institution. Already it has reasserted itself as an industrial and business center. Not so many years ago, there was much talk of decentralizing to campus-like offices, and a wholesale exodus of business to the countryside seemed imminent. But a business pastoral is something of a contradiction in terms, and for the simple reason that the city is the center of things because it is a center, the suburban heresy never came off. Many industrial campuses have been built, but the overwhelming proportion of new office building has been taking place in the big cities. But the rebuilding of downtown is not enough; a city deserted at night by its leading citizens is only half a city. If it is to continue as the dominant cultural force in American life, the city must have a core of people to support its theatres and museums, its shops and its restaurants—even a Bohemia of sorts can be of help. For it is the people who like living in the city who make it an attraction to the visitors who don't. It is the city dwellers who support its style; without them there is nothing to come downtown to.
    The cities have a magnificent opportunity. There are definite signs of a small but significant move back from suburbia. There is also evidence that many people who will be moving to suburbia would prefer to stay in the city—and it would not take too much more in amenities to make them stay. But the cities seem on the verge of muffing their opportunity and muffing it for generations to come. In a striking failure to apply marketing principles and an even more striking failure of aesthetics, the cities are freezing on a design for living ideally calculated to keep everybody in suburbia. These vast, barracks-like superblocks are not designed for people who like cities, but for people who have no other choice. A few imaginative architects and planners have shown that redeveloped blocks don't have to be repellent to make money, but so far their ideas have had little effect. The institutional approach is dominant, and, unless the assumptions embalmed in it are re-examined, the city is going to be turned into a gigantic bore.

1. The author would NOT be pleased with
   A. a crowded, varied, stimulating city
   B. the dedication of new funds to the reconstruction of the cities
   C. a more detailed understanding of the poor
   D. the elimination of assumptions which do not reflect the function of the city
   E. the adoption of a laissez-faire attitude by those in charge of redevelopment

2. "The rebuilding of downtown" (1st sentence, 3rd paragraph) refers to
   A. huge redevelopment projects to come
   B. the application of marketing and aesthetic principles to rejuvenating the city
   C. keeping the city as the center of business
   D. attracting a core of people to support the city's functions
   E. the doing away with barracks-like structures

3. According to the author the city, in order to better itself, *must*
   A. increase its downtown population
   B. attract an interested core of people to support its cultural institutions
   C. adhere to an institutional approach rather than be satisfied with the status quo
   D. erect campus-like business complexes
   E. establish an ideal for orderly future growth

4. The MAIN purpose of the passage is to
   A. show that the present people inhabiting the city do not make the city viable
   B. discuss the types of construction which should and should not take place in the city's future
   C. indicate that imaginative architects and planners have shown that redeveloped areas don't have to be ugly to make money
   D. discuss the human element in the city
   E. point out the lack of understanding by many city planners of the city's functions

5. The author's thesis would be LESS supportable if
   I. city planners presently understood that stereotyped reconstruction is doomed to ultimate failure
   II. the institutional approach referred to in the passage was based upon assumptions which took into account the function of the city
   III. there were signs that a shift back to the city from suburbia were occurring
   The CORRECT answer is:
   A. II only   B. II and III   C. I and II   D. I only   E. III only

KEY (CORRECT ANSWERS)

1. D
2. C
3. B
4. E
5. C

TEST 7

DIRECTIONS: Each question or incomplete statement is followed by several suggested answers or completions. Select the one that BEST answers the question or completes the statement. *PRINT THE LETTER OF THE CORRECT ANSWER IN THE SPACE AT THE RIGHT.*

     In estimating the child's conceptions of the world, the first question is to decide whether external reality is as external and objective for the child as it is for adults. In other words, can the child distinguish the self from the external world? So long as the child supposes that everyone necessarily thinks like himself, he will not spontaneously seek to convince others, nor to accept common truths, nor, above all, to prove or test his opinions. If his logic lacks exactitude and objectivity, it is because the social impulses of mature years are counteracted by an innate egocentricity. In studying the child's thought, not in this case in relation to others but to things, one is faced at the outset with the analogous problem of the child's capacity to dissociate thought from self in order to form an objective conception of reality.
     The child, like the uncultured adult, appears exclusively concerned with things. He is indifferent to the life of thought and the originality of individual points of view escape him. His earliest interests, his first games, his drawings are all concerned solely with the imitation of what is. In short, the child's thought has every appearance of being exclusively realistic.
     But realism is of two types, or, rather, objectivity must be distinguished from realism. Objectivity consists in so fully realizing the countless intrusions of the self in everyday thought and the countless illusions which result—illusions of sense, language, point of view, value, etc.—that the preliminary step to every judgment is the effort to exclude the intrusive self. Realism, on the contrary, consists in ignoring the existence of self and thence regarding one's own perspective as immediately objective and absolute. Realism is thus anthropocentric illusion, finality—in short, all those illusions which teem in the history of science. So long as thought has not become conscious of self, it is a prey to perpetual confusions between objective and subjective, between the real and the ostensible; it values the entire content of consciousness on a single lane in which ostensible realities and the unconscious interventions of the self are inextricably mixed. It is thus not futile, but, on the contrary, indispensable to establish clearly and before all else the boundary the child draws between the self and the external world.

1. The result of a child's not learning that others think differently than he does is that   1.____
   A. the child will not be able to function as an adult
   B. when the child has matured, he will be innately egocentric
   C. when the child has matured, his reasoning will be poor
   D. upon maturity, the child will not be able to distinguish thought from objects
   E. upon maturity, the child will not be able to make non-ego-influenced value

2. Objectivity is the ability to   2.____
   A. distinguish ego from the external world
   B. dissociate oneself from others
   C. realize that others have a different point of view
   D. dissociate ego from thought

3. When thought is not conscious of self,
    A. one is able to draw the correct conclusions from his perceptions
    B. the apparent may not be distinguishable from the actual
    C. conscious thought may not be distinguishable from the unconscious
    D. the ego may influence the actual
    E. ontogeny recapitulates phylogony

4. The MAIN purpose of the passage is to
    A. argue that the child should be made to realize that others may not think like he does
    B. estimate the child's conception of the world
    C. explain the importance of distinguishing the mind from external objects
    D. emphasize the importance of non-ego-influenced perspective
    E. show how the child establishes the boundary between himself and the external world

5. The author *implies* that, if an adult is to think logically,
    A. his reasoning, as he matures, must be tempered by other viewpoints
    B. he must be able to distinguish one physical object from another
    C. he must be exclusively concerned with thought instead of things
    D. he must be able to perceive reality without the intrusions of the self
    E. he must not value the content of consciousness on a single plain

6. Realism, according to the passage, is
    A. the realization of the countless intrusions of the self
    B. final and complete objectivity
    C. a desire to be truly objective and absolute
    D. the ability to be perceptive and discerning
    E. none of the above

7. The child who is exclusively concerned with things
    A. thinks only objectivity
    B. is concerned with imitating the things he sees
    C. must learn to distinguish between realism and anthropomorphism
    D. has no innate ability
    E. will, through interaction with others, often prove his opinions

KEY (CORRECT ANSWERS)

1.	C	5.	A
2.	E	6.	E
3.	B	7.	B
4.	D		

TEST 8

DIRECTIONS: Each question or incomplete statement is followed by several suggested answers or completions. Select the one that BEST answers the question or completes the statement. *PRINT THE LETTER OF THE CORRECT ANSWER IN THE SPACE AT THE RIGHT.*

Democracy is not logically antipathetic to most doctrines of natural rights, fundamental or higher law, individual rights, or any similar ideals—but merely asks citizens to take note of the fact that the preservation of these rights rests with the majority, in political processes, and does not depend upon a legal or constitutional Maginot line. Democracy may, then, be supported by believers in individual rights providing they believe that rights—or any transcendental ends—are likely to be better safeguarded under such a system. Support for democracy on such instrumental ground may, of course, lead to the dilemma of loyalty to the system vs. loyalty to a natural right—but the same kind of dilemma may arise for anyone, over any prized value, and in any political system, and is insoluble in advance.

There is unanimous agreement that—as a matter of fact and law, not of conjecture—no single right can be realized, except at the expense of other rights and claims. For that reason their absolute status, in some philosophic sense, is of little political relevance. Political policies involve much more than very generable principles or rights. The main error of the older natural rights school was not that it had an absolute right, but that it had too many absolute rights. There must be compromise, and, as any compromise destroys the claim to absoluteness, the natural outcome of experience was the repudiation of all of them. And now the name of "natural right" can only creep into sight with the reassuring placard, "changing content guaranteed." Nor is it at all easy to see how many doctrine of inalienable, natural, individual rights can be reconciled with a political doctrine of common consent—except in an anarchist society, or one of saints. Every natural right ever put forward, and the lists are elusive and capricious, is every day invaded by governments, in the public interest and with widespread public approval.

To talk of relatively attainable justice or rights in politics is not to plump for a moral relativism—in the sense that all values are equally good. But while values may be objective, the specific value judgments and policies are inevitably relative to a context, and is only when a judgment divorces context from general principle that it looks like moral relativism. Neither, of course, does the fact of moral diversity invalidate all moral rules.

Any political system, then, deals only with relatively attainable rights, as with relative justice and freedoms. Hence, we may differ in given instances on specific policies, despite agreement on broad basic principles such as a right or a moral "ought"; and, per contra, we may agree on specific policies while differing on fundamental principles or long-range objectives or natural rights. Politics and through politics, law and policies, give these rights—and moral principles—their substance and limits. There is no getting away from the political nature of this or any other prescriptive ideal in a free society.

1. With which of the following would the author *agree*? 1._____
   A. Natural and individual rights can exist at all only under a democracy.
   B. While natural rights may exist, they are only relatively attainable.
   C. Civil disobedience has no place in a democracy where natural rights have no philosophic relevance.
   D. Utilitarianism, which draws its criteria from the happiness and welfare of individuals, cannot logically be a goal of a democratic state.
   E. Some natural rights should never be compromised for the sake of political policy.

2. It can be *inferred* that a democratic form of government
   A. can be supported by natural rightists as the best pragmatic method of achieving their aims
   B. is a form of government wherein fundamental or higher law is irrelevant
   C. will inn time repudiate all inalienable rights
   D. forces a rejection of moral absolutism
   E. will soon exist in undeveloped areas of the world

3. The MAIN purpose of the passage is to
   A. discuss natural rights doctrine
   B. compare and contrast democracy to individual rights
   C. discuss the reconciliation of a doctrine of inalienable natural rights with a political system
   D. discuss the safeguarding of natural rights in a democratic society
   E. indicate that moral relativism is antipathetic to democracy

4. The author indicates that natural rights
   I. are sometimes difficult to define
   II. are easily definable but at times unreconcilable with a system of government predicated upon majority rule
   III. form a basis for moral relativism
   The CORRECT answer is:
   A. I only   B. II only   C. I and II   D. III only   E. II and III

5. The fact that any political system deals with relatively attainable rights
   A. shows that all values are equally good or bad
   B. is cause for divorcing political reality from moral rules
   C. shows that the list of natural rights is elusive and capricious
   D. is inconsistent with the author's thesis
   E. does not necessarily mean that natural rights do not exist

6. The passage indicates that an important conflict which can exist in a democracy is the rights of competing groups, i.e., labor versus management
   A. adherence to the democratic process versus non-democratic actions by government
   B. difficulty in choosing between two effective compromises
   C. adherence to the democratic process versus the desire to support a specific right
   D. difficulty in reconciling conflict by natural rights

KEY (CORRECT ANSWERS)

1. B   4. A
2. A   5. E
3. C   6. D

READING COMPREHENSION
UNDERSTANDING AND INTERPRETING WRITTEN MATERIAL
EXAMINATION SECTION
TEST 1

DIRECTIONS: Each question or incomplete statement is followed by several suggested answers or completions. Select the one that BEST answers the question or completes the statement. *PRINT THE LETTER OF THE CORRECT ANSWER IN THE SPACE AT THE RIGHT.*

1. The question *Who shall now teach Hegel?* is shorthand for the question *Who is going to teach this genre—all the so-called Continental philosophers?* The obvious answer to this question is *Whoever cares to study them.* This is also the right answer, but we can only accept it whole heartedly if we clear away a set of factitious questions. On such question is: *Are these Continental philosophers really philosophers?* Analytic philosophers, because they identify philosophical ability with argumentative skill and notice that there is nothing they would consider an argument in the bulk of Heidegger or Foucault, suggest that these must be people who tried to be philosophers and failed-incompetent philosophers. This is as silly as saying that Plato was an incompetent sophist, or that a hedgehog is an incompetent fox. Hegel knew what he thought about philosophers who imitated the method and style of mathematics. He thought they were incompetent. These reciprocal charges of incompetence do nobody any good. We should just drop the questions of what philosophy really is or who really counts as a philosopher.
Which sentence is BEST supported by the above paragraph?
   A. The study of Hegel's philosophy is less popular now than in the past.
   B. Philosophers must stop questioning the competence of other philosophers.
   C. Philosophers should try to be as tolerant as Foucault and Heidegger.
   D. Analytic philosophers tend to be more argumentative than other philosophers.

1.____

2. It is an interesting question: the ease with which organizations of different kinds at different stages in their history can continue to function with ineffectual leadership at the top, or even function without a clear system of authority. Certainly, the success of some experiments in worker self-management shows that bosses are not always necessary, as some contemporary Marxists argue. Indeed, sometimes the function of those at the top is merely to symbolize organizational accountability, especially in dealing with outside authorities, but not to guide the actions of those within the organization. A vice president of a large insurance company remarked to us that *Presidents are powerless; no one needs them. They should all be sent off to do public relations for the company.* While this is clearly a self-serving statement from someone next in line to command, it does give meaning to the expression *being kicked upstairs.* According to the author,

2.____

A. organizations function very smoothly without bosses
B. the function of those at the top is sometimes only to symbolize organizational accountability
C. company presidents are often inept at guiding the actions of those within the organization
D. presidents of companies have less power than one might assume they have

3. The goal of a problem is a terminal expression one wishes to cause to exist in the world of the problem. There are two types of goals: specified goal expressions in proof problems and incompletely specified goal expressions in find problems. For example, consider the problem of finding the value of X, given the expression 4X+5 = 17. In this problem, one can regard the goal expression as being of the form X = _____, the goal expression. The goal expression in a find problem of this type is incompletely specified. If the goal expression were specified completely—for example, X = 3—then the problem would be a proof problem, with only the sequence of operations to be determined in order to solve the problem. Of course, if one were not guaranteed that the goal expression X = 3 was true, then the terminal goal expression should really be considered to be incompletely specified—something like the statement X = 3 (true or false).
According to the preceding paragraph,
A. the goal of the equation 4X+5 = 17 is true, not false
B. if the goal expression was specified as being equal to 3, the problem 4X+5 = 17 would be a proof problem
C. if the sequence of operations of the problem given in the paragraph is predetermined, the goal of the problem becomes one of terminal expression, or the number 17
D. X cannot be found unless X is converted into a proof problem

3.____

4. We have human psychology and animal psychology, but no plant psychology. Why? Because we believe that plants have no perceptions or intentions. Some plants exhibit *behavior* and have been credited with *habits*. If you stroke the midrib of the compound leaf of a sensitive plant, the leaflets close. The sunflower changes with the diurnal changes in the source of light. The lowest animals have not much more complicated forms of behavior. The sea anemone traps and digests the small creatures that the water brings to it; the pitcher plant does the same thing and even more, for it presents a cup of liquid that attracts insects, instead of letting the surrounding medium drift them into its trap. Here as everywhere in nature where the great, general classes of living things diverge, the lines between them are not perfectly clear. A sponge is an animal; the pitcher plant is a flowering plant, but it comes nearer to *feeding itself* than the animal. Yet the fact is that we credit all animals, and only the animals, with some degree of feeling.
Of the following, the MAIN idea expressed in the above paragraph is:
A. The classification of plants has been based on beliefs about their capacity to perceive and feel
B. Many plants are more evolved than species considered animals

4.____

C. The lines that divide the classes of living things are never clear.
D. The abilities and qualities of plants are undervalued.

5. Quantitative indexes are not necessarily adequate measures of true economic significance or influence. But even the raw quantitative data speak loudly of the importance of the new transnationalized economy. The United Nations estimated value added in this new sector of the world economy at $500 billion in 2001, mounting to one-fifth of total GNP of the non-socialist world and exceeding the GNP of any one other country except the United States. Furthermore, all observers agree that the share of this sector in the world economy is growing rapidly. At least since 1980, its annual rate of growth has been high and remarkably steady at 10 percent compared to 4 percent for noninternationalized output in the Western developed countries.
One spokesman for the new system franklin envisages that within a generation some 400 to 500 multinational corporations will own close to two-thirds of the world's fixed assets.
According to the author, all of the following are true EXCEPT
   A. Quantitative indexes are not necessarily adequate measures of actual economic influence.
   B. The transnational sector of the world economy is growing rapidly.
   C. Since 1980, the rate of growth of transnationals has been 10% compared to 4% for internationalized output in the Western developed countries.
   D. Continued growth for multinational corporations is likely.

5.____

6. A bill may be sent to the Governor when it has passed both houses. During the session, he is given ten days to act on bills that reach his desk. Bills sent to him within ten days of the end of the session must be acted on within 30 days after the last day of the session. If the Governor takes no action on a ten day bill, it automatically becomes a law. If he disapproves or vetoes a ten day bill, it can become law only if it is re-passed by two-thirds vote in each house. If he fails to act on a 30 day bill, the bill is said to have received a *pocket veto*. It is customary for the Governor to act, however, on all bills submitted to him, and give his reason in writing for approving or disapproving important legislation.
According to the above paragraph, all of the following are true EXCEPT:
   A. Bills sent to the Governor in the last ten days of the session must be acted on within thirty days after the last day of the session,
   B. If the Governor takes no action on a 10 day bill, it is said to have received a *pocket veto*.
   C. It is customary for the Governor to act on all bills submitted to him.
   D. If the Governor vetoes a ten day bill, it can become law only if passed by a two-thirds vote of the Legislature.

6.____

7. It is particularly when I see a child going through the mechanical process of manipulating numbers without any intuitive sense of what it is all about that I recall the lines of Lewis Carroll: *Reeling and Writhing, of course, to begin with…and then the different branches of Arithmetic-Ambition, Distraction, Uglification, and Derision.* Or, as Max Beberman has put it, much more gently: *Somewhat related to the notion of discovery in teaching is our insistence that*

7.____

the student become aware of a concept before a name has been assigned to the concept. I am quite aware that the issue of intuitive understanding is a very live one among teachers of mathematics, and even a casual reading of the yearbook of the National Council of Teachers of Mathematics makes it clear that they are also very mindful of the gap that exists between proclaiming the importance of such understanding and actually producing it in the classroom.
The MAIN idea expressed in the above paragraph is:
   A. Math teachers are concerned about the difficulties inherent in producing an understanding of mathematics in their students.
   B. It is important that an intuitive sense in approaching math problems be developed, rather than relying on rote, mechanical learning.
   C. Mathematics, by its very nature, encourages rote, mechanical learning.
   D. Lewis Carroll was absolutely correct in his assessment of the true nature of mathematics.

8. Heisenberg's *Principle of Uncertainty*, which states that events at the atomic level cannot be observed with certainty, can be compared to this: In the world of everyday experience, we can observe any phenomenon and measure its properties without influencing the phenomenon in question to any significant extent. To be sure, if we try to measure the temperature of a demitasse with a bathtub thermometer, the instrument will absorb so much heat from the coffee that it will change the coffee's temperature substantially. But with a small chemical thermometer, we may get a sufficiently accurate reading. We can measure the temperature of a living cell with a miniature thermometer, which has almost negligible heat capacity. But in the atomic world, we can never overlook the disturbance caused by the introduction of the measuring apparatus.
Which sentence is BEST supported by the above paragraph?
   A. There is little we do not alter by the mere act of observation.
   B. It is always a good idea to use the smallest measuring device possible.
   C. Chemical thermometers are more accurate than bathtub thermometers.
   D. It is not possible to observe events at the atomic level and be sure that the same events would occur if we were not observing them.

8.____

9. It is a myth that American workers are pricing themselves out of the market, relative to workers in other industrialized countries of the world. The wages of American manufacturing workers increased at a slower rate in the 1990s than those of workers in other major western countries. In terms of American dollars, between 1990 and 2000, hourly compensation increased 489 percent in Japan and 464 percent in Germany, compared to 128 percent in the United States. Even though these countries experienced faster productivity growth, their unit labor costs still rose faster than in the United States, according to the Bureau of Labor Statistics. During the 1990s, unit labor costs rose 192 percent in Japan, 252 percent in Germany, and only 78 percent in the United States.
According to the above passage,
   A. unit labor costs in the 1990s were higher in Japan than they were in Germany or the United States
   B. the wages of American workers need to be increased to be consistent with other countries

9.____

C. American worker are more productive than Japanese or German workers
D. the wages of American workers in manufacturing increased at a slower rate in the 1990s than the wages of workers in Japan or Germany

10. No people have invented more ways to enjoy life than the Chinese, perhaps to balance floods, famines, warlords, and other ills of fate. The clang of gongs, clashing cymbals, and beating of drums sound through their long history. No month is without fairs and theatricals when streets are hung with fantasies of painted lanterns and crowded with *carriages that flow like water, horses like roaming dragons*. Night skies are illumined by firecrackers—a Chinese invention—bursting in the form of flowerpots, peonies, fiery devils. The ways of pleasure are myriad. Music plays in the air through bamboo whistles of different pitch tied to the wings of circling pigeons. To skim a frozen lake in an ice sleigh with a group of friends on a day when the sun is warm is rapture, like *moving in a cup of jade*. What more delightful than the ancient festival called *Half an Immortal*, when everyone from palace officials to the common man took a ride on a swing? When high in the air, one felt like an Immortal, when back to earth once again human—no more than to be for an instant a god.
According to the above passage,
    A. if the Chinese hadn't had so many misfortunes, they wouldn't have created so many pleasurable past times
    B. the Chinese invented flowerpots
    C. every month the Chinese have fairs and theatricals
    D. pigeons are required to play the game *Half an Immortal*

10.____

11. In our century, instead, poor Diphilus is lost in the crowd of his peers. We flood one another. No one recognizes him as he loads his basket in the supermarket. What grevious fits of melancholy have I not suffered in one of our larger urban bookstores, gazing at the hundreds, thousands, tens of thousands of books on shelve and tables? And what are they to the hundreds of thousands, the millions that stand in our research libraries? More books than Noah saw raindrops. How many readers will read a given one of them—mine, yours—in their lifetimes? And how will it be in the distant future? Incomprehensible masses of books, Pelion upon Ossa, hordes of books, each piteously calling for attention, respect, love, in competition with the vast disgorgements of the past and with one another in the present. Neither is it at all helpful that books can even now be reduced to the size of a postage stamp. Avanti! Place the Bible on a pinhead! Crowding more books into small spaces does not cram more books into our heads. Here I come to the sticking point that unnerves the modern Diphilus. The number of books a person can read in a given time is, roughly speaking, a historical constant. It does not change significantly even when the number of books available for reading does. Constants are pitted against variables to confound both writer and reader.
Of the following, the MAIN idea in this passage is:
    A. It is difficult to attain immortality because so many books are being published.
    B. Too many books are being published, so fewer people are reading them.

11.____

C. Because so many books are being published, the quality of the writing is poorer.
D. Because so many books are available, but only a fixed amount of time to read them, frustration results for both the reader and the writer.

12. Until recently, consciousness of sexual harassment has been low. But workers have become aware of it as more women have arrived at levels of authority in the workplace, feminist groups have focused attention on rape and other violence against women, and students have felt freer to report perceived abuse by professors. In the last 5 years, studies have shown that sexual misconduct at the workplace is a big problem. For example, in a recently published survey of federal employees, 42% of 694,000 women and 15% of 1,168,000 men said they had experienced some form of harassment. According to the author,   12.____
    A. the awareness of sexual harassment at the workplace is increasing
    B. the incidence of harassment is higher in universities than workplaces
    C. sexual harassment is much more commonly experienced by women than men
    D. it is rare for men to experience sexual harassment

Questions 13-17.

DIRECTIONS: Questions 13 through 17 are to be answered SOLELY on the basis of the following paragraph.

Since discounts are in common use in the commercial world and apply to purchases made by government agencies as well as business firms, it is essential that individuals in both public and private employment who prepare bills, check invoices, prepare payment vouchers, or write checks to pay bills have an understanding of the terms used. These include cash or time discount, trade discount, and discount series. A cash or time discount offers a reduction in price to the buyer for the prompt payment of the bill and is usually expressed as a percentage with a time requirement, stated in days, within which the bill must be paid in order to earn the discount. An example would be 3/10, meaning a 3% discount may be applied to the bill if the payment is forwarded to the vendor within 10 days. On an invoice, the cash discount terms are usually followed by the net terms, which is the time in days allowed for ordinary payment of the bill. Thus, 3/10, Net 30 means that full payment is expected in thirty days if the cash discount of 3% is not taken for having paid the bill within ten days. When the expression Terms Net Cash is listed on a bill, it means that no deduction for early payment is allowed. A trade discount is normally applied to list prices by a manufacturer to show the actual price to retailers so that they may know their cost and determine markups that will allow them to operate competitively and at a profit. A trade discount is applied by the seller to the list price and is independent of a cash or time discount. Discounts may also be used by manufacturers to adjust prices charged to retailers without changing list prices. This is usually done by series discounting and is expressed as a series of percentages. To compute a series discount, such as 40%, 20%, 10%, first apply the 40% discount to the list price, then apply the 20% discount to the remainder, and finally apply the 10% discount to the second remainder.

13. According to the above paragraph, trade discounts are 13.____
    A. applied by the buyer
    B. independent of cash discounts
    C. restricted to cash sales
    D. used to secure rapid payment of bills

14. According to the above paragraph, if the sales terms 5/10, Net 60 appear on a 14.____
    bill in the amount of $100 dated December 5 and the buyer submits his
    payment on December 15, his PROPER payment should be
    A. $60   B. $90   C. $95   D. $100

15. According to the above paragraph, if a manufacturer gives a trade discount of 15.____
    40% for an item with a list price of $250 and the terms are Net Cash, the price
    a retail merchant is required to pay for this item is
    A. $250   B. $210   C. $150   D. $100

16. According to the above paragraph, a series discount of 25%, 20%, 10% applied 16.____
    to a list price of $200 results in an ACTUAL price to the buyer of
    A. $88   B. $90   C. $108   D. $110

17. According to the above paragraph, if a manufacturer gives a trade discount 17.____
    of 50% and the terms are 6/10, Net 30, the cost to a retail merchant of an item
    with a list price of $500 and for which he takes the time discount, is
    A. $220   B. $235   C. $240   D. $250

Questions 18-22.

DIRECTIONS: Questions 18 through 22 are to be answered SOLELY on the basis of the
             following paragraph.

   The city may issue its own bonds or it may purchase bonds as an investment. Bonds may
be issued in various denominations, and the face value of the bond is its par value. Before
purchasing a bond, the investor desires to know the rate of income that the investment will yield.
In computing the yield on a bond, it is assumed that the investor will keep the bond until the date
of maturity, except for callable bonds which are not considered in this paragraph. To compute
exact yield is a complicated mathematical problem, and scientifically prepared tables are
generally used to avoid such computation. However, the approximate yield can be computed
much more easily. In computing approximate yield, the accrued interest on the date of
purchase should be ignored, because the buyer who pays accrued interest to the seller receives
it again at the next interest date. Bonds bought at a premium (which cost more) yield a lower
rate of income than the same bonds bought at par (face value), and bonds bought at a discount
(which cost less) yield a higher rate of income than the same bonds bought at par.

18. An investor bought a $10,000 city bond paying 6% interest. 18.____
    Which of the following purchase prices would indicate that the bond was
    bought at a PREMIUM?
    A. $9,000   B. $9,400   C. $10,000   D. $10,600

19. During the year, a particular $10,000 bond paying 74% sold at fluctuating prices.
   Which of the following prices would indicate that the bond was bought at a DISCOUNT?
   A. $9,800   B. $10,000   C. $10,200   D. $10,750

20. A certain group of bonds was sold in denominations of $5,000, $10,000, $20,000 and $50,000.
   In the following list of four purchase prices, which one is MOST likely to represent a bond sold at par value?
   A. $10,500   B. $20,000   C. $22,000   D. $49,000

21. When computing the approximate yield on a bond, it is DESIRABLE to
   A. assume the bond was purchased at par
   B. consult scientifically prepared tables
   C. ignore accrued interest on the date of purchase
   D. wait until the bond reaches maturity

22. Which of the following is MOST likely to be an exception to the information provided in the above paragraph? Bonds
   A. purchased at a premium   B. sold at par
   C. sold before maturity   D. which are callable

Questions 23-25

DIRECTIONS: Questions 23 through 25 are to be answered SOLELY on the basis of the following paragraph.

There is one bad habit of drivers that often causes chain collisions at traffic lights. It is the habit of keeping one foot poised over the accelerator pedal, ready to step on the gas the instant the light turns green. A driver who is watching the light, instead of watching the cars in front of him, may *jump the gun* and bump the car in front of him, and this car in turn may bump the next car. If a driver is resting his foot on the accelerator, his foot will be slammed down when he bumps into the car ahead. This makes the collision worse and makes it very likely that cars further ahead in the line are going to get involved in a series of violent bumps.

23. Which of the following conclusions can MOST reasonably drawn from the information given in the above paragraph?
   A. American drivers have a great many bad driving habits.
   B. Drivers should step on the gas as soon as the light turns green.
   C. A driver with poor driving habits should be arrested and fined.
   D. A driver should not rest his foot on the accelerator when the car is stopped for a traffic light.

24. From the information given in the above paragraph, a reader should be able to tell that a chain collision may be defined as a collision
   A. caused by bad driving habits at traffic lights
   B. in which one car hits another, this second car hits a third car, and so on

C. caused by drivers who fail to use their accelerators
D. that takes place at an intersection where there is a traffic light

25. The above passage states that a driver who watches the light instead of paying attention to traffic may
    A. be involved in an accident
    B. end up in jail
    C. lose his license
    D. develop bad driving habits

KEY (CORRECT ANSWERS)

1.	B		11.	D
2.	B		12.	A
3.	B		13.	B
4.	A		14.	C
5.	C		15.	C
6.	B		16.	C
7.	B		17.	B
8.	D		18.	D
9.	D		19.	A
10.	C		20.	B

21. C
22. D
23. D
24. B
25. A

TEST 2

DIRECTIONS: Each question or incomplete statement is followed by several suggested answers or completions. Select the one that BEST answers the question or completes the statement. *PRINT THE LETTER OF THE CORRECT ANSWER IN THE SPACE AT THE RIGHT.*

Questions 1-4.

DIRECTIONS: Each of the statements in this section is followed by several labeled choices. In the space at the right, write the letter of the sentence which means MOST NEARLY what is stated or implied in the passage.

1. It may be said that the problem in adult education seems to be not the piling up of facts but practice in thinking.
   This statement means MOST NEARLY that
   A. educational methods for adults and young people should differ
   B. adults seem to think more than young people
   C. a well-educated adult is one who thinks but does not have a store of information
   D. adult education should stress ability to think

   1.____

2. Last year approximately 19,000 fatal accidents were sustained in industry. There were approximately 130 non-fatal injuries to each fatal injury.
   According to the above statement, the number of non-fatal accidents was
   A. 146,000   B. 190,000   C. 1,150,000   D. 2,500,000

   2.____

3. No employer expects his stenographer to be a walking encyclopedia, but it is not unreasonable for him to expect her to know where to look for necessary information on a variety of topics.
   The above statement means MOST NEARLY that the stenographer should
   A. be a college graduate
   B. be familiar with standard office reference books
   C. keep a scrapbook of all interesting happenings
   D. go to the library regularly

   3.____

4. For the United States, Canada has become the most important country in the world, yet there are few countries about which Americans know less. Canada is the third largest country in the world; only Russia and China are larger. The area of Canada is more than a quarter of the whole British Empire.
   According to the above statement, the
   A. British Empire is smaller than Russia or China
   B. territory of China is greater than that of Canada
   C. Americans know more about Canada than they do about China or Russia
   D. Canadian population is more than one-quarter the population of the British Empire

   4.____

Questions 5-8.

DIRECTIONS: Questions 5 through 8 are to be answered SOLELY on the basis of the following paragraph.

A few people who live in old tenements have had the bad habit of throwing garbage out of their windows, especially if there is an empty lot near their building. Sometimes the garbage is food; sometimes the garbage is half-empty soda cans. Sometimes the garbage is a little bit of both mixed together. These people just don't care about keeping the lot clean.

5. The above paragraph states that throwing garbage out of windows is a
   A. bad habit
   B. dangerous thing to do
   C. good thing to do
   D. good way to feed rats

6. According to the above paragraph, an empty lot next to an old tenement is sometimes used as a place to
   A. hold local gang meetings
   B. play ball
   C. throw garbage
   D. walk dogs

7. According to the above paragraph, which of the following throw garbage out of their windows?
   A. Nobody
   B. Everybody
   C. Most people
   D. Some people

8. According to the above paragraph, the kinds of garbage thrown out of windows are
   A. candy and cigarette butts
   B. food and half-empty soda cans
   C. fruit and vegetables
   D. rice and bread

Questions 9-12.

DIRECTIONS: Questions 9 through 12 are to be answered SOLELY on the basis of the following paragraph.

The game that is recognized all over the world as an all-American game is the game of baseball. As a matter of fact, baseball heroes like Joe DiMaggio, Willie Mays, and Babe Ruth were as famous in their day as movie stars Robert Redford, Paul Newman, and Clint Eastwood are now. All these men have had the experience of being mobbed by fans whenever they put in an appearance anywhere in the world. Such unusual popularity makes it possible for stars like these to earn at least as much money off the job as on the job. It didn't take manufacturers and advertising men long to discover that their sales of shaving lotion, for instance, increased when they got famous stars to advertise their product for them on radio and television.

9. According to the above paragraph, baseball is known everywhere as a(n) _____ game.
   A. all-American   B. fast   C. unusual   D. tough

10. According to the above paragraph, being so well known means that it is possible for people like Willie Mays and Babe Ruth to
    A. ask for anything and get it
    B. make as much money off the job as on it
    C. travel anywhere free of charge
    D. watch any game free of charge

10.____

11. According to the above paragraph, which of the following are known all over the world?
    A. Baseball heroes
    B. Advertising men
    C. Manufacturers
    D. Basketball heroes

11.____

12. According to the above paragraph, it is possible to sell much more shaving lotion on television and radio if
    A. the commercials are in color instead of black and white
    B. you can get a prize with each bottle of shaving lotion
    C. the shaving lotion makes you smell nicer than usual
    D. the shaving lotion is advertised by famous stars

12.____

Questions 13-15.

DIRECTIONS: Questions 13 through 15 are to be answered SOLELY on the basis of the following passage.

That music gives pleasure is axiomatic. Because this is so, the pleasures of music may seem a rather elementary subject for discussion. Yet the source of that pleasure, our musical instinct, is not at all elementary. It is, in fact, one of the prime puzzles of consciousness. Why is it that we are able to make sense out of these nerve signals so that we emerge from engulfment in the orderly presentation of sound stimuli as if we had lived through an image of life?

If music has impact for the mere listener, it follows that it will have much greater impact for those who sing it or play it themselves with proficiency. Any educated person in Elizabethan times was expected to read musical notation and take part in a madrigalsing. Passive listeners, numbered in the millions, are a comparatively recent innovation.

Everyone is aware that so-called serious music has made great strikes in general public acceptance in recent years, but the term itself still connotes something forbidding and hermetic to the mass audience. They attribute to the professional musician a kind of initiation into secrets that are forever hidden from the outsider. Nothing could be more misleading. We all listen to music, professionals, and non-professionals alike in the same sort of way, in a dumb sort of way, really, because simple or sophisticated music attracts all of us in the first instance, on the primordial level of sheer rhythmic and sonic appeal. Musicians are flattered, no doubt, by the deferential attitude of the layman in regard to what he imagines to be our secret understanding of music. But in all honesty, we musicians know that in the main we listen basically as others do, because music hits us with an immediacy that we recognize in the reactions of the most simple minded of music listeners.

13. A suitable title for the above passage would be
    A. HOW TO LISTEN TO MUSIC
    B. LEARNING MUSIC APPRECIATION
    C. THE PLEASURES OF MUSIC
    D. THE WORLD OF THE MUSICIAN

    13.____

14. The author implies that the passive listener is one who
    A. cannot read or play music
    B. does not appreciate serious music
    C. does not keep time to the music by hand or toe tapping
    D. will not attend a concert if he has to pay for the privilege

    14.____

15. The author of the above passage is apparently inconsistent when he discusses
    A. the distinction between the listener who pays for the privilege and the one who does not
    B. the historical development of musical forms
    C. the pleasures derived from music by the musician
    D. why it is that we listen to music

    15.____

Questions 16-18.

DIRECTIONS: Questions 16 through 18 are to be answered SOLELY on the basis of the following passage.

Who are the clerisy? They are people who like to read books. The use of a word so unusual, so out of fashion, can only be excused on the ground that it has no familiar synonym. The word is little known because what it describes has disappeared, though I do not believe is gone forever. The clerisy are those who read for pleasure, but not for idleness; who read for pastime, but not to kill time; who love books, but do not live by books.

Let us consider the actual business of reading—the interpretive act of getting the words off the age and into your head in the most effective way. The most effective way is not the quickest way of reading; and for those who think that speed is the greatest good, there are plenty of manuals on how to read a book which profess to tell how to strip off the husk and guzzle the milk, like a chimp attacking a coconut. Who among today's readers would whisk through a poem, eyes aflicker, and say that he had read it? The answer to that last question must unfortunately be: far too many. For reading is not respected for the art it is.

Doubtless there are philosophical terms for the attitude of mind of which nasty reading is one manifestation, but here let us call it end-gaining, for its victims put ends before means; they value not reading, but having read. In this, the end-gainers make mischief and spoil all they do; end-gaining is one of the curses of our nervously tense, intellectually flabby civilization. In reading, as in all arts, it is the means, and not the end, which gives delight and brings the true reward. Not straining forward toward the completion, but the pleasure of every page as it comes, is the secret of reading. We must desire to read a book, rather than to have read it. This change in attitude, so simple to describe, is by no means simple to achieve,, if one has lived the life of an end-gainer.

16. A suitable title for the above passage would be
    A. READING FOR ENLIGHTENMENT
    B. THE ART OF RAPID READING
    C. THE WELL-EDUCATED READER
    D. VALUES IN READING

17. The author does NOT believe that most people read because they
    A. are bored
    B. have nothing better to do
    C. love books
    D. wish to say that they have read certain books

18. The change in attitude to which the author refers in the last sentence of the above passage implies a change from
    A. dawdling while reading so that the reader can read a greater number of books
    B. reading light fiction to reading serious fiction and non-fiction
    C. reading works which do not amuse the reader
    D. skimming through a book to reading it with care

Questions 19-22.

DIRECTIONS: Questions 19 through 22 are to be answered SOLELY on the basis of the following passage.

Violence is not new to literature. The writings of Shakespeare and Cervantes are full of it. But those classic writers did not condone violence. They viewed it as a just retribution for sins against the divine order or as a sacrifice sanctioned by heroism. What is peculiar to the modern literature is violence for the sake of violence. Perhaps our reverence for life has been dulled by mass slaughter, though mass slaughter has not been exceptional in the history of mankind. What is exceptional is the boredom that now alternates with war. The basic emotion in peacetime has become a horror of emptiness: a fear of being alone, of having nothing to do, a neurosis whose symptoms are restlessness, an unmotivated and undirected rage, sinking at times into vapid listlessness. This neurotic syndrome is intensified by the prevailing sense of insecurity. The threat of atomic war has corrupted our faith in life itself.

This universal neurosis has developed with the progress of technology. It is the neurosis of men whose chief expenditure of energy is to pull a lever or push a button, of men who have ceased to make things with their hands. Such inactivity applies not only to muscles and nerves but to the creative processes that once engaged the mind. If one could contrast visually, by time-and-motion studies, the daily actions of an eighteenth-century carpenter with a twentieth-century machinist, the latter would appear as a <u>confined, repetitive clot</u>, the former as a free and even fantastic pattern. But the most significant contrast could not be visualized—the contrast between a mind suspended aimlessly above an autonomous movement and a mind consciously bent on the shaping of a material substance according to the persistent evidence of the senses.

19. A suitable title for the above passage would be
    A. INCREASING PRODUCTION BY MEANS OF SYSTEMATIZATION
    B. LACK OF A SENSE OF CREATIVENESS AND ITS CONSEQUENCE
    C. TECHNOLOGICAL ACHIEVEMENT IN MODERN SOCIETY
    D. WHAT CAN BE DONE ABOUT SENSELESS VIOLENCE

19.____

20. According to the author, Shakespeare treated violence as a
    A. basically sinful act not in keeping with religious thinking
    B. just punishment of transgressors against moral law
    C. means of achieving dramatic excitement
    D. solution to a problem provided no other solution was available

20.____

21. According to the author, boredom may lead to
    A. a greater interest in leisure-time activities
    B. chronic fatigue
    C. senseless anger
    D. the acceptance of a job which does not provide a sense of creativity

21.____

22. The underlined phrase refers to the
    A. hand movements made by the carpenter
    B. hand movements made by the machinist
    C. relative ignorance of the carpenter
    D. relative ignorance of the machinist

22.____

23. The concentration of women and female-headed families in the city is both cause and consequence of the city's fiscal woes. Women live in cities because it is easier and cheaper for them to do so, but because fewer women are employed, and those that are receive lower pay than men, they do not make the same contribution to the tax base that an equivalent population of men would. Concomitantly, they are more dependent on public resources, such as transportation and housing. For these reasons alone, urban finances would be improved by increasing women's employment opportunities and pay. Yet nothing in our current urban policy is specifically geared to improving women's financial resources. There are some proposed incentives to create more jobs, but not necessarily ones that would utilize the skills women currently have. The most innovative proposal was a tax credit for new hires from certain groups with particularly high unemployment rates. None of the seven targeted groups were women.
    Which sentence is BEST supported by the above paragraph?
    A. Innovative programs are rapidly improving conditions for seven targeted groups with traditionally high unemployment rates.
    B. The contribution of women to a city's tax base reflects their superior economic position.
    C. Improving the economic position of women who live in cities would help the financial conditions of the cities themselves.
    D. Most women in this country live in large cities.

23.____

24. None of this would be worth saying if Descartes had been right in positing a one-to-one correspondence between stimuli and sensations. But we know that nothing of the sort exists. The perception of a given color can be evoked by an infinite number of differently combined wavelengths. Conversely, a given stimulus can evoke a variety of sensations, the image of a duck in one recipient, the image of a rabbit in another. Nor are responses like these entirely innate. One can learn to discriminate colors or patterns which were indistinguishable prior to training. To an extent still unknown, the production of data from stimuli is a learned procedure. After the learning process, the same stimulus evokes a different datum. I conclude that, though data are the minimal elements of our individual experience, they need be shared responses to a given stimulus only within the membership of a relatively homogeneous community: educational, scientific, or linguistic.
Which sentence is BEST supported by the above paragraph?
    A. One stimulus can give rise to a number of different sensations.
    B. There is a one-to-one correspondence between stimuli and sensations.
    C. It is not possible to produce data from stimuli by using a learned procedure.
    D. It is not necessary for a group to be relatively homogeneous in order to share responses to stimuli.

25. Workers who want to move in the direction of participative structures will need to confront the issues of power and control. The process of change needs to be mutually shared by all involved, or the outcome will not be a really participative model. The demand for a structural redistribution of power is not sufficient to address the problem of change toward a humanistic, as against a technological, workplace. If we are to change our institutional arrangements from hierarchy to participation, particularly in our workplaces, we will need to look to transformations in ourselves as well. As long as we are imbued with the legitimacy of hierarchical authority, with the sovereignty of the status quo, we will never be able to generate the new and original forms that we seek. This means if we are to be equal to the task of reorganizing our workplaces, we need to think about how we can reeducate ourselves and become aware of our assumptions about the nature of our social life together. Unless the issue is approached in terms of these complexities, I fear that all the worker participation and quality of work life efforts will fail.
According to the above paragraph, which of the following is NOT true?
    A. Self-education concerning social roles must go hand in hand with workplace reorganization.
    B. The structural changing of the workplace, alone, will not bring about the necessary changes in the quality of work life.
    C. Individuals can easily overcome their attitudes towards hierarchical authority.
    D. Changing the quality of work life will require the participation of all involved.

KEY (CORRECT ANSWERS)

1.	D	11.	A
2.	D	12.	D
3.	B	13.	C
4.	B	14.	A
5.	A	15.	C
6.	C	16.	D
7.	D	17.	C
8.	B	18.	D
9.	A	19.	B
10.	B	20.	B

21. C
22. B
23. C
24. A
25. C

READING COMPREHENSION
UNDERSTANDING AND INTERPRETING WRITTEN MATERIAL
EXAMINATION SECTION
TEST 1

DIRECTIONS: Each question or incomplete statement is followed by several suggested answers or completions. Select the one that BEST answers the question or completes the statement. *PRINT THE LETTER OF THE CORRECT ANSWER IN THE SPACE AT THE RIGHT.*

Questions 1-4.

DIRECTIONS: Questions 1 through 4 are to be answered SOLELY on the basis of the following passage.

Those engaged in the exercise of First Amendment rights by pickets, marches, parades, and open-air assemblies are not exempted from obeying valid local traffic ordinances. In a recent pronouncement, Mr. Justice Baxter, speaking for the Supreme Court, wrote:

The rights of free speech and assembly, while fundamental to our democratic society, still do not mean that everyone with opinions or beliefs to express may address a group at any public place and at any time. The constitutional guarantee of liberty implies the existence of an organized society maintaining public order, without which liberty itself would be lost in the excesses of anarchy. The control of travel on the streets is a clear example of governmental responsibility to insure this necessary order. A restriction in that relation, designed to promote the public convenience in the interest of all, and not susceptible to abuses of discriminatory application, cannot be disregarded by the attempted exercise of some civil rights which, in other circumstances, would be entitled to protection. One would not be justified in ignoring the familiar red light because this was thought to be a means of social protest. Governmental authorities have the duty and responsibility to keep their streets open and available for movement. A group of demonstrators could not insist upon the right to cordon off a street, or entrance to a public or private building, and allow no one to pass who did not agree to listen to their exhortations.

1. Which of the following statements BEST reflects Mr. Justice Baxter's view of the relationship between liberty and public order?

    A. Public order cannot exist without liberty.
    B. Liberty cannot exist without public order.
    C. The existence of liberty undermines the existence of public order.
    D. The maintenance of public order insures the existence of liberty.

1._____

2. According to the above passage, local traffic ordinances result from

    A. governmental limitations on individual liberty
    B. governmental responsibility to insure public order
    C. majority rule as determined by democratic procedures
    D. restrictions on expression of dissent

2._____

3. The above passage suggests that government would be acting improperly if a local traffic ordinance

   A. was enforced in a discriminatory manner
   B. resulted in public inconvenience
   C. violated the right of free speech and assembly
   D. was not essential to public order

4. Of the following, the MOST appropriate title for the above passage is

   A. THE RIGHTS OF FREE SPEECH AND ASSEMBLY
   B. ENFORCEMENT OF LOCAL TRAFFIC ORDINANCES
   C. FIRST AMENDMENT RIGHTS AND LOCAL TRAFFIC ORDINANCES
   D. LIBERTY AND ANARCHY

Questions 5-8

DIRECTIONS: Questions 5 through 8 are to be answered SOLELY on the basis of the following passage

On November 8, 1976, the Supreme Court refused to block the payment of Medicaid funds for elective abortions. The Court's action means that a new Federal statute that bars the use of Federal funds for abortions unless abortion is necessary to save the life of the mother will not go into effect for many months, if at all.

A Federal District Court in Brooklyn ruled the following month that the statute was unconstitutional and ordered that Federal reimbursement for the costs of abortions continue on the same basis as reimbursements for the costs of pregnancy and childbirth-related services.

Technically, what the Court did today was to deny a request by Senator Howard Ramsdell and others for a stay blocking enforcement of the District Court order pending appeal. The Court's action was a victory for New York City. The City's Health and Hospitals Corporation initiated one of the two lawsuits challenging the new statute that led to the District Court's decision. The Corporation also opposed the request for a Supreme Court stay of that decision, telling the Court in a memorandum that a stay would subject the Corporation to a *grave and irreparable injury*.

5. According to the above passage, it would be CORRECT to state that the Health and Hospitals Corporation

   A. joined Senator Ramsdell in his request for a stay
   B. opposed the statute which limited reimbursement for the cost of abortions
   C. claimed that it would experience a loss if the District Court order was enforced
   D. appealed the District Court decision

6. The above passage indicates that the Supreme Court acted in DIRECT response to

   A. a lawsuit initiated by the Health and Hospitals Corporation
   B. a ruling by a Federal District Court
   C. a request for a stay
   D. the passage of a new Federal statute

7. According to the above passage, it would be CORRECT to state that the Supreme Court

   A. blocked enforcement of the District Court order
   B. refused a request for a stay to block enforcement of the Federal statute
   C. ruled that the new Federal statute was unconstitutional
   D. permitted payment of Federal funds for abortion to continue

8. Following are three statements concerning abortion that might be correct:
   I. Abortion costs are no longer to be Federally reimbursed on the same basis as those for pregnancy and childbirth
   II. Federal funds have not been available for abortions except to save the life of the mother
   III. Medicaid has paid for elective abortions in the past

   According to the passage above, which of the following CORRECTLY classifies the above statements into those that are true and those that are not true?

   A. I is true, but II and III are not.
   B. I and III are true, but II is not.
   C. I and II are true, but III is not.
   D. III is true, but I and II are not.

Questions 9-12.

DIRECTIONS: Questions 9 through 12 are to be answered SOLELY on the basis of the following passage.

A person may use physical force upon another person when and to the extent he reasonably believes such to be necessary to defend himself or a third person from what he reasonably believes to be the use or imminent use of unlawful physical force by such other person, unless (a) the latter's conduct was provoked by the actor himself with intent to cause physical injury to another person; or (b) the actor was the initial aggressor; or (c) the physical force involved is the product of a combat by agreement not specifically authorized by law.

A person may not use deadly physical force upon another person under the circumstances specified above unless (a) he reasonably believes that such other person is using or is about to use deadly physical force. Even in such case, however, the actor may not use deadly physical force if he knows he can, with complete safety, as to himself and others avoid the necessity of doing so by retreating; except that he is under no duty to retreat if he is in his dwelling and is not the initial aggressor; or (b) he reasonably believes that such other person is committing or attempting to commit a kidnapping, forcible rape, or forcible sodomy.

9. Jones and Smith, who have not met before, get into an argument in a tavern. Smith takes a punch at Jones, but misses. Jones then hits Smith on the chin with his fist. Smith falls to the floor and suffers minor injuries.
   According to the above passage, it would be CORRECT to state that _____ justified in using physical force.

   A. only Smith was
   B. only Jones was
   C. both Smith and Jones were
   D. neither Smith nor Jones was

10. While walking down the street, Brady observes Miller striking Mrs. Adams on the head with his fist in an attempt to steal her purse.
    According to the above passage, it would be CORRECT to state that Brady would

    A. not be justified in using deadly physical force against Miller since Brady can safely retreat
    B. be justified in using physical force against Miller but not deadly physical force
    C. not be justified in using physical force against Miller since Brady himself is not being attacked
    D. be justified in using deadly physical force

11. Winters is attacked from behind by Sharp, who attempts to beat up Winters with a blackjack. Winters disarms Sharp and succeeds in subduing him with a series of blows to the head. Sharp stops fighting and explains that he thought Winters was the person who had robbed his apartment a few minutes before, but now realizes his mistake.
    According to the above passage, it would be CORRECT to state that

    A. Winters was justified in using physical force on Sharp only to the extent necessary to defend himself
    B. Winters was not justified in using physical force on Sharp since Sharp's attack was provoked by what he believed to be Winters' behavior
    C. Sharp was justified in using physical force on Winters since he reasonably believed that Winters had unlawfully robbed him
    D. Winters was justified in using physical force on Sharp only because Sharp was acting mistakenly in attacking him

12. Roberts hears a noise in the cellar of his home, and, upon investigation, discovers an intruder, Welch. Welch moves towards Roberts in a threatening manner, thrusts his hand into a bulging pocket, and withdraws what appears to be a gun. Roberts thereupon strikes Welch over the head with a golf club. He then sees that the *gun* is a toy. Welch later dies of head injuries. According to the above passage, it would be CORRECT to state that Roberts was

    A. justified in using deadly physical force because he reasonably believed Welch was about to use deadly physical force
    B. not justified in using deadly physical force
    C. justified in using deadly physical force only because he did not provoke Welch's conduct
    D. justified in using deadly physical force only because he was not the initial aggressor

Questions 13-16.

DIRECTIONS: Questions 13 through 16 are to be answered SOLELY on the basis of the following passage.

From the beginning, the Supreme Court has supervised the fairness of trials conducted by the Federal government. But the Constitution, as originally drafted, gave the court no such general authority in state cases. The court's power to deal with state cases comes from the Fourteenth Amendment, which became part of the Constitution in 1868. The crucial provision forbids any state to *deprive any person of life, liberty, or property without due process of law.*

The guarantee of *due process* would seem, at the least, to require fair procedure in criminal trials. But curiously the Supreme Court did not speak on the question for many decades. During that time, however, the due process clause was interpreted to bar *unreasonable* state economic regulations, such as minimum wage laws.

In 1915, there came the case of Leo M. Frank, a Georgian convicted of murder in a trial that he contended was dominated by mob hysteria. Historians now agree that there was such hysteria, with overtones of anti-semitism.

The Supreme Court held that it could not look past the findings of the Georgia courts that there had been no mob atmosphere at the trial. Justices Oliver Wendell Holmes and Charles Evans Hughes dissented, arguing that the constitutional guarantee would be *a barren one* if the Federal courts could not make their own inferences from the facts.

In 1923, the case of Moore v. Dempsey involved five Arkansas Blacks convicted of murder and sentenced to death in a community so aroused against them that at one point they were saved from lynching only by Federal troops. Witnesses against them were said to have been beaten into testifying.

The court, though not actually setting aside the convictions, directed a lower Federal court to hold a habeas corpus hearing to find out whether the trial had been fair, or whether the whole proceeding had been a *mask—that counsel, jury, and judge were swept to the fatal end by an irresistible wave of public passion.*

13. According to the above passage, the Supreme Court's INITIAL interpretation of the Fourteenth Amendment

    A. protected state supremacy in economic matters
    B. increased the scope of Federal jurisdiction
    C. required fair procedures in criminal trials
    D. prohibited the enactment of minimum wage laws

14. According to the above passage, the Supreme Court in the Frank case

    A. denied that there had been mob hysteria at the trial
    B. decided that the guilty verdict was supported by the evidence
    C. declined to question the state court's determination of the facts
    D. found that Leo Frank had not received *due process*

15. According to the above passage, the dissenting judges in the Frank case maintained that

    A. due process was an empty promise in the circumstances of that case
    B. the Federal courts could not guarantee certain provisions of the Constitution
    C. the Federal courts should not make their own inferences from the facts in state cases
    D. the Supreme Court had rendered the Constitution *barren*

16. Of the following, the MOST appropriate title for the above passage is   16._____
   A. THE CONDUCT OF FEDERAL TRIALS
   B. THE DEVELOPMENT OF STATES' RIGHTS: 1868-1923
   C. MOORE V. DEMPSEY: A CASE STUDY IN CRIMINAL JUSTICE
   D. DUE PROCESS-THE EVOLUTION OF A CONSTITUTIONAL CORNERSTONE

Questions 17-20.

DIRECTIONS: Questions 17 through 20 are to be answered SOLELY on the basis of the following passage.

The difficulty experienced in determining which party has the burden of proving payment or non-payment is due largely to a lack of consistency between the rules of pleading and the rules of proof. In some cases, a plaintiff is obligated by a rule of pleading to allege non-payment on his complaint, yet is not obligated to prove non-payment on the trial. An action upon a contract for the payment of money will serve as an illustration. In such a case, the plaintiff must allege non-payment in his complaint, but the burden of proving payment on the trial is upon the defendant. An important and frequently cited case on this problem is Conkling v. Weatherwax. In that case, the action was brought to establish and enforce a legacy as a lien upon real property. The defendant alleged in her answer that the legacy had been paid. There was no witness competent to testify for the plaintiff to show that the legacy had not been paid. Therefore, the question of the burden of proof became of primary importance since, if the plaintiff had the burden of proving non-payment, she must fail in her action; whereas if the burden of proof was on the defendant to prove payment, the plaintiff might win. The Court of Appeals held that the burden of proof was on the plaintiff. In the course of his opinion, Judge Vann attempted to harmonize the conflicting cases on this subject, and for that purpose formulated three rules. These rules have been construed and applied to numerous subsequent cases. As so construed and applied, these may be summarized as follows:

Rule 1. In an action upon a contract for the payment of money only, where the complaint does not allege a balance due over and above all payments made, the plaintiff must allege nonpayment in his complaint, but the burden of proving payment is upon the defendant. In such a case, payment is an affirmative defense which the defendant must plead in his answer. If the defendant fails to plead payment, but pleads a general denial instead, he will not be permitted to introduce evidence of payment.

Rule 2. Where the complaint sets forth a balance in excess of all payments, owing to the structure of the pleading, burden is upon the plaintiff to prove his allegation. In this case, the defendant is not required to plead payment as a defense in his answer but may introduce evidence of payment under a general denial.

Rule 3. When the action is not upon contract for the payment of money, but is upon an obligation created by operation of law, or is for the enforcement of a lien where non-payment of the amount secured is part of the cause of action, it is necessary both to allege and prove the fact of nonpayment.

17. In the above passage, the case of Conkling v. Weatherwax was cited PRIMARILY to illustrate   17.____

    A. a case where the burden of proof was on the defendant to prove payment
    B. how the question of the burden of proof can affect the outcome of a case
    C. the effect of a legacy as a lien upon real property
    D. how conflicting cases concerning the burden of proof were harmonized

18. According to the above passage, the pleading of payment is a defense in Rule(s)   18.____

    A. 1, but not Rules 2 and 3
    B. 2, but not Rules 1 and 3
    C. 1 and 3, but not Rule 2
    D. 2 and 3, but not Rule 1

19. The facts in Conkling v. Weatherwax CLOSELY resemble the conditions described in   19.____

    A. Rule #1
    B. Rule #2
    C. Rule #3
    D. none of the rules

20. The MAJOR topic of the above passage may BEST be described as   20.____

    A. determining the ownership of property
    B. providing a legal definition
    C. placing the burden of proof
    D. formulating rules for deciding cases

Questions 21-25.

DIRECTIONS: Questions 21 through 25 are to be answered SOLELY on the basis of the following passage.

The law is quite clear that evidence obtained in violation of Section 605 of the Federal Communications Act is not admissible in Federal court. However, the law as to the admissibility of evidence in state court is far from clear. Had the Supreme Court of the United States made the wiretap exclusionary rule applicable to the states, such confusion would not exist.

In the case of Alton v. Texas, the Supreme Court was called upon to determine whether wiretapping by state and local officers came within the proscription of the Federal statute and, if so, whether Section 605 required the same remedies for its vindication in state courts. In answer to the first question, Mr. Justice Minton, speaking for the court, flatly stated that Section 605 made it a federal crime for anyone to intercept telephone messages and divulge what he learned. The court went on to say that a state officer who testified in state court concerning the existence, contents, substance, purport, effect, or meaning of an intercepted conversation violated the Federal law and committed a criminal act. In regard to the second question, how-ever, the Supreme Court felt constrained by due regard for federal-state relations to answer in the negative. Mr. Justice Minton stated that the court would not presume, in the absence of a clear manifestation of congressional intent, that Congress intended to supersede state rules of evidence.

Because the Supreme Court refused to apply the exclusionary rule to wiretap evidence that was being used in state courts, the states respectively made this decision for themselves. According to hearings held before a congressional committee in 1975, six states authorize wiretapping by statute, 33 states impose total bans on wiretapping, and 11 states have no definite statute on the subject. For examples of extremes, a statute in Pennsylvania will be compared with a statute in New York.

The Pennsylvania statute provides that no communications by telephone or telegraph can be intercepted without permission of both parties. It also specifically prohibits such interception by public officials and provides that evidence obtained cannot be used in court.

The lawmakers in New York, recognizing the need for legal wire-tapping, authorized wire-tapping by statute. A New York law authorizes the issuance of an ex parte order upon oath or affirmation for limited wiretapping. The aim of the New York law is to allow court-ordered wiretapping and to encourage the testimony of state officers concerning such wiretapping in court. The New York law was found to be constitutional by the New York State Supreme Court in 1975. Other states, including Oregon, Maryland, Nevada, and Massachusetts, enacted similar laws which authorize court-ordered wiretapping.

To add to this legal disarray, the vast majority of the states, including New Jersey and New York, permit wiretapping evidence to be received in court even though obtained in violation of the state laws and of Section 605 of the Federal act. However, some states, such as Rhode Island, have enacted statutory exclusionary rules which provide that illegally procured wiretap evidence is incompetent in civil as well as criminal actions.

21. According to the above passage, a state officer who testifies in New York State court concerning the contents of a conversation he overheard through a court-ordered wire-tap is in violation of _____ law.

    A. state law but not federal
    B. federal law but not state
    C. federal law and state
    D. neither federal nor state

22. According to the above passage, which of the following statements concerning states statutes on wiretapping is CORRECT?

    A. The number of states that impose total bans on wiretapping is three times as great as the number of states with no definite statute on wiretapping.
    B. The number of states having no definite statute on wiretapping is more than twice the number of states authorizing wiretapping.
    C. The number of states which authorize wiretapping by statute and the number of states having no definite statute on wiretapping exceed the number of states imposing total bans on wiretapping.
    D. More states authorize wiretapping by statute than impose total bans on wiretapping.

23. Following are three statements concerning wiretapping that might be valid:
    I. In Pennsylvania, only public officials may legally intercept telephone communications.
    II. In Rhode Island, evidence obtained through an illegal wiretap is incompetent in criminal, but not civil, actions.
    III. Neither Massachusetts nor Pennsylvania authorizes wiretapping by public officials.

    According to the above passage, which of the following CORRECTLY classifies these statements into those that are valid and those that are not?

    A. I is valid, but II and III are not.
    B. II is valid, but I and III are not.
    C. II and III are valid, but I is not.
    D. None of the statements is valid.

24. According to the above passage, evidence obtained in violation of Section 605 of the Federal Communications Act is inadmissible in

    A. federal court but not in any state courts
    B. federal court and all state courts
    C. all state courts but not in federal court
    D. federal court and some state courts

25. In regard to state rules of evidence, Mr. Justice Minton expressed the Court's opinion that Congress

    A. intended to supersede state rules of evidence, as manifested by Section 605 of the Federal Communications Act
    B. assumed that federal statutes would govern state rules of evidence in all wiretap cases
    C. left unclear whether it intended to supersede state rules of evidence
    D. precluded itself from superseding state rules of evidence through its regard for federal-state relations

KEY (CORRECT ANSWERS)

1. B
2. B
3. A
4. C
5. B
6. C
7. D
8. D
9. B
10. B
11. A
12. A
13. D
14. C
15. A
16. D
17. B
18. A
19. C
20. C
21. B
22. A
23. D
24. D
25. C

TEST 2

DIRECTIONS: Each question or incomplete statement is followed by several suggested answers or completions. Select the one that BEST answers the question or completes the Statement. *PRINT THE LETTER OF THE CORRECT ANSWER IN THE SPACE AT THE RIGHT.*

Questions 1-3.

DIRECTIONS: Questions 1 through 3 are to be answered SOLELY on the basis of the following passage.

    The State Assembly has passed a bill that would require all state agencies, public authorities, and local governments to refuse bids in excess of $2,000 from any foreign firm or corporation. The only exceptions to this outright prohibition against public buying of foreign goods or services would be for products not available in this country, goods of a quality unobtainable from an American supplier, and products using foreign materials that are *substantially* manufactured in the United States.

    This bill is a flagrant violation of the United States' officially espoused trade principles. It would add to the costs of state and local governments. It could provoke retaliatory action from many foreign governments against the state and other American producers, and foreign governments would be fully entitled to take such retaliatory action under the General Agreement on Tariffs and Trade, which the United States has signed.

    The State Senate, which now has the Assembly bill before it, should reject this protectionist legislation out of enlightened regard for the interests of the taxpayers and producers of the State—as well as for those of the nation and its trading partners generally. In this time of unemployment and international monetary disorder, the State—with its reputation for intelligent and progressive law-making—should avoid contributing to what could become a tidal wave of protectionism here and overseas.

1. Under the requirements of the bill passed by the State Assembly, a bid from a foreign manufacturer in excess of $2,000 can be accepted by a state agency or local government only if it meets which one of the following requirements?
The

   A. bid is approved individually by the State Legislature
   B. bidder is willing to accept payment in United States currency
   C. bid is for an item of a quality unobtainable from an American supplier
   D. bid is for an item which would be more expensive if it were purchased from an American supplier

1.____

2. The author of the above passage feels that the bill passed by the State Assembly should be

   A. passed by the State Senate and put into effect
   B. passed by the State Senate but vetoed by the Governor
   C. reintroduced into the State Assembly and rejected
   D. rejected by the State Senate

2.____

3. The author of the above passage calls the practice of prohibiting purchase of products manufactured by foreign countries

   A. prohibition
   B. protectionism
   C. retaliatory action
   D. isolationism

Questions 4-7.

DIRECTIONS: Questions 4 through 7 are to be answered SOLELY on the basis of the following passage.

Data processing is by no means a new invention. In one form or another, it has been carried on throughout the entire history of civilization. In its most general sense, data processing means organizing data so that it can be used for a specific purpose-a procedure commonly known simply as *record-keeping* or *paperwork*. With the development of modern office equipment, and particularly with the recent introduction of computers, the techniques of data processing have become highly elaborate and sophisticated, but the basic purpose remains the same: Turning raw data into useful information.

The key concept here is usefulness. The data, or input, that is to be processed can be compared to the raw material that is to go into a manufacturing process. The information, or output, that results from data processing—like the finished product of a manufacturer—should be clearly usable. A collection of data has little value unless it is converted into information that serves a specific function.

4. The expression *paperwork,* as it is used in this passage,

   A. shows that the author regards such operations as a waste of time
   B. has the same general meaning as *data processing*
   C. refers to methods of record-keeping that are no longer in use
   D. indicates that the public does not understand the purpose of data processing

5. The above passage indicates that the use of computers has

   A. greatly simplified the clerical work in an office
   B. led to more complicated systems for the handling of data
   C. had no effect whatsoever on data processing
   D. made other modern office machines obsolete

6. Which of the following BEST expresses the basic principle of data processing as it is described in the above passage?

   A. Input-processing-output
   B. Historical record-keeping-modern techniques -specific functions
   C. Office equipment-computer-accurate data
   D. Raw material-manufacturer-retailer

7. According to the above passage, data processing may be described as

   A. a new management technique
   B. computer technology
   C. information output
   D. record-keeping

Questions 8-10.

DIRECTIONS: Questions 8 through 10 are to be answered SOLELY on the basis of the following passage.

A loan receipt is an instrument devised to permit the insurance company to bring an action against the wrongdoer in the name of the insured despite the fact that the insured no longer has any financial interest in the outcome. It provides, in effect, that the amount of the loss is advanced to the insured as a loan which is repayable only up to the extent of any recovery made from the wrongdoer. The insured further agrees to enter and prosecute suit against the wrongdoer in his own name. Such a receipt substitutes a loan for a payment for the purpose of permitting the insurance company to press its action against the wrongdoer in the name of the insured.

8. According to the above passage, the purpose behind the use of a loan receipt is to 8._____

    A. guarantee that the insurance company gets repayment from the person insured
    B. insure repayment of all expenditures to the named insured
    C. make it possible for the insurance company to sue in the name of the policyowner
    D. prevent the wrongdoer from escaping the natural consequences of his act

9. According to the above passage, the amount of the loan which must be paid back to the insurance company equals but does NOT exceed the amount 9._____

    A. of the loss
    B. on the face of the policy
    C. paid to the insured
    D. recovered from the wrongdoer

10. According to the above passage, by giving a loan receipt, the person insured agrees to 10._____

    A. a suit against the wrongdoer in his own name
    B. forego any financial gain from the outcome of the suit
    C. institute an action on behalf of the insurance company
    D. repay the insurance company for the loan received

Questions 11-12.

DIRECTIONS: Questions 11 and 12 are to be answered SOLELY on the basis of the following passage.

Open air markets originally came into existence spontaneously when groups of pushcart peddlers congregated in spots where business was good. Good business induced them to return to these spots daily and, thus, unofficial open air markets arose. These peddlers paid no fees, and the city received no revenue from them. Confusion and disorder reigned in these unsupervised markets; the earliest arrivals secured the best locations, unless or until forcibly ejected by stronger or tougher peddlers. Although the open air markets supplied a definite need in the community, there were many detrimental factors involved in their operation. They were unsightly, created unsanitary conditions in market streets by the deposit of garbage and waste and were a definite obstruction to traffic, as well as a fire hazard.

11. On the basis of the above passage, the MOST accurate of the following statements is:

    A. Each peddler in the original open air markets had his own fixed location.
    B. Open air markets were originally organized by means of agreements between groups of pushcart peddlers.
    C. The locations of these markets depended upon the amount of business the vendors were able to do.
    D. There was confusion and disorder in these open air markets because the peddlers were not required to pay any fees to the city.

12. Of the following, the MOST valid implication which can be made on the basis of the above passage is that the

    A. detrimental aspect of the operations of open air markets was the probable reason for the creation of enclosed markets under the supervision of the Department of Markets
    B. open air markets could not supply any community need without proper supervision
    C. original open air markets were good examples of the operation of fair competition in business
    D. possibility of obtaining a source of revenue was probably the most important reason for the city's ultimate undertaking of the supervision of open air markets

Questions 13-14.

DIRECTIONS: Questions 13 and 14 are to be answered SOLELY on the basis of the following passage.

A person who displays on his window, door, or in his place of business words or letters in Hebraic characters other than the word *kosher,* or any sign, emblem, insignia, six-pointed star, symbol or mark in simulation of same, without displaying in conjunction there-with in English letters of at least the same size as such characters, signs, emblems, insignia or marks, the words *we sell kosher meat and food only* or *we sell non-kosher meat and food only* or *we sell both kosher and non-kosher meat and food,* as the case may be, is guilty of a misdemeanor. Possession of non-kosher meat and food in any place of business advertising the sale of kosher meat and food only is presumptive evidence that the person in possession exposes the same for sale with intent to defraud, in violation of the provisions of this section.

13. Of the following, the MOST valid implication that can be made on the basis of the above passage is that a person who

    A. displays on his window a six-pointed star in addition to the word *kosher* in Hebraic letters is guilty of intent to defraud
    B. displays on his window the word *kosher* in Hebraic characters intends to indicate that he has only kosher food for sale
    C. sells both kosher and non-kosher food in the same place of business is guilty of a misdemeanor
    D. sells only that type of food which can be characterized as neither kosher nor non-kosher, such as fruit and vegetables, without an explanatory sign in English is guilty of intent to defraud

14. Of the following, the one which would constitute a violation of the rules of the above passage is a case in which a person 14.____

    A. displays the word *kosher* on his window in Hebraic letters has only kosher meat and food in the store but has some non-kosher meat in the rear of the establishment
    B. selling both kosher and non-kosher meat and food uses words in Hebraic letters, other than the word *kosher,* on his window and a sign of the same size letters in English stating *we sell both kosher and non-kosher meat and food*
    C. selling only kosher meat and food uses words in Hebraic letters, other than the word *kosher,* on his window and a sign of the same size letters in English stating *we sell kosher meat and food only*
    D. selling only non-kosher meat and food displays a six-pointed star on his window and a sign of the same size letters in English stating *we sell only non-kosher meat and food*

Questions 15-16.

DIRECTIONS: Questions 15 and 16 are to be answered SOLELY on the basis of the following passage.

COMMODITIES IN GLASS BOTTLES OR JARS

The contents of the bottle may be stated in terms of weight or of fluid measure, the weight being indicated in terms of pounds and ounces and the fluid measure being indicated in terms of gallons, quarts, pints, half-pints, gills, or fluid ounces. When contents are liquid, the amount should not be stated in terms of weight. The marking indicating content is to be on a tag attached to the bottle or upon a label. The letters shall be in bold-faced type at least one-ninth of an inch (1/9") in height for bottles or jars having a capacity of a gill, half-pint, pint, or multiples of a pint, and letters at least three-sixteenths of an inch (3/16") in height for bottles of other capacities, on a part of the tag or label free from other printing or ornamentation, leaving a clear space around the marking which indicates the contents.

15. Of the following, the one which does NOT meet the requirements of the above passage is a 15.____

    A. bottle of cooking oil with a label stating *contents—16 fluid ounces* in appropriate sized letters
    B. bottle of vinegar with a label stating *contents—8 ounces avoir.* in appropriate sized letters
    C. glass jar filled with instant coffee with a label stating *contents—1 lb. 3 ozs. avoir.* in appropriate sized letters
    D. glass jar filled with liquid bleach with a label stating *contents—1 quart* in appropriate sized letters

16. Of the following, the one which does meet the requirements of the above passage is a 16.____

    A. bottle filled with a low-calorie liquid sweetener with a label stating *contents—3 fluid ounces* in letters 1/12" high
    B. bottle filled with ammonia solution for cleaning with a label stating *contents—1 pint* in letters 1/10" high

C. jar filled with baking powder with a label stating *contents—$\frac{1}{2}$ pint* in letters $\frac{1}{4}$" high

D. jar filled with hard candy with a label stating *contents—1 lb. avoir.* in letters $\frac{1}{2}$" high

Question 17.

DIRECTIONS: Question 17 is to be answered SOLELY on the basis of the information contained in the following passage.

DEALERS IN SECOND HAND DEVICES

1. It shall be unlawful for any person to engage in or conduct the business of dealing in, trading in, selling, receiving, or repairing condemned, rebuilt, or used weighing or measuring devices without a permit therefor.

2. Such permit shall expire on the twenty-eighth day of February next succeeding the date of issuance thereof.

3. Every person engaged in the above business, within five days after the making of a repair, or the sale and delivery of a repaired, rebuilt, or used weighing or measuring device, shall serve notice in writing on the commissioner giving the name and address of the person for whom the repair has been made or to whom a repaired, rebuilt, or used weighing or measuring device has been sold or delivered, and shall include a statement that such device has been so altered, repaired, or rebuilt as to conform to the regulations of the department.

17. According to the above passage, the MOST accurate of the following statements is: 17.___

   A. A permit issued to engage in the business mentioned above, first issued on April 23, 1968, expired on February 28, 1969.
   B. A rebuilt or repaired weighing or measuring device should not operate with less error than the tolerances permitted by the regulations of the department.
   C. If a used scale in good condition is sold, it is not necessary for the seller to notify the commissioner of the name and address of the buyer.
   D. There is a difference in the time required to notify the commissioner of a repair or of a sale of a repaired device.

Questions 18-19.

DIRECTIONS: Questions 18 and 19 are to be answered SOLELY on the basis of the following passage.

   A. It shall be unlawful for any person, firm, or corporation to sell or offer for sale at retail for use in internal combustion engines in motor vehicles any gasoline unless such seller shall post and keep continuously posted on the individual pump or other dispensing device from which such gasoline is sold or offered for sale a sign or placard not less than seven inches in height and eight inches in width nor larger than twelve inches in height and twelve inches in width and stating clearly in numbers of uniform size the selling price or prices per gallon of such gasoline so sold or offered for sale from such pump or other dispensing device.

B. The amount of governmental tax to be collected in connection with the sale of such gasoline shall be stated on such sign or placard and separately and apart from such selling price or prices.

18. The one of the following price signs posted on a gasoline pump which would be in violation of the above passage is a sign _____ square inches in size and _____ inches high.

   A. 144; 12   B. 84; 7   C. 72; 12   D. 60; 8

19. According to the above passage, the LEAST accurate of the following statements is:

   A. Gasoline may be sold from a dispensing device other than a pump.
   B. If two different pumps are used to sell the same grade of gasoline, a price sign must appear on each pump.
   C. The amount of governmental tax and the price of the gasoline must not be stated on the same sign.
   D. The sizes of the numbers used on a sign to indicate the price of gasoline must be the same.

Questions 20-21.

DIRECTIONS: Questions 20 and 21 are to be answered SOLELY on the basis of the following passage.

In all systems of weights and measures based on one or more arbitrary fundamental units, the concrete representation of the unit in the form of a standard is necessary, and the construction and preservation of such a standard is a matter of primary importance. Therefore, it is essential that the standard should be so constructed as to be as nearly permanent and invariable as human ingenuity can contrive. The reference of all measures to an original standard is essential for their correctness, and such a standard must be maintained and preserved in its integrity by some responsible authority which is thus able to provide against the use of false weights and measures. Accordingly, from earliest times, standards were constructed and preserved under the direction of kings and priests, and the temples were a favorite place for their deposit. Later, this duty was assumed by the government, and today we find the integrity of standards of weights and measures safeguarded by international agreement.

20. Of the following, the MOST valid implication which can be made on the basis of the above passage is that

   A. fundamental units of systems of weights and measures should be represented by quantities so constructed that they are specific and constant
   B. in the earliest times, standards were so constructed that they were as permanent and invariable as modern ones
   C. international agreement has practically relieved the U.S. government of the necessity of preserving standards of weights and measures
   D. the preservation of standards is of less importance than the ingenuity used in their construction

21. Of the following, the MOST appropriate title for the above passage is   21.____

   A. THE CONSTRUCTION AND PRESERVATION OF STANDARDS OF WEIGHTS AND MEASURES
   B. THE FIXING OF RESPONSIBILITY FOR THE ESTABLISHMENT OF STANDARDS OF WEIGHTS AND MEASURES
   C. THE HISTORY OF SYSTEMS OF WEIGHTS AND MEASURES
   D. THE VALUE OF PROPER STANDARDS IN PROVIDING CORRECT WEIGHTS AND MEASURES

Questions 22-23.

DIRECTIONS: Questions 22 and 23 are to be answered SOLELY on the basis of the following passage.

   Accurate weighing and good scales insure that excess is not given just for the sake of good measure. No more striking example of the fundamental importance of correct weighing to the business man is found than in the simple and usual relation where a charge or value is obtained by multiplying a weight by a unit price. For example, a scale may weigh *light,* that is, the actual quantity delivered is in excess by 1 percent. The actual result is that the seller taxes himself. If his profit is supposed to be 10 percent of total sales, an overweight of 1 percent represents 10 percent of that profit. Under these conditions, the situation is as though the seller were required to pay a sales tax equivalent to what he is taxing himself.

22. Of the following, the MOST valid implication which can be made on the basis of the above passage is that   22.____

   A. consistent use of scales that weigh *light* will reduce sellers' profits
   B. no good businessman would give any buyer more than the weight required even if his scale is accurate
   C. the kind of situation described in the above passage could not arise if sales were being made of merchandise sold by the yard
   D. the use of incorrect scales is one of the reasons causing governments to impose sales taxes

23. According to the above passage, the MOST accurate of the following statements is: 23.____

   A. If his scale weighs *light* by an amount of 2 percent, the seller would deliver only 98 pounds when 100 pounds was the amount agreed upon.
   B. If the seller's scale weighs *heavy,* the buyer will receive an amount in excess of what he intended to purchase.
   C. If the seller's scale weighs *light* by an amount of 1 percent, a buyer who agreed to purchase 50 pounds of merchandise would actually receive $50 \frac{1}{2}$ pounds.
   D. The use of a scale which delivers an amount which is in excess of that required is an example of deliberate fraud.

Questions 24-25.

DIRECTIONS: Questions 24 and 25 are to be answered SOLELY on the basis of the following passage.

Food shall be deemed to be misbranded:
1. If its labeling is false or misleading in any particular.

2. If any word, statement, or other information required by or under authority of this article to appear on the label or labeling is not prominently placed thereon with such conspicuousness (as compared with other words, statements, designs, or devices in the labeling) and in such terms as to render it likely to be read and understood by the ordinary individual under customary conditions of purchase and use.

3. If it purports to be or is represented as a food for which a standard of quality has been prescribed and its quality falls below such standard, unless its label bears a statement that it falls below such standard.

24. According to the above passage, the MOST accurate of the following statements is:

    A. A food may be considered misbranded if the label contains a considerable amount of information which is not required.
    B. If a consumer purchased one type of canned food, although he intended to buy another, the food is probably misbranded.
    C. If a food is used in large amounts by a group of people of certain foreign origin, it can be considered misbranded unless the label is in the foreign language with which they are familiar.
    D. The required information on a label is likely to be in larger print than other information which may appear on it.

25. According to the above passage, the one of the following foods which may be considered to be misbranded is a

    A. can of peaches with a label which carries the brand name of the packer but states *Below Standard in Quality*
    B. can of vegetables with a label on which is printed a shield which states *U.S. Grade B*
    C. package of frozen food which has some pertinent information printed on it in very small type which a customer cannot read and which the store manager cannot read when asked to do so by the customer
    D. package of margarine of the same size as the usual package of butter, kept near the butter, but clearly labeled as margarine

10 (#2)

KEY (CORRECT ANSWERS)

1.	C	11.	C
2.	D	12.	A
3.	B	13.	B
4.	B	14.	A
5.	B	15.	B
6.	A	16.	D
7.	D	17.	A
8.	C	18.	C
9.	D	19.	C
10.	A	20.	A

21. D
22. A
23. C
24. D
25. C

READING COMPREHENSION
UNDERSTANDING AND INTERPRETING WRITTEN MATERIAL

EXAMINATION SECTION
TEST 1

DIRECTIONS: Each question or incomplete statement is followed by several suggested answers or completions. Select the one that BEST answers the question or completes the statement. *PRINT THE LETTER OF THE CORRECT ANSWER IN THE SPACE AT THE RIGHT*

Questions 1-5.

DIRECTIONS: The following passage is to be used as the SOLE basis for answering Questions 1 to 5. Read the passage carefully and base your answers ONLY on the information contained therein.

PASSAGE
LOW EXPLOSIVES

The following represent explosives of a military, commercial, and homemade origin which the police officer would be most likely to encounter.

BLACK POWDER
Black powder is the oldest known explosive. Its origin is, in fact, lost to history. The Chinese, the Arabs, and the Hindus are all credited in various histories with its invention, and it was used by them prior to its use in Europe. Through the 1880's, black powder was the explosive used for blasting and for propelling and bursting charges in munitions. Black powder is a mixture of potassium or sodium nitrate (75 percent), charcoal (15 percent), and sulfur (10 percent). Black powder is extremely sensitive to friction, spark, and heat, and will ignite at around 300°C. Commercial black powder is approximately 55 percent as strong as TNT, which is a high explosive, but homemade black powder is even less powerful. The quality of the charcoal, inaccurate measuring, the inability to "weld" or secure a finely pulverized mixture of the ingredients result in much slower burning of the homemade mixtures.

SMOKELESS POWDERS
These are the propellant powders used in small arms ammunition, and are known as nitro-cellulose explosives. Two types are predominantly used as small arms ammunition propellants and they are known as either single-base or double-base propellants. The bomb constructor secures smokeless powder through bulk-loading ammunition supply sources, or by extracting the powder from purchased ammunition.

Single-Base Propellant - This is used in the majority of small arms cartridges and consists of nitrated cotton, called nitrocellulose. It is manufactured in various sizes and forms as flakes, pellets, and cylindrical grains. The grains may be sold, or have a perforation designed to increase the burning surface area and control the burning speed. Single-base propellant ignites at approximately 315°C., and is relatively insensitive. Depending on the manufacturer, the color may be amber, grey, or black. It is stronger than black powder, it is safer, and it produces pressure up to 60,000 pounds per square inch. It will give up to 900 cubic centimeters of gas per gram, compared with approximately 300 cubic centimeters per gram for black powder.

Double-Base Propellant - This is a nitrocellulose, single-base propellant, to which 30-40 percent nitroglycerine has been added. The nitrocellulose-nitroglycerine mixture is more sensitive, burns faster, produces more heat and gas, and has a lower ignition temperature (150°C.) than single-base smokeless powder. However, double-base propellant has a disadvantage in that the residue in the gun tube after firing is very corrosive when compared with single-base propellant residue. For this reason double-base propellant is used only when the gain in power is considered to offset the disadvantages of corrosion and cleaning problems. Double-base propellant is used in .45 caliber and shotgun ammunition.

1. According to the passage, which one of the following BEST states a major disadvantage of black powder as compared with single-base propellant smokeless powder, especially when used in homemade explosives?   1._____

   A. Its extreme sensitivity
   B. Its very corrosive nature
   C. Its higher ignition temperature
   D. The fact that it is 55% less powerful than either form of smokeless powder
   E. The fact that the sodium nitrate used in making it is extremely expensive

2. According to the passage, which one of the following is MOST properly considered to be the reason for stating that a single-base propellant is safer than black powder? Single-base propellant   2._____

   A. is stronger than black powder
   B. ignites at a lower temperature than black powder
   C. is less sensitive to friction, spark, and heat than black powder
   D. is almost always produced by experts, while black powder is frequently produced by amateurs
   E. has been in use longer than black powder, so that safety procedures for handling a single-base propellant are more sophisticated

3. According to the passage, which one of the following techniques is employed to increase the burning surface area and to control the burning speed of nitrocellulose when used as a single-base propellant?   3._____

   A. Flaking the grains of nitrocellulose
   B. Pelletizing the grains of nitrocellulose
   C. Perforating the grains of nitrocellulose
   D. Adding nitroglycerine to the nitrocellulose
   E. Using a greater proportion of sodium nitrate in the powder mixture

4. According to the passage, which one of the following BEST makes an accurate comparison between a single-base propellant and a double-base propellant? 4._____

   A. A single-base propellant is more expensive to produce than a double-base propellant
   B. A single-base propellant ignites at a higher temperature than a double-base propellant
   C. A single-base propellant contains black powder, while a double-base propellant does not
   D. The color of a single-base propellant may be amber, gray, or black, while the color of a double-base propellant is almost always black
   E. A single-base propellant is manufactured as either flakes or cylindrical grains, while a double-base propellant is manufactured only as pellets

5. According to the passage, the addition of which one of the following to single-base propellant for the purpose of producing double-base propellant results in the residue in the gun being more corrosive than single-base propellant residue? 5._____

   A. Black powder
   B. Sodium nitrate
   C. Nitrocellulose
   D. Nitroglycerine
   E. Nitrated cotton

Questions 6-10.

DIRECTIONS: The following passage is to be used as the SOLE basis for answering Questions 6 to 10. Read the passage carefully and base your answers ONLY on the information contained therein.

PASSAGE
DOUBLE JEOPARDY

Double jeopardy can arise from a second prosecution for one criminal act by one authority (single sovereignty double jeopardy). A second prosecution for the same offense by the federal government is prohibited by the Fifth Amendment to the Federal Constitution. Such a second prosecution is also prohibited by the constitutions of forty-five states and, in the five states where no constitutional bar exists, there is a common law rule to the same effect.

Double jeopardy can also arise from a second prosecution by an authority other than the one that first prosecuted (dual sovereignty double jeopardy). In dual sovereignty situations, the constitutional bars do not apply, for "A single act which violates both federal and state criminal laws is generally held to result in a distinct offense against the two separate governments and may be punished by both." Thus, "In the absence of a contrary statute, the rule against double jeopardy applies only to offenses against the same sovereignty."

A majority of the states recognize the rule that an accused may be tried twice for the same criminal act by the state and the federal government, but in eighteen states, a state prosecution is barred by statute if there has been a prior federal prosecution for the same crime.

6. A certain person is prosecuted in the courts of a certain state for a particular criminal act. Subsequently, he is prosecuted in a federal court for the same criminal act. According to the passage, which one of the following choices MOST accurately states the extent of the legality of this second prosecution?

   A. The second prosecution is entirely legal because the constitutional bar does not apply
   B. The second prosecution is illegal because it is barred by the Fifth Amendment to the Federal Constitution
   C. The prosecution is legal, but only if the first prosecution has occurred in one of the five states which has no bar to a second prosecution in their constitutions
   D. The second prosecution is illegal, but only if the first prosecution had occurred in one of the 18 states which bar state prosecution if there has been a prior federal prosecution for the first crime
   E. A second prosecution is legal, but only if the first prosecution had occurred in one of the 38 states which recognize the rule that the accused may be tried twice for the same criminal act

7. Which one of the following statements concerning the prohibition of double jeopardy is MOST adequately supported by the passage?

   A. The state constitution takes precedence over any state statute in the matter of double jeopardy
   B. In all 50 states, the state is prohibited from a second prosecution for the same criminal act for which that state had previously prosecuted
   C. In 45 states, the common law rule does not prohibit the state from a second prosecution for the same criminal act for which that state had previously prosecuted
   D. The constitutions of 18 states prohibit a second prosecution for the same criminal act for which the accused had previously been prosecuted by the federal government
   E. In 32 states, the state is prohibited from a second prosecution for the same criminal act for which the accused had been previously prosecuted by the federal government

8. According to the passage, which one of the following phrases can MOST probably be substituted properly for the word "rule" (underlined on line 10) WITHOUT altering the meaning of the sentence?

   A. The common law rule
   B. State statutes
   C. Federal statutes
   D. The state constitution rule
   E. The federal constitution rule

9. According to the passage, which one of the following second prosecutions for one criminal act would most definitely NOT be permissible?
    A. In Utah, a second prosecution, by the State, for a criminal act solely against the State statute
    B. In Maine, a second prosecution, by the State, for a criminal act against both State and Federal statutes
    C. In Florida, a second prosecution, by the federal government, for a criminal act against both a State and Federal statute
    D. A second prosecution in Federal court for a criminal act for which the accused had previously been prosecuted in a Texas State court
    E. A second prosecution in an Idaho State court for a criminal act for which the accused had previously been prosecuted in a Federal court

10. The newspapers frequently report a second prosecution for a single criminal act by the same state when the first prosecution ended in a mistrial because the jurors could not agree on a verdict.
    According to the passage, which one of the following conclusions about such second prosecutions is MOST probable?

    A. Such second prosecutions are probably in violation of the accused's rights
    B. The newspaper accounts of such second prosecutions are probably erroneous
    C. Such second prosecutions probably occurred only in the 32 states that permit an accused to be tried, twice
    D. Such second prosecutions are clearly permitted, according to the passage
    E. The passage fails to state clearly that the prohibition of double jeopardy does not apply to an incomplete prosecution which did not end either in conviction or acquittal

KEY (CORRECT ANSWERS)

1. A   6. A
2. C   7. B
3. C   8. A
4. B   9. A
5. D   10. E

TEST 2

DIRECTIONS: Each question or incomplete statement is followed by several suggested answers or completions. Select the one that BEST answers the question or completes the statement. *PRINT THE LETTER OF THE CORRECT ANSWER IN THE SPACE AT THE RIGHT.*

Questions 1-3.

DIRECTIONS: Answer Questions 1 through 3 SOLELY on the basis of the following passage.

PASSAGE

In dealing with people, police officers should realize that personality is what makes each person different, each person an individual. Although most persons have adequate personalities, some have inadequate personalities. It is the latter group, those persons with inadequate personalities, with whom police officers interact very often, and in trying situations. In addition, as managers, each one of you should be aware and observant of the personality traits exhibited by your subordinates, and watch for signs that would indicate the presence of psychological problems. Persons with inadequate personalities fall into two major types. In type one, neurosis, persons have mental problems that occur intermittently but do not dominate the entire personality. These problems occur in a personality that is basically healthy and cause the individuals to experience moderate adjustment problems and to misinterpret reality in minor ways. They may imagine people are their "enemies;" they experience severe anxiety from time to time and occasional periods of depression from which they can recover. These individuals usually realize they are having problems. In type two, psychosis, people experience extreme adjustment problems. They are incapable of functioning in a normal setting. They replace reality with their own imaginary world. They feel so worthless and inadequate that they actually desire death. They want to harm their "enemies," have continuously occurring problems, and experience depressions so intense that they are severely incapacitated for months or even years. They experience anxiety so severe that it can produce hallucinations and delusions. These individuals are unaware that they are having problems. Thoughts and language do not consistently make any sense. Emotions are always distorted and not appropriate for the occasion. Time sequences are confused, and hallucinations are frequent occurrences. There are a number of patterns that have been identified as fairly indicative of abnormal behavior: (I) We have the situation where a person builds up a fear of something where there is no concrete cause for the fear, or there is a slight cause which has been highly exaggerated. For example, there is the officer who fears being killed to the extent that he feels he will be next, or suspects those he encounters are out to kill him. (II) An individual has delusions, or false beliefs, which he believes are true. (III) An individual experiences fear over an object that is not a real source of danger. (IV) An individual's behavior is no longer guided by what the mind and senses perceive. Instead of working as an integrated whole, the personality is shattered in such a way that one part, or parts, do not act in harmony with the other parts. Finally, we have the situation in which an individual exhibits extreme disturbance on both ends of the emotional spectrum. Either he is extremely depressed, so much so that he must be protected against suicidal tendencies, or becomes so excited or elated that his speech and actions are uncontrollably boisterous.

1. Which one of the following officers MOST likely would be considered neurotic, as described in the above passage? An officer

   A. states he can't trust his fellow officers because they are plotting to kill him
   B. unjustifiably feels that his sergeant is treating him unfairly
   C. hears voices telling him what to do
   D. consistently displays inappropriate emotional responses to all situations

2. Which one of the following officers would MOST likely be considered psychotic, as described in the above passage? An officer

   A. experiences depression so severe that it incapacitates him for a week
   B. experiences feelings of inferiority and inadequacy
   C. consistently imagines that he is a ranking officer of the department
   D. is afraid of heights and believes that such a fear is normal

3. Based on the above passage, which one of the following officers is MOST likely to attempt to commit suicide? He

   A. alternates between extreme optimism and extreme depression
   B. is excessively fearful of large gatherings of people
   C. constantly thinks about death
   D. feels that he will be the next officer shot

Questions 4-10.

DIRECTIONS: Answer Questions 4 through 10 based SOLELY on the information contained in the following passage.

PASSAGE

On February 7, the defendant entered a liquor store in Prince County and, after asking the owner for change to use the pay phone across the street, drew a gun and demanded all the money in the cash register. After being given all the cash, the defendant left the store.

When the police arrived moments later, the owner of the store described the robber to a detective and accompanied the detective to the police station where he subsequently identified photos of the defendant as the woman who held him up. The store owner indicated, however, he would have to see the defendant in person to be certain of a positive identification.

Nine weeks later, the defendant was being held in Prince County on charges unrelated to the liquor store holdup. The defendant was not under arrest at that time although a photo identification had been made. The defendant was placed in a line-up with four stand-ins and, because of a request for legal representation; a Legal Aid lawyer was present and assigned to represent the defendant. The owner identified the defendant as the robber and the defendant's attorney left. After the Legal Aid lawyer left, a police officer asked the detective if he wished to speak to the defendant. Despite his admitted knowledge that the defendant was now represented by counsel on the robbery charge, the detective indicated he would like to speak to the defendant. The detective had not told the lawyer he was going to speak to his client nor had he made any effort to contact the lawyer before talking to the defendant. At the police officer's request, the defendant signed an undescribed waiver (which the detective testified he had never seen) and agreed to talk to the detective. The defendant was then brought into an interview room.

The defendant was advised of her rights and indicated an understanding of them. The detective asked the defendant, "Do you wish to contact an attorney?" The defendant said, "No." The detective then asked, "Having these rights in mind, do you wish to talk to me now without a lawyer?" The defendant said, "Yes." The defendant asked the detective if the owner of the liquor store had identified her as the perpetrator and, when informed the owner had, expressed a desire to "clear up everything" and, in effect, confessed to the robbery.

4. The positive identification of the defendant as the perpetrator of the liquor store holdup was made by the

   A. cashier at the store
   B. owner of the store
   C. police officer conducting the line-up
   D. detective

5. Which of the following can NOT be deduced from the above passage? The defendant
   A. had been wanted for committing a robbery two weeks earlier when the liquor store was robbed
   B. possessed a gun at the time of the robbery
   C. left the liquor store with all of the cash that had been in the cash register at the time of the robbery
   D. was a woman

6. Which one of the following statements MOST accurately reflects the defendant's status at the time of the line-up? The

   A. defendant was not then represented by counsel
   B. witness had positively identified the defendant from a photograph
   C. detective had spoken to the defendant concerning the liquor store holdup
   D. defendant had not yet been arrested for committing the liquor store holdup

7. Of the following, it is MOST accurate to conclude that the defendant learned of the witness' identification of the defendant from the

   A. witness to the holdup
   B. defense attorney present at the line-up
   C. detective investigating the holdup
   D. police officer conducting the line-up

8. Based solely on the above passage, it is MOST appropriate to conclude that the defendant confessed to the hold-up because the

   A. defendant was already being held on a more serious charge at the time the confession to the crime was made
   B. detective's astute questioning produced a confession that the defendant had not wished to make
   C. defendant knew that the Legal Aid lawyer would advise a plea of guilty
   D. defendant knew that the witness had made a positive identification at the line-up

9. Which one of the following statements is MOST accurate concerning the role of the   9._____
   Legal Aid lawyer in this case? He

   A. was present at the line-up because the defendant had requested legal counsel
   B. advised the defendant to plead guilty to a holdup charge
   C. declined to represent the defendant after the defendant confessed to the crime
   D. was not present at the time of questioning because the defendant had told him
      that his presence was not desired at that time

10. Which one of the following topics is NOT delineated or treated in the passage?   10._____

    A. The inadequate personality
    B. Misinterpretation of reality
    C. Adjustment problems
    D. The adequate personality

KEY (CORRECT ANSWERS)

1. B   6. D
2. C   7. C
3. A   8. D
4. B   9. A
5. A   10. D

LOGICAL REASONING
EVALUATING CONCLUSIONS IN LIGHT OF KNOWN FACTS
EXAMINATION SECTION
TEST 1

COMMENTARY

This section is designed to provide practice questions in evaluating conclusions when you are given specific data to work with.

We suggest you do the questions three at a time, consulting the answer key and then the solution section for any questions you may have missed. It's a good idea to try the questions again a week before the exam.

In the validity of conclusion type of question, you are first given a reading passage which describes a particular situation. The passage may be on any topic, as it is not your knowledge of the topic that is being tested, but your reasoning abilities. The passage is likely to detail several proposed courses of action and factors affecting these proposals. The reading passage is followed by a conclusion based on the facts in the passage, or a description of a decision taken regarding the situation. The conclusion is followed by a number of statements which have a possible connection to the conclusion. For each statement, you are to determine whether:

- A. The statement proves the conclusion.
- B. The statement supports the conclusion but does not prove it.
- C. The statement disproves the conclusion.
- D. The statement weakens the conclusion but does not disprove it.
- E. The statement has no relevance to the conclusion.

Remember that the conclusion after the passage is to be accepted as the outcome of what actually happened, and that you are being asked to evaluate the impact each statement would have had on the conclusion.

Questions 1-8.

DIRECTIONS: Questions 1 through 8 are based on the following paragraph.

In May of 2018, Mr. Bryan inherited a clothing store on Main Street in a small New England town. The store has specialized in selling quality men's and women's clothing since 1920. Business has been stable throughout the years, neither increasing nor decreasing. He has an opportunity to buy two adjacent stores which would enable him to add a wider range and style of clothing. In order to do this, he would have to borrow a substantial amount of money. He also risks losing the goodwill of his present clientele.

CONCLUSION: On November 7, 2018, Mr. Bryan tells the owner of the two adjacent stores that he has decided not to purchase them. He feels that it would be best to simply maintain his present marketing position, as there would not be enough new business to support an expansion.

A. The statement proves the conclusion.
B. The statement supports the conclusion but does not prove it.
C. The statement disproves the conclusion.
D. The statement weakens the conclusion.
E. The statement is irrelevant to the conclusion.

1. A large new branch of the county's community college holds its first classes in September. 1._____

2. The town's largest factory shuts down with no indication that it will reopen. 2._____

3. The United States Census showed that the number of children per household dropped from 2.4 to 2.1 since the last census. 3._____

4. Mr. Bryan's brother tells him of a new clothing boutique specializing in casual women's clothing which is opening soon. 4._____

5. Mr. Bryan's sister buys her baby several items for Christmas at Mr. Bryan's store. 5._____

6. Mrs. McIntyre, the President of the Town Council, brings Mr. Bryan a home-baked pumpkin pie in honor of his store's 100th anniversary. They discuss the changes that have taken place in the town, and she comments on how his store has maintained the same look and feel over the years. 6._____

7. In October, Mr. Bryan's aunt lends him $50,000. 7._____

8. The Town Council has just announced that the town is eligible for funding from a federal project designed to encourage the location of new businesses in the central districts of cities and towns. 8._____

Questions 9-18.

DIRECTIONS: Questions 9 through 18 are based on the following paragraph.

A proposal was put before the legislative body of a country to require air bags in all automobiles manufactured for domestic use in that country after 2019. The air bag, made of nylon or plastic, is designed to inflate automatically within a car at the impact of a collision, thus protecting front-seat occupants from being thrown forward. There has been much support of the measure from consumer groups, the insurance industry, key legislators, and the general public. The country's automobile manufacturers, who contend the new crash equipment would add up to $1,000 to car prices and provide no more protection than existing seat belts, are against the proposed legislation

CONCLUSION: On April 21, 2014, the legislation requiring air bags in all automobiles manufactured for domestic use in that country after 2019.

A. The statement proves the conclusion.
B. The statement supports the conclusion but does not prove it.
C. The statement disproves the conclusion.
D. The statement weakens the conclusion.
E. The statement is irrelevant to the conclusion.

9. A study has shown that 59% of car occupants do not use seat belts.   9._____

10. The country's Department of Transportation has estimated that the crash protection equipment would save up to 5,900 lives each year.   10._____

11. On April 27, 2013, Augusta Raneoni was named head of an advisory committee to gather and analyze data on the costs, benefits, and feasibility of the proposed legislation on air bags in automobiles.   11._____

12. Consumer groups and the insurance industry accuse the legislature of rejecting passage of the regulation for political reasons.   12._____

13. A study by the Committee on Imports and Exports projected that the sales of imported cars would rise dramatically in 2019 because imported cars do not have to include air bags, and can be sold more cheaply.   13._____

14. Research has shown that air bags, if produced on a large scale, would cost about $200 apiece, and would provide more reliable protection than any other type of seat belt.   14._____

15. Auto sales in 2011 increased 3% over the previous year.   15._____

16. A Department of Transportation report in July of 2020 credits a drop in automobile deaths of 4,100 to the use of air bags.   16._____

17. In June of 2014, the lobbyist of the largest insurance company receives a bonus for her work on the passage of the air bag legislation.   17._____

18. In 2020, the stock in crash protection equipment has risen three-fold over the previous year.   18._____

Questions 19-25.

DIRECTIONS: Questions 19 through 25 are based on the following paragraph.

On a national television talk show, Joan Rivera, a famous comedienne, has recently insulted the physical appearances of a famous actress and the dead wife of an ex-President. There has been a flurry of controversy over her comments, and much discussion of the incident has appeared in the press. Most of the comments have been negative. It appears that this tie she might have gone too far. There have been cancellations of two of her five scheduled performances in the two weeks since the show was televised, and Joan's been receiving a lot of negative mail. Because of the controversy, she has an interview with a national news magazine at the end of the week, and her press agent is strongly urging her to apologize publicly. She feels strongly that her comments were no worse than any other she has ever made, and that the whole incident will *blow over* soon. She respects her press agent's judgment, however, as his assessment of public sentiment tends to be very accurate.

CONCLUSION: Joan does not apologize publicly, and during the interview she challenges the actress to a weight-losing contest. For every pound the actress loses, Joan says she will donate $1 to the Cellulite Prevention League.

    A. The statement proves the conclusion.
        B. The statement supports the conclusion but does not prove it.
        C. The statement disproves the conclusion.
        D. The statement weakens the conclusion.
        E. The statement is irrelevant to the conclusion.

19. Joan's mother, who she is very fond of, is very upset with Joan's comments.   19.____

20. Six months after the interview, Joan's income has doubled.   20.____

21. Joan's agent is pleased with the way Joan handles the interview.   21.____

22. Joan's sister has been appointed Treasurer of the Cellulite Prevention League   22.____
    In her report, she states that Joan's $12 contribution is the only amount that
    has been donated to the League in its first six months.

23. The magazine receives many letters commending Joan for the courage it   23.____
    took for her to apologize publicly in the interview.

24. Immediately after the interview appears, another one of Joan's performances   24.____
    is cancelled.

25. Due to a printers' strike, the article was not published until the following week.   25.____

Questions 26-30.

DIRECTIONS: Questions 25 through 30 are based on the following paragraph.

The law-making body of Country X must decide what to do about the issue of recording television shows for home use. There is currently no law against recording shows directly from the TV as long as the DVDs are not used for commercial purposes. The increasing popularity of pay TV and satellite systems, combined with the increasing number of homes that own recording equipment, has caused a great deal of concern in some segments of the entertainment industry. Companies that own the rights to films, popular television shows, and sporting events feel that their copyright privileges are being violated, and they are seeking compensation or the banning of TV recording. Legislation has been introduced to make it illegal to record television programs for home use. Separate proposed legislation is also pending that would continue to allow recording of TV shows for home use, but would place a tax of 10% on each DVD that is purchased for home use. The income from that tax would then be proportionately distributed as royalties to those owning the rights to programs being aired. A weighted point system coupled with the averaging of several national viewing rating systems would be used to determine the royalties. There is a great deal of lobbying being done for both bills, as the manufacturers of DVDs and recording equipment are against the passage of the bills.

CONCLUSION: The legislature of Country X rejects both bills by a wide margin.

A. The statement proves the conclusion.
  B. The statement supports the conclusion but does not prove it.
  C. The statement disproves the conclusion.
  D. The statement weakens the conclusion.
  E. The statement is irrelevant to the conclusion.

26. Country X's Department of Taxation hires 500 new employees to handle the increased paperwork created by the new tax on DVDs. 26.____

27. A study conducted by the country's most prestigious accounting firm shows that the cost of implementing the proposed new DVD tax would be greater than the income expected from it. 27.____

28. It is estimated that 80% of all those working in the entertainment industry, excluding performers, own DVD recorders. 28.____

29. The head of Country X's law enforcement agency states that legislation banning the home recording of TV shows would be unenforceable. 29.____

30. Financial experts predict that unless a tax is placed on DVDs, several large companies in the entertainment industry will have to file for bankruptcy. 30.____

Questions 31-38.

DIRECTIONS: Questions 31 through 38 are variations on the type of question you just had. It is important that you read the question very carefully to determine exactly what is required.

31. In this question, select the choice that is MOST relevant to the conclusion. 31.____
    I. The Buffalo Bills football team is in second place in its division.
    II. The New England Patriots are in first place in the same division.
    III. There are two games left to play in the season, and the Bills will not play the Patriots again.
    IV. The New England Patriots won ten games and lost four games, and the Buffalo Bills have won eight games and lost six games.
    CONCLUSION: The Buffalo Bills win their division.
      A. The conclusion is proved by sentences I-IV.
      B. The conclusion is disproved by sentences I-IV.
      C. The facts are not sufficient to prove or disprove the conclusion.

32. In this question, select the choice that is MOST relevant to the conclusion. 32._____
   I. On the planet of Zeinon there are only two different eye colors and only two different hair colors.
   II. Half of those beings with purple hair have golden eyes.
   III. There are more inhabitants with purple hair than there are inhabitants with silver hair.
   IV. One-third of those with silver hair have green eyes.
   CONCLUSION: There are more golden-eyed beings on Zeinon than green-eyed ones.
   A. The conclusion is proved by sentences I-IV.
   B. The conclusion is disproved by sentences I-IV.
   C. The facts are not sufficient to prove or disprove the conclusion.

33. In this question, select the choice that is MOST relevant to the conclusion. 33._____
   John and Kevin are leaving Amaranth to go to school in Bethany. They've decided to rent a small truck to move their possessions. Joe's Truck Rental charges $100 plus 30¢ a mile. National Movers charges $50 more but gives free mileage for the first 100 miles. After the first 100 miles, they charge 25¢ a mile.
   CONCLUSION: John and Kevin rent their truck from National Movers because it is cheaper.
   A. The conclusion is proved by the facts in the above paragraph.
   B. The conclusion is disproved by the facts in the above paragraph.
   C. The facts are not sufficient to prove or disprove the conclusion.

34. For this question, select the choice that supports the information given in the passage. 34._____

   Municipalities in Country X are divided into villages, towns, and cities. A village has a population of 5,000 or less. The population of a town ranges from 5,001 to 15,000. In order to be incorporated as a city, the municipality must have a population over 15,000. If, after a village becomes a town, or a town becomes a city, the population drops below the minimum required (for example, the population of a city goes below 15,000), and stays below the minimum for more than ten years, it loses its current status, and drops to the next category. As soon as a municipality rises in population to the next category (village to town, for example), however, it is immediately reclassified to the next category.

   In the 2000 census, Plainfield had a population of 12,000. Between 2000 and 2010, Plainfield grew 10%, and between 2010 and 2020 Plainfield grew another 20%. The population of Springdale doubled from 2000 to 2010, and increased 25% from 2010 to 2020. The city of Smallville's population, 20,283, has not changed significantly in recent years. Granton had a population of 25,000 people in 1990, and has decreased 25% in each ten year period since then. Ellenville had a population of 4,283 in 1990, and grew 5% in each ten year period since 1990.

In 2020,
  A. Plainfield, Smallville, and Granton are cities.
  B. Smallville is a city, Granton is a town, and Ellenville is a village.
  C. Springdale, Granton, and Ellenville are towns.
  D. Plainfield and Smallville are cities, and Ellenville is a town.

35. For this question, select the choice that is MOST relevant to the conclusion.
    A study was done for a major food-distributing firm to determine if there is any difference in the kind of caffeine containing products used by people of different ages. A sample of one thousand people between the ages of twenty and fifty were drawn from selected areas in the country. They were divided equally into three groups.
    Those individuals who were 20-29 were designated Group A, those 30-39 were Group B, and those 40-50 were placed in Group C.
    It was found that on the average, Group A drank 1.8 cups of coffee, Group B 3.1, and Group C 2.5 cups of coffee daily. Group A drank 2.1 cups of tea, Group B drank 1.2, and Group C drank 2.6 cups of tea daily. Group A drank 3 1.8 ounces glasses of cola, Group B drank 1.9, and Group C drank 1.5 glasses of cola daily.
    CONCLUSION: According to the study, the average person in the 20-29 age group drinks less tea daily than the average person in the 40-50 age group, but drinks more coffee daily than the average person in the 30-39 age group drinks cola.
      A. The conclusion is proved by the facts in the above paragraph.
      B. The conclusion is disproved by the facts in the above paragraph.
      C. The facts are not sufficient to prove or disprove the conclusion.

36. For this question, select the choice that is MOST relevant to the conclusion
    I. Mary is taller than Jane but shorter than Dale.
    II. Fred is taller than Mary but shorter than Steven.
    III. Dale is shorter than Steven but taller than Elizabeth.
    IV. Elizabeth is taller than Mary but not as tall as Fred.
    CONCLUSION: Dale is taller than Fred.
      A. The conclusion is proved by sentences I-IV.
      B. The conclusion is disproved by sentences I-IV.
      C. The facts are not sufficient to prove or disprove the conclusion.

37. For this question, select the choice that is MOST relevant to the conclusion.
    I. Main Street is between Spring Street and Glenn Blvd.
    II. Hawley Avenue is one block south of Spring Street and three blocks north of Main Street.
    III. Glenn Street is five blocks south of Elm and four blocks south of Main.
    IV. All the streets mentioned are parallel to one another.
    CONCLUSION: Elm Street is between Hawley Avenue and Glenn Blvd.
      A. The conclusion is proved by the facts in sentences I-IV.
      B. The conclusion is disproved by the facts in sentences I-IV.
      C. The facts are not sufficient to prove or disprove the conclusion.

38. For this question, select the choice that is MOST relevant to the conclusion.
    I. Train A leaves the town of Hampshire every day at 5:50 A.M. and arrives in New London at 6:42 A.M.
    II. Train A leaves New London at 7:00 A.M. and arrives in Kellogsville at 8:42 A.M.
    III. Train B leaves Kellogsville at 8:00 A.M. and arrives in Hampshire at 10:45 A.M.
    IV. Due to the need for repairs, there is just one railroad track between New London and Hampshire.
    CONCLUSION: It is impossible for Train A and Train B to follow these schedules without colliding.
    A. The conclusion is proved by the facts in sentences I-IV.
    B. The conclusion is disproved by the facts in sentences I-IV.
    C. The facts are not sufficient to prove or disprove the conclusion.

KEY (CORRECT ANSWERS)

1.	D	11.	C	21.	D	31.	C
2.	B	12.	C	22.	A	32.	A
3.	E	13.	D	23.	C	33.	C
4.	B	14.	B	24.	B	34.	B
5.	C	15.	E	25.	E	35.	B
6.	A	16.	B	26.	C	36.	C
7.	D	17.	A	27.	B	37.	A
8.	B	18.	B	28.	E	38.	B
9.	B	19.	D	29.	B		
10.	B	20.	E	30.	D		

SOLUTIONS TO QUESTIONS

1. The answer is D. This statement weakens the conclusion, but does not disprove it. If a new branch of the community college opened in September, it could possibly bring in new business for Mr. Bryant. Since it states in the conclusion that Mr. Bryant felt there would not be enough new business to support the additional stores, this would tend to disprove the conclusion. Choice C would not be correct because it's possible that he felt that the students would not have enough additional money to support his new venture, or would not be interested in his clothing styles. It's also possible that the majority of the students already live in the area, so that they wouldn't really be a new customer population. This type of question is tricky, and can initially be very confusing, so don't feel badly if you missed it. Most people need to practice with a few of these types of questions before they feel comfortable recognizing exactly what they're being asked to do.

2. The answer is B. It supports the conclusion because the closing of the factory would probably take money and customers out of the town, causing Mr. Bryant to lose some of his present business. It doesn't prove the conclusion, however, because we don't know how large the factory was. It's possible that only a small percentage of the population was employed there, or that they found other jobs.

3. The answer is E. The fact that the number of children per household dropped slightly nationwide in the decade is irrelevant. Statistics showing a drop nationwide doesn't mean that there was a drop in the number of children per household in Mr. Bryant's hometown. This is a tricky question, as choice B, supporting the conclusion but not proving it, may seem reasonable. If the number of children per household declined nationwide, then it may not seem unreasonable to feel that this would support Mr. Bryant's decision not to expand his business. However, we're preparing you for promotional exams, not "real life." One of the difficult things about taking exams is that sometimes you're forced to make a choice between two statements that both seem like they could be the possible answer. What you need to do in that case is choose the best choice. Becoming annoyed or frustrated with the question won't really help much. If there's a review of the exam, you can certainly appeal the question. There have been many cases where, after an appeal, two possible choices have been allowed as correct answers. We've included this question, however, to help you see what to do should you get a question like this. It's most important not to get rattled, and to select the BEST choice. In this case, the connection between the statistical information and Mr. Bryant's decision is pretty remote. If the question had said that the number of children in Mr. Bryant's <u>town</u> had decreased, then choice B would have been a more reasonable choice. It could also help in this situation to visualize the situation. Picture Mr. Bryant in his armchair reading that, nationwide, the average number of children per household has declined slightly. How likely would this be to influence his decision, especially since he sells men's and women's clothing? It would take a while for this decline in population to show up, and we're not even sure if it applies to Mr. Bryant's hometown. Don't feel badly if you missed this; it was tricky. The more of these you do, the more comfortable you'll feel.

4. The answer is B. If a new clothing boutique specializing in casual women's clothing were to open soon, this would lend support to Mr. Bryant's decision not to expand, but would not prove that he had actually made the decision to expand. A new women's clothing boutique would most likely be in competition with his existing business, thus making any possible expansion a riskier venture. We can't be sure from this, however, that he didn't go ahead and expand his business despite the increased competition. Choice A, proves the conclusion, would only be the answer if we could be absolutely sure from the statement that Mr. Bryant had actually not expanded his business.

5. The answer is C. This statement disproves the conclusion. In order for his sister to buy several items for her baby at Mr. Bryant's store, he would have to have changed his business to include children's clothing.

6. The answer is A. It definitely proves the conclusion. The passage states that Mr. Bryan's store had been in business since 1920. A pie baked in honor of his store's 100th anniversary would have to be presented sometime in 2020. The conclusion states that he made his decision not to expand on November 7, 2018. If, more than a year later Mrs. MacIntyre comments that his store has maintained the same look and feel over the years, it could not have been expanded, or otherwise significantly changed.

7. The answer is D. If Mr. Bryant's aunt lent him $50,000 in October, this would tend to weaken the conclusion, which took place in November. Because it was stated that Mr. Bryant would need to borrow money in order to expand his business, it would be logical to assume that if he borrowed money he had decided to expand his business, weakening the conclusion. The reason C, disproves the conclusion, is not the correct answer is because we can't be sure Mr. Bryant didn't borrow the money for another reason.

8. The answer is B. If Mr. Bryant's town is eligible for federal funds to encourage the location of new businesses in the central district, this would tend to support his decision not to expand his business. Funds to encourage new business would increase the likelihood of there being additional competition for Mr. Bryant's store to contend with. Since we can't say for sure that there would be direct competition from a new business, however, choice A would be incorrect. Note that this is also a tricky question. You might have thought that the new funds weakened the conclusion because it would mean that Mr. Bryant could easily get the money he needed. Mr. Bryant is expanding his present business, not creating a new business. Therefore, he is not eligible for the funding.

9. The answer is B. This is a very tricky question. It's stated that 59% of car occupants don't use seat belts. The legislature is considering the use of air bags because of safety issues. The advantage of air bags over seat belts is that they inflate upon impact, and don't require car occupants to do anything with them ahead of time. Since the population has strongly resisted using seat belts, the air bags could become even more important in saving lives. Since saving lives is the purpose of the proposed legislation, the information that a small percentage of people use seat belts could be helpful to the passage of the legislation. We can't be sure that this is reason enough for the legislature to vote for the legislation, however, so choice A in incorrect.

10. The answer is B, as the information that 5,900 lives could be saved would tend to support the conclusion. Saving that many lives through the use of air bags could be a very persuasive reason to vote for the legislation. Since we don't know for sure that it's enough of a compelling reason for the legislature to vote for the legislation, however, choice A could not be the answer.

11. The answer is C, disproves the conclusion. If the legislation had been passed as stated in the conclusion, there would be no reason to appoint someone head of an advisory committee six days later to analyze the "feasibility of the proposed legislation." The key word here is "proposed." If it has been proposed, it means it hasn't been passed. This contradicts the conclusion and, therefore, disproves it.

12. The answer is C, disproves the conclusion. If the legislation had passed, there would be no reason for supporters of the legislation to accuse the legislature of rejecting the legislation for political reasons. This question may have seemed so obvious that you might have thought there was a trick to it. Exams usually have a few obvious questions, which will trip you up if you begin reading too much into them.

13. The answer is D, as this would tend to disprove the conclusion. A projected dramatic rise in imported cars could be very harmful to the country's economy and could be a very good reason for some legislators to vote against the proposed legislation. It would be assuming too much to choose C, however, because we don't know if they actually did vote against it.

14. The answer is B. This information would tend to support the passage of the legislation. The estimate of the cost of the air bags is $800 less than the cost estimated by opponents, and it's stated that the protection would be more reliable than any other type of seat belt. Both of these would be good arguments in favor of passing the legislation. Since we don't know for sure, however, how persuasive they actually were, choice A would not be the correct choice.

15. The answer is E, as this is irrelevant information. It really doesn't matter whether auto sales in 2001 have increased slightly over the previous year. If the air bag legislation were to go into effect in 2004, that might make the information somehow more relevant. But the air bag legislation would not take effect until 2009, so the information is irrelevant, since it tells us nothing about the state of the auto industry then.

16. The answer is B, supports the conclusion. This is a tricky question. While at first it might seem to prove the conclusion, we can't be sure that the air bag legislation is responsible for the drop in automobile deaths. It's possible air bags came into popular use without the legislation, or with different legislation. There's no way we can be sure that it was the proposed legislation mandating the use of air bags that was responsible.

17. The answer is A. If, in June of 2009, the lobbyist received a bonus "for her work on the air bag legislation," we can be sure that the legislation passed. This proves the conclusion.

18. The answer is B. This is another tricky question. A three-fold stock increase would strongly suggest that the legislation had been passed, but it's possible that factors other than the air bag legislation caused the increase. Note that the stock is in "crash protection

equipment." Nowhere in the statement does it say air bags. Seat belts, motorcycle helmets, and collapsible bumpers are all crash protection equipment and could have contributed to the increase. This is just another reminder to read carefully because the questions are often designed to mislead you.

19. The answer is D. This would tend to weaken the conclusion because Joan is very fond of her mother and she would not want to upset her unnecessarily. It does not prove it, however, because if Joan strongly feels she is right, she probably wouldn't let her mother's opinion sway her. Choice E would also not be correct, because we cannot assume that Joan's mother's opinion is of so little importance to her as to be considered irrelevant.

20. The answer is E. The statement is irrelevant. We are told that Joan's income has doubled but we are not old why. The phrase "six months after the interview" can be misleading in that it leads us to assume that the increase and the interview are related. Her income could have doubled because she regained her popularity but it could also have come from stocks or some other business venture. Because we are not given any reason for her income doubling, it would be impossible to say whether or not this statement proves or disproves the conclusion. Choice E is the best choice of the five possible choices. One of the problems with promotional exams is that sometimes you need to select a choice you're not crazy about. In this case, "not having enough information to made a determination" would be the best choice. However, that's not an option, so you're forced to work with what you've got. On these exams it's sometimes like voting for President; you have to pick the "lesser of the two evils" or the least awful choice. In this case, the information is more irrelevant to the conclusion than it is anything else.

21. The answer is D, weakens the conclusion. We've been told that Joan's agent feels that she should apologize. If he is pleased with her interview, then it would tend to weaken the conclusion but not disprove it. We can't be sure that he hasn't had a change of heart, or that there weren't other parts of the interview he liked so much that they outweighed her unwillingness to apologize.

22. The answer is A. The conclusion states that Joan will donate $1 to the Cellulite Prevention League for every pound the actress loses. Joan's sister's financial report on the League's activities directly supports and proves the conclusion.

23. The answer is C, disproves the conclusion. If the magazine receives many letters commending Joan for her courage in apologizing, this directly contradicts the conclusion, which states that Joan didn't apologize.

24. The answer is B. It was stated in the passage that two of Joan's performances were cancelled after the controversy first occurred. The cancellation of another performance immediately after her interview was published would tend to support the conclusion that she refused to apologize. Because we can't be sure, however, that her performance wasn't cancelled for another reason, choice A would be incorrect.

25. The answer is E, as this information is irrelevant. Postponing the article an extra week does not affect Joan's decision or the public's reaction to it.

26. The answer is C. If 500 new employees are hired to handle the "increased paperwork created by the new tax on DVDs," this would directly contradict the conclusion, which states that the legislature defeated both bills. (They should all be this easy.)

27. The answer is B. The results of the study would support the conclusion. If implementing the legislation was going to be so costly, it is likely that the legislature would vote against it. Choice A is not the answer, however, because we can't be sure that the legislature didn't pass it anyway.

28. The answer is E. It's irrelevant to the conclusion that 80% of all those working in the entertainment industry own DVD recorders. Sometimes if you're not sure about these, it can help a lot to try and visualize the situation. Why would someone voting on this legislation care about this fact? It doesn't seem to be the kind of information that would make any difference or impact upon the conclusion.

29. The answer is B. The head of the law enforcement agency's statement that the legislation would be unenforceable would support the conclusion. It's possible that many legislators would question why they should bother to pass legislation that would be impossible to enforce. Choice A would be incorrect, however, because we can't be sure that the legislation wasn't passed in spite of his statement.

30. The answer is D. This would tend to weaken the conclusion because the prospect of several large companies going bankrupt would seem to be a good argument in favor of the legislation. The possible loss of jobs and businesses would be a good reason for some people to vote for the legislation. We can't be sure, however, that this would be a competing enough reason to ensure passage of the legislation so choice C is incorrect.

This concludes our section on the "Validity of Conclusion" type of questions. We hope these weren't too horrible for you. It's important to keep in mind exactly what you've been given and exactly what they want you to do with it. It's also necessary to remember that you may have to choose between two possible answers. In that case, you must choose the one that seems the best. Sometimes you may think there is no good answer. You will probably be right, but you can't let that upset you. Just choose the one you dislike the least.

We want to repeat that it is unlikely that this exact format will appear on the exam. The skills required to answer these questions, however, are the same as those you'll need for the exam so we suggest that you review this section before taking the actual exam.

31. The answer is C. This next set of questions requires you to "switch gears" slightly, and get used to different formats. In this type of question, you have to decide whether the conclusion is proved by the facts give, disproved by the facts given, or neither because note enough information has been provided. Fortunately, unlike the previous questions, you don't have to decide whether particular facts support or don't support the conclusion. This type of question is more straight forward, but the reasoning behind it is the same. We are told that the Bills have won two games less than the Patriots, and that the Patriots are in first place and the Bills are in second place. We are also told that there are two games left to play, and that they won't play each other again. The conclusion states that the Bills won the division. Is there anything in the four statements that would prove this? We have

no idea what the outcome of the last two games of the season was. The Bills and Patriots could have ended up tied at the end of the season, or the Bills could have lost both or one of their last games while the Patriots did the same. There might even be another team tied for first or second place with the Bills or Patriots. Since we don't know for sure, Choice A is incorrect. Choice B is trickier. It might seem at first glance that the best the Bills could do would be to tie the Patriots if the Patriots lost their last two games and the Bills won their last two games. But it would be too much to assume that there is no procedure for a tiebreaker that wouldn't give the Bills the division championship. Since we don't know what the rules are in the event of a tie (for example, what if a tie was decided on the results of what happened when the two teams had played each other, or on the best record in the division, or on most points scored?), we can't say for sure that it would be impossible for the Bills to win their division. For this reason, choice C is the answer, as we don't have enough information to prove or disprove the conclusion. This question looked more difficult than it actually was. It's important to disregard any factors outside of the actual question, and to focus only on what you've been given. In this case, as on all of these types of questions, what you know or don't know about a subject is actually irrelevant. It's best to concentrate only on the actual facts given.

32. The answer is A. The conclusion is proved by the facts given.

    In this type of problem, it is usually best to pull as many facts as possible from the sentences and then put them into a simpler form. The phrasing and the order of exam questions are designed to be confusing so you need to restate things as clearly as possible by eliminating the extras.

    Sentence I tells us that there are only two possible colors for eyes and two for hair. Looking at the other sentences we learn that eyes are either green or gold and that hair is either silver or purple. If half the beings with purple hair have golden eyes, then the other half must have green eyes since it is the only other eye color. Likewise, if one-third of those with silver hair have green eyes, the other two-thirds must have golden eyes.

    This information makes it clear that there are more golden-eyed beings on Zeinon than green-eyed ones. It doesn't matter that we don't know exactly how many are actually living on the planet. The number of those with gold eyes (1/2 plus 2/3) will always be greater than the number of those with green eyes (1/2 plus 1/3), no matter what the actual figures might be. Sentence III is totally irrelevant because even if there were more silver-haired inhabitants it would not affect the conclusion.

33. The answer is C. The conclusion is neither proved nor disproved by the facts because we don't know how many miles Bethany is from Amoranth.

    With this type of question, if you're not sure how to approach it, you can always substitute in a range of "real numbers" to see what the result would be. If they were 200 miles apart, Joe's Truck Rental would be cheaper because they would charge a total of $160 while National Movers would charge $175.

    Joe's - $100 plus .30 x 200 (or $60) = $160
    National - $150 plus .25 x 100 (or $25) = $175

    If the towns were 600 miles apart, however, National Movers would be cheaper. The cost of renting from National would be $275 compared to the $280 charged by Joe's Trucking.

    Joe's - $100 plus .30 x 600 (or $180) = $280
    National - $150 plus .25 x 500 (or $125) = $275

15 (#1)

34. The answer is B. We've varied the format once more, but the reasoning is similar. This is a tedious question that is more like a math question, but we wanted to give you some practice with this type, just in case. You won't be able to do this question if you've forgotten how to do percents. Many exams require this knowledge, so if you feel you need a review we suggest you read Booklets 1, 2 or 3 in this series.

   The only way to attack this problem is to go through each choice until you find the one that is correct. Choice A states that Plainfield, Smallville, and Granton are cities. Let's begin with Plainfield. The passage states that in 1990 Plainfield had a population of 12,000, and that it grew 10% between 1990 and 2000, and another 20% between 2000 and 2010. Ten percent of 12,000 is 1200 (12,000 x .10 = 1200). Therefore, the population grew from 12,000 in 1990 to 12,000 + 1200 between 1990 and 2000. At the time of the 2000 Census, Plainfield's population was 13,200. It then grew another 20% between 2000 and 2010, so, 13,200 x .20 = 2640. 13,200 plus the additional increase of 2640 would make the population of Plainfield 15,840. This would qualify it as a city, since its population is over 15,000. Since a change upward in the population of a municipality is re-classified immediately, Plainfield would have become a city right away. So far, statement A is true. The passage states that Smallville's population has not changed significantly in the last twenty years. Since Smallville's population was 20,283, Smallville would still be a city. Granton had a population of 25,000 (what a coincidence that so any of these places have such nice, even numbers) in 1980. The population has decreased 25% in each ten year period since that time. So from 1980 to 1990, the population decreased 25%. 25,000 x .25 = 6,250. 25,000 minus 6,250 = 18,750. So the population of Granton in 1990 would have been 18,750. (Or, you could have saved a step and multiplied 25,000 by .75 to get 18,750.) The population from 1990 to 2000 decreased an additional 25%. So: 18,750 x .25 = 4,687.50. 18,750 minus 4,687.50 = 14,062.50. Or: 18,750 x .75 = 14,062.50. (Don't let the fact that a half of a person is involved confuse you; these are exam questions, not real life.) From 2000 to 2010 the population decreased an additional 25%. This would mean that Granton's population was below 15,000 for more than ten years, so it's status as a city would have changed to that of a town, which would make choice A incorrect.

   Choice B states that Smallville is a city and Granton is a town, which we know to be true from the information above. Choice B is correct so far. We next need to determine if Ellenville is a village. Ellenville had a population of 4,283 in 1980, and increased 5% in each ten year period since 1980. 4,283 x .05 = 214.15. 4,283 plus 214.15 = 4,497.15, so Ellenville's population from 1980 to 1990 increased to 4,497.15. (Or: 4,283 x 1.05 – 4,497.15.) From 1990 to 2000 Ellenville's population increased another 5%: 4,497.15 x .05 = 224.86. 4,497.15 plus 224.86 = 4,772.01 (or: 4,497.15 x 1.05 = 4,722.01.) From 2000 to 2010, Ellenville's population increased another 5%: 4,722.01 x .05 = 236.10. 4,722.01 plus 236.10 = 4,958.11. (Or: 4,722.01 x 1.05 = 4,958.11.).
   Ellenville's population is still under 5,000 in 2010, so it would continue to be classified as a village. Since all three statements in choice B are true, choice B must be the answer. However, we'll go through the other choices. Choice C states that Springdale is a town. The passage tells us that the population of Springdale doubled from 1990 to 2000, and increased 25% from 2000 to 2010. It doesn't give us any actual population figures, however, so it's impossible to know what the population of Springdale is, making choice C incorrect. Choice C also states that Granton is a town, which is true, and that Ellenville is

a town, which is false (from choice B we know it's a village). Choice D states that Plainfield and Smallville are cities, which is information we already know is true, and that Ellenville is a town. Since Ellenville is a village, choice D is also incorrect.

This was a lot of work for just one question and we doubt you'll get one like this on this section of the exam, but we included it just in case. On an exam, you can always put a check mark next to a question like this and come back to it later, if you feel you're pressed for time and cold spend your time more productively on other, less time-consuming problems.

35. The answer is B. This question requires very careful reading. It's best to break the conclusion down into smaller parts in order to solve the problem. The first half of the conclusion states that the average person in the 20-29 age group (Group A) drinks less tea daily than the average person in the 40-50 age group (Group C). The average person in Group A drinks 2.1 cups of tea daily, while the average person in Group C drinks 2.6 cups of tea daily. Since 2.1 is less than 2.6, the conclusion is correct so far. The second half of the conclusion states that the average person in Group A drinks more coffee daily than the average person in the 30-39 age group (Group B) drinks cola. The average person in Group A drinks 1.8 cups of coffee daily, while the average person in Group B drinks 1.9 glasses of cola. This disproves the conclusion, which states that the average person in Group A drinks more coffee daily than the average person in Group B drinks cola.

36. The answer is C. The easiest way to approach a problem that deals with the relationship between a number of different people or things is to set up a diagram. This type of problem is usually too confusing to do in your head. For this particular problem, the "diagram" could be a line, one end of which would be labeled tall and the other end labeled short. Then, taking one sentence at a time, place the people on the line to see where they fall in relation to one another.

The diagram of the first sentence would look like this:

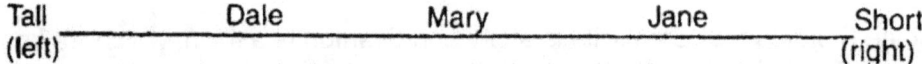

Mary is taller than Jane but shorter than Dale, so she would fall somewhere between the two of them. We have placed tall on the left and labeled it left just to make the explanation easier. You could just as easily have reversed the position.

The second sentence places Fred somewhere to the left of Mary because he is taller than she is. Steven would be to the left of Fred for the same reason. At this point we don't know whether Steven and Fred are taller or shorter than Dale. The new diagram would look like this:

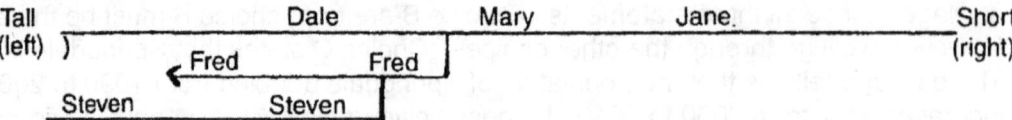

17 (#1)

The third sentence introduces Elizabeth, presenting a new problem. Elizabeth can be anywhere to the right of Dale. Don't make the mistake of assuming she falls between Dale and Mary. At this point we don't know where she fits in relation to Mary, Jane, or even Fred.

We do get information about Steven, however. He is taller than Dale so he would be to the left of Dale. Since he is also taller than Fred (see sentence II), we know that Steven is the tallest person thus far. The diagram would now look like this:

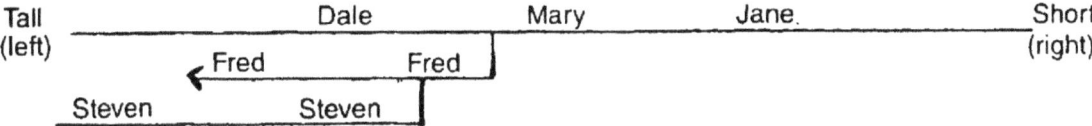

Fred's height is somewhere between Steven and Mary, Elizabeth's anywhere between Dale and the end of the line.

The fourth sentence tells us where Elizabeth stands, in relation to Fred and the others in the problem. The fact that she is taller than Mary means she is also taller than Jane. The final diagram would look like this:

Tall (left)	Steven	Dale	Elizabeth	Mary	Jane	Short (right)
		Fred				

We still don't know whether Dale or Fred is taller, however. Therefore, the conclusion that Dale is taller than Fred can't be proved. It also can't be disproved because we don't know for sure that he isn't. The answer has to be choice C, as the conclusion can't be proved or disproved.

37. The answer is A. This is another problem that is easiest for most people if they make a diagram. Sentence I states that Main Street is between Spring Street and Glenn Blvd. At this point we don't know if they are next to each other or if they are separated by a number of streets. Therefore, you should leave space between streets as you plot your first diagram.

The order of the streets could go either:

    Spring St.   or   Glenn Blvd.
    Main St.   Main St.
    Glenn Blvd.   Spring St.

Sentence II states that Hawley Street is one block south of Spring Street and 3 blocks north of Main Street. Because most people think in terms of north as above and south as below and because it was stated that Hawley is one block south of Spring Street and three blocks north of Main Street, the next diagram could look like this:

<u>Spring</u>
<u>Hawley</u>
_____

_____
<u>Main</u>
<u>Glenn</u>

The third sentence states that Glenn Street is five blocks south of Elm and four blocks south of Main. It could look like this:

<u>Spring</u>
<u>Hawley</u>

<u>Elm</u>
<u>Main</u>

_____
_____

<u>Glenn</u>

The conclusion states that Elm Street is between Hawley Avenue and Glenn Blvd. From the above diagram, we can see that this is the case.

38. The answer is B. For most people, the best way to do this problem is to draw a diagram, plotting the course of both trains. Sentence I states that Train A leaves Hampshire at 5:50 A.M. and reaches New London at 6:42. Your first diagram might look like this:

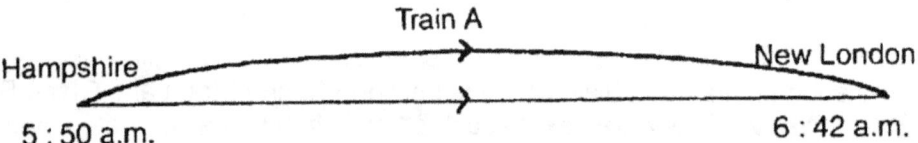

Sentence II states that the train leaves New London at 7:00 a.m. and arrives in Kellogsville at 8:42 a.m. The diagram might now look like this:

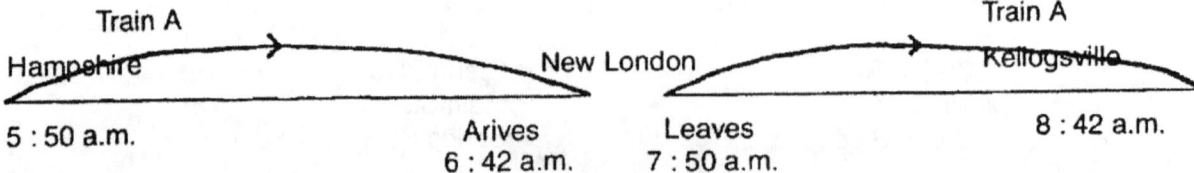

Sentence III gives us the rest of the information that must be included in the diagram. It introduces Train B, which moves in the opposite direction, leaving Kellogsville at 8:00 a.m. and arriving at Hampshire at 10:42 a.m. The final diagram might look like this:

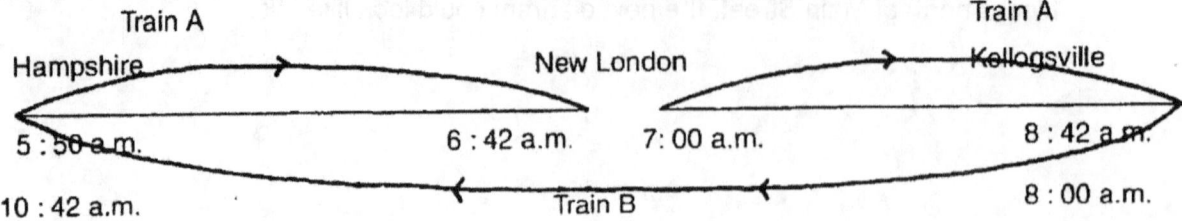

19 (#1)

As you can see from the diagram, the routes of the two trains will overlap somewhere between Kellogsville and New London. If you read sentence IV quickly and assumed that that was the section with only one track, you probably would have assumed that there would have had to be a collision. Sentence IV states, however, that there is only one railroad track between New London and Hampshire. That is the only section, then, where the two trains could collide. By the time Train B gets to that section, however, Train A will have passed it. The two trains will pass each other somewhere between New London and Kellogsville, not New London and Hampshire.

ANALYTICAL REASONING

COMMENTARY

This unique type of question focuses on the ability to understand a structure of relationships and to draw conclusions about that structure. The examinee is asked to understand the conditions used to establish the structure of the relationship and to deduce new information from them. Each group of questions consists of (1) a set of several related conditions (and sometimes other explanatory material) describing a structure of relationships, and (2) three or more questions that test understanding of the implications of that structure. Although each question in a group is based on the same set of conditions, the questions are independent of one another; answering one question in a group does not depend on answering any other question.

Each group of questions is based on a set of conditions that establish relationships among persons, places, things, or events. The relationships are common ones such as temporal order

> (A arrived before B but after C);spatial order
> (X always sits in front of Y and behind Z);
> group membership (If Professor Smith serves on
> the committee, then Professor Jones must also
> serve); and family structure (Jane is John's
> mother and Beth's sister).

The conditions should be read carefully to determine the exact nature of the relationships involved. Some relationships are fixed (J and K always sit at the same table). Other relationships are variable (S must be assigned to either table 1 or table 3). Some relationships that are not stated in the conditions can be deduced from those that are stated (if one condition about books on a shelf specifies that Book M is to the left of Book N, and another specifies that Book O is to the left of Book M then it can be deduced that Book O is to the left of Book N.)

No knowledge of formal logic is required for solving these problems. These questions are intended to be answered using knowledge, skills, and reasoning ability which are expected of college students and graduates.

SUGGESTED APPROACH

Some persons may prefer to answer first those questions in a group that seem to pose little difficulty and then to return to those that seem troublesome. It is best not to start one group before finishing another because much time can be lost in returning to a question group and reestablishing familiarity with its relationships. Do not assume that, because the conditions for a set look long or complicated, the questions based on those conditions will be especially difficult.

In reading the conditions, do not introduce unwarranted assumptions; for instance, in a set establishing relationships of height and weight among the members of a team, do not assume that a person who is taller than another person must weigh more than that person.

It is intended that the conditions be as clear as possible; do not interpret them as if they were designed to trick you. For example, if a question asks how many people could be eligible to serve on a committee, consider only those people named in the explanatory material unless directed otherwise. When in doubt, read the conditions in their most obvious sense. However, the language in the conditions is intended to be read for precise meaning. It is essential, for instance, to pay particular attention to words that describe or limit relationships, such as *only, exactly, never, always, must be, cannot be,* and the like. The result of the careful reading described above should be a clear picture of the structure of relationships involved, including what kinds of relationships are permitted, who or what the participants in the relationships are, and what is and is not known about the structure of the relationships. For instance, following a careful reading it can often be determined whether only a single configuration of relationships is permitted by the conditions or whether alternative configurations are permitted.

Each question should be considered separately from the other questions in its group; no information, except what is given in the original conditions, should be carried over from one question to another. In some cases a question will simply ask for conclusions to be drawn from the conditions as originally given. An individual question can, however, add information to the original conditions or temporarily suspend one of the original conditions for the purpose of that question only. For example, if Question 1 adds the information "if P is setting at table 2 ....," this information should NOT be carried over to any other question in the group.

Many people find it useful to underline key points in the conditions.

As the directions for this type of question suggest, it may prove very helpful to draw a diagram representing the configuration to assist you in answering the question.

Even though some people find diagrams to be very helpful, other people seldom use them. And among those who do regularly use diagrams in solving these problems, there is by no means universal agreement on which kind of diagram is best for which problem or in which cases a diagram is most useful. Therefore, do not be concerned if a particular problem in the test seems to be best approached without the use of diagrams.

EXAMINATION SECTION
TEST 1

DIRECTIONS: Each question or incomplete statement is followed by several suggested answers or completions. Select the one that BEST answers the question or completes the statement. *PRINT THE LETTER OF THE CORRECT ANSWER IN THE SPACE AT THE RIGHT.*

QUESTIONS 1-5.

Questions 1-5 refer to the following factual conditions.

Mrs. Jones is a teacher with a class of only five students, whose names are Alice, Bob, Carol, Donald, and Edna. There is only one row consisting of six seats, numbered 1 through 6 from front to back. No girl will sit behind all the other children. Also, due to conflicting personalities, Alice and Carol must not be assigned to consecutive seats.

1. Which of the following arrangements is(are) acceptable for seats #3 through #6?
    I. Empty, Alice, Carol, Bob
    II. Carol, Donald, Edna, Empty
    III. Carol, Edna, Empty, Bob
   The CORRECT answer is:

   A. I only
   B. II only
   C. III only
   D. I and II
   E. II and III

2. If Alice is assigned to the fourth seat, and the two boys are assigned to the first and second seats, in how many ways can the remaining two girls be seated?

   A. 1
   B. 2
   C. 3
   D. 4
   E. None of these

3. If Edna, Donald, and Carol will be seated in consecutive seats (from front to back), in that order, in how many ways can all the students be arranged?

   A. 2   B. 3   C. 4   D. 5   E. 6 or more

4. If Mrs. Jones decides that the sixth seat shall be vacant and that Alice needs to sit in either the first or second seat, which of the following statements must be TRUE?

   A. The first seat will be occupied by a girl
   B. If Alice sits in the second seat, Edna will sit in either the first or third seats
   C. If Alice sits in the first seat, Carol will sit in the third seat
   D. The two boys will occupy the fourth and fifth seats
   E. None of the above

5. Suppose Edna is assigned the fifth seat and Donald is assigned the third seat. Which of the following represents the complete and accurate list of seat numbers which may be vacant?

   A. 2 and 4
   B. 1 *only*
   C. 4 and 6
   D. 1 and 2
   E. 2 *only*

115

QUESTIONS 6-10.

Questions 6-10 refer to the following factual conditions.

John wishes to arrange seven textbooks on a shelf, which contains exactly seven slots numbered 1 through 7 from left to right. Three texts are math books, two are history books, one is a science book, and one is a logic book. He has decided that no two math books will occupy adjacent slots and that the number of slots between the two history books must equal the number of slots between the logic and science books. This number may be zero.

6. Which of the following arrangements for the first three slots is (are) NOT acceptable?
   I. History, History, Math
   II. History, Logic, History
   III. Science, Math, Logic
   The CORRECT answer is:

   A. I only
   B. II only
   C. III only
   D. I and II
   E. I and III

7. If the slots numbered 2, 6, and 7 are occupied by the texts history, science, and logic respectively, which of the following statements is CORRECT?

   A. A math book must be in slot 1
   B. The other history book must be in slot 3
   C. Both statements A and B
   D. Any arrangement of the remaining books is acceptable
   E. There is no possible arrangement that satisfies these conditions

8. If no math book is placed in slots 5 or 7, then:

   A. A math book is placed in slot 1
   B. The two history books must be in slot 3
   C. Both statement A and B
   D. Any arrangement of the remaining books is acceptable
   E. There is no possible arrangement that satisfies these condition

9. If the third, fourth, and fifth slots are occupied by a logic book, math book, and history book respectively, then in which of the following pairs of slots would it NOT be possible to place the other two math books?

   A. 2 and 6
   B. 2 and 7
   C. 1 and 7
   D. 1 and 6
   E. More than one choice among A, B, C, D

10. If two of the math books occupy slots 1 and 4 and a history book occupies slot 6, then which of the following is a complete list of types of books which may occupy slot 5?

    A. History
    B. Logic
    C. Science
    D. Two of the above
    E. All of the above

QUESTIONS 11-15.

Questions 11-15 refer to the following factual conditions.

A family consists of 6 members: Mother, Father, 2 sons, Frank and George, and 2 daughters, Helen and Ida. The dining room table is circular with six seats numbered 1 through 6. Seat 1 is located at the 12 o'clock position and the seats are numbered consecutively clockwise, and are evenly spaced. (e.g., seat 4 is at 6 o'clock).
The family has some peculiar rules when they sit at this table, i.e.:
1. None of the sons will sit in seat 4;
2. Mother and Father must be three seats apart;
3. Helen will not sit next to Ida; and
4. Frank insists on sitting next to Mother.

11. If Father sits in seat 2 and Ida sits in seat 4, which of the following is a complete list of the people who can occupy seat 3?

    A. George and Helen
    B. Frank *only*
    C. George *only*
    D. Frank and George
    E. Mother *only*

12. If Frank sits in an even-numbered seat, which of the following is(are) TRUE?
    I. Father sits in an even-numbered seat
    II. George sits next to Father
    III. Ida sits next to George or Frank
    IV. Mother sits in an odd-numbered seat
    The CORRECT answer is:

    A. I, II
    B. II, IV
    C. I, III
    D. II, III, IV
    E. I, III, IV

13. Which of the following is an IMPOSSIBLE arrangement of the occupants of seats 1 through 3 respectively?

    A. George, Helen, Father
    B. Frank, Ida, Father
    C. Mother, Helen, George
    D. Ida, George, Mother
    E. None of these

14. If one of the daughters is assigned to seat 6, and Mother is assigned to seat 4, which of the following choices lists ALL the seats which could be occupied by Helen?

    A. 1, 3, 5
    B. 2, 3, 6
    C. 2, 6
    D. 1, 2, 3
    E. 1, 3, 6

15. If George and Father decide to sit next to each other, and Father sits in seat 5, which of the following selections MOST accurately describes who may sit next to George (besides Father)?

    A. Helen or Frank
    B. Only Frank
    C. Ida or Helen
    D. Ida, Helen, or Frank
    E. Only Ida

QUESTIONS 16-20.

Questions 16-20 refer to the following factual conditions.

A company is moving to a new building and is going to rearrange the location of each of its departments. The list of departments are: Marketing, Personnel, Engineering, Research, Advertising, and Sales. The new building will contain eight floors, and each of the six departments will occupy a complete floor, (numbered 1 through 8 from bottom to top). The company president has issued several restrictions:
1. No department shall be situated such that there is a vacant floor both one floor below it and one floor above it simultaneously.
2. If a department is located on the 8th floor, it is permissible to have a vacancy on the 7th floor, but not on both the 6th and 7th floors simultaneously.
3. The 1st floor shall never be vacant
4. The Personnel department shall be located no higher than the 3rd floor.
5. The Sales department must be situated on either the 4th floor or the 5th floor.

16. Suppose the Marketing department is assigned to the 8th floor, and the Advertising department is assigned to the 2nd floor. Which of the following statements is ACCURATE?

    A. If the Engineering department is on a higher floor than Personnel, then the Engineering department cannot be on the 3rd floor
    B. The Research department will necessarily be on a higher floor than Personnel
    C. If the 6th floor is occupied by Research, then the 7th floor must be occupied by Engineering
    D. If personnel is assigned to the 3rd floor, some department will be assigned to the 5th floor or there will be 2 consecutive vacancies
    E. If the 4th floor is vacant, then exactly two departments are situated on higher floors than Sales

17. Which of the following is a possible arrangement for the 1st floor through the 4th floor respectively?
    I. Marketing, Vacant, Personnel, Sales
    II. Personnel, Vacant, Engineering, Vacant
    III. Research, Personnel, Sales, Marketing

    The CORRECT answer is:

    A. I only
    B. II only
    C. III only
    D. II, III
    E. I, II, III

18. Which of the following is a possible arrangement for floors 5 through 8, respectively?
    I. Vacant, Sales, Advertising, Engineering
    II. Vacant, Reaserch, Engineering, Vacant
    III. Sales, Marketing, Research, Advertising
    IV. Sales, Vacant, Vacant, Research

    The CORRECT answer is:

    A. I, II, III, IV
    B. Exactly one of I, II, III, IV
    C. Exactly two of I, II, III, IV
    D. Exactly three of I, II, III, IV
    E. None of the above

19. Suppose that Marketing is assigned to the 7th floor, and Advertising is assigned to the 3rd floor. After each of the other departments are then assigned to their respective floors, which of the following is a pair of floors for which vacancies can exist *simultaneously*?

   A. 1, 2   B. 4, 5   C. 2, 4   D. 6, 8   E. 5, 6

20. Assume that the Research department must be on a higher floor than Engineering but on a lower floor than Sales, and Personnel is below each of the other 5 departments.
    If Research occupies a floor no higher than the 5th, which of the following is a complete and accurate list of the floors on which it is possible to find Research?

   A. 2   B. 3 or 4   C. 3, 4, or 5
   D. 3   E. 4 or 5

QUESTIONS 21-25.

Questions 21-25 refer to the following factual conditions.

A music teacher needs to select four students to play in a small band. The selected students will sit in seats 1 through 4, from left to right. The instruments being played from seat 1 to seat 4 IN ORDER are: trumpet, trombone, saxophone, and drum. Students A and B can only play trumpet. Student C can play trumpet or saxophone. Student D can play trombone or drum. Student E can only play trombone. Students G and H can only play saxophone. Students J and K can only play drums. (Assume that any one person cannot be chosen to play 2 instruments simultaneously.) Additionally, 2 other stipulations prevail:
   1. D will not participate if J is chosen to play.
   2. B will participate only if H is also chosen.

21. Which of the following is a possible selection for seats 1 to 4, respectively?
    I.   A, D, H, J
    II. B, E, H, D
    III. C, D, H, K

    The CORRECT answer is:

    A. I *only*   B. II *only*
    C. III *only*   D. Exactly 2 choices of I, II, III
    E. I, II, III

22. If B is chosen to play trumpet, in how many different ways can the other three players be chosen?

    A. 3   B. 4   C. 5   D. 6   E. 7

23. Which of the following statements would be sufficient to imply that A will play trumpet?

    A. C is chosen for saxophone
    B. E is chosen for trombone, and G is chosen for saxophone
    C. D is chosen for trombone
    D. All of the above
    E. None of the above

24. If H is chosen for saxophone, and K is chosen for drum, this implies
    A. C is chosen for trumpet
    B. B is chosen for trumpet
    C. E is chosen for trombone
    D. Exactly 2 of A, B, or C must be correct
    E. None of A, B, C must necessarily be correct

25. Which of the following statements is ACCURATE?
    A. If A plays trumpet, then C plays saxophone
    B. If D plays trombone, then K play drum
    C. If G plays saxophone, then C plays trumpet
    D. If K plays drum, then E plays trombone
    E. None of the above

KEY (CORRECT ANSWERS)

1.	C	11.	C
2.	E	12.	E
3.	D	13.	D
4.	B	14.	B
5.	D	15.	C
6.	D	16.	D
7.	E	17.	A
8.	A	18.	C
9.	E	19.	E
10.	E	20.	B

21. D
22. B
23. A
24. E
25. B

---

7 (#1)

SOLUTIONS TO PROBLEMS

1. CHOICE I is not acceptable since Alice and Carol sit in consecutive seats.
   CHOICE II is not acceptable since Edna would be sitting behind everyone else, violating the condition that no girl shall sit behind all the other children.
   CHOICE III is acceptable, for it allows the following complete seating arrangement: Alice, Donald, Carol, Edna, Empty, Bob.

   (Answer C)

2. Regardless of how Carol and Edna are seated, one girl will be sitting behind all the other children, which is not a per-missable condition.

   (Answer E)

3. The allowable arrangements are:
   Alice, Empty, Edna, Donald, Carol, Bob
   Empty, Alice, Edna, Donald, Carol, Bob
   Edna, Donald, Carol, Empty, Alice, Bob
   Alice, Edna, Donald, Carol, Empty, Bob
   Alice, Edna, Donald, Carol, Bob, Empty

   (Answer D)

4. CHOICE A is not necessarily true, since Alice could be assigned to the second seat, and either Donald or Bob could be assigned the first seat.
   CHOICE B must take place; since, if Edna sat in the fourth seat, Carol would be forced into either the first, second, or fifth seats. This would violate one of the required conditions that either Alice and Carol cannot occupy consecutive seats, or that no girl shall sit behind all the other children.
   CHOICE C need not happen, since a possible arrangement is: Alice, Bob, Edna, Carol, Donald, Empty.
   CHOICE D is not necessarily true, as seen in the explanation of CHOICE C.

   (Answer B)

5. Bob must be assigned to the sixth seat, in order not to violate the required conditions. If seat 4 were vacant, it would force Alice and Carol to sit in consecutive seats. If the first seat were vacant, Alice and Carol could occupy seats 2 and 4. Likewise, if the second seat were vacant, Alice and Carol could occupy seats 1 and 4. Thus, CHOICE D is correct and complete.

   (Answer D)

6. CHOICE I would force the other two math books into slots 5 and 7 and thus the logic and science books would be 2 slots apart. Since the history books are not 2 slots apart also, this is incorrect.
   CHOICE II implies that the science book would occupy slot 4 and this situation would force the math books to occupy adjacent slots.
   CHOICE III is acceptable, with the following complete arrangement: Science, Math, Logic, Math, History, Math, History.

   (Answer D)

7. From the stated conditions in the paragraph governing this question, a history book must be placed in either slot 1 or slot 3. In either event, as least one pair of adjacent slots (numbers 4 and 5) will both contain math books.

(Answer E)

8. CHOICE A implies that the other two math books will be found in slots 1 and 6. Since the number of slots between the two history books must equal the number of slots between the number of slots between the science and logic books, the history books can be placed in slots 2 and 4, with the science and logic books in slots 5 and 7.
CHOICE B is not necessarily true since a possible arrangement is: Logic, Math, History, Math, Science, Math, History.
CHOICE C would place the math books in slots 1, 4, and 6. Thus the science and logic books could not be adjacent to each other.
CHOICE D would create a five-slot gap requirement for the two history books, which is impossible.
CHOICE E can be countered by this arrangement: Math, History, Math, History, Logic, Math, Science.

(Answer A)

9. CHOICES B and D would be impossible. For CHOICE B, we have _____, Math, Logic, Math, History, _____, Math. No matter how the other history and science books are filled in, a violation of the original conditions will prevail. For CHOICE D, we would have Math, _____ Logic, Math, History, Math, _____. Again no possible arrangement of the remaining two books is permissible.

(Answer E)

10. CHOICE A allows this arrangement: Math, Logic, Science, Math, History, History, Math. Also the logic and science books may be interchanged.
CHOICE B allows: Math, Science, History, Math, Logic, History, Math.
CHOICE C allows: Math, Logic, History, Math, Science, History, Math.
Thus all 3 of the subjects history, logic, and science are allowed.

(Answer E)

11. Condition 3 eliminates Helen from seat 3. Frank cannot occupy seat 3 either because of condition 4. If Mother were to occupy seat 3, then Frank would be forced into seat 5 or seat 6, — again violating condition 4. George could be assigned seat 3 and an acceptable arrangement becomes: Helen, Father, George, Ida, Mother, Frank.

(Answer C)

12. Due to condition 1, Frank must sit in seat 2 or seat 6. By condition 4, Mother will definitely sit in an odd-numbered seat. By condition 2, this implies that Father will sit three seats away from Mother and this will be an even-numbered seat. Statement II is not necessarily true as the following arrangement shows: Mother, Frank, Helen, Father, Ida, George. Thus, statements I, III, and IV must be true.

(Answer E)

13. CHOICE D will violate one of the four conditions. By condition 4, Frank would be forced into seat 4. However, this situation would violate condition 1. Each of choices a, b, c are possible, as indicated with the following complete arrangements associated with each of these choices.
    For CHOICE A: George, Helen, Father, Ida, Frank, Mother
    For CHOICE B: Frank, Ida, Father, Helen, George, Mother
    For CHOICE C: Mother, Helen, George, Father, Ida, Frank

    (Answer D)

14. Certainly Helen could occupy seat 6, from the given information. If Ida is assigned seat 6, then Helen cannot occupy seats 1 or 5. Since Mother is already in seat 4, Helen is then obliged to take seats 2 or 3. Thus, seats 2, 3, or 6 are the only ones which Helen may occupy.

    (Answer B)

15. Condition 4 forces Frank to sit in seat 1 or seat 3, which follows from condition 2 placing Mother in seat 2. The only arrangements which would then allow Frank to sit next to George would be as follows (seats 1 to 6 in order):
    1. Frank, Mother, _____, _____, Father, George; or
    2. _____, Mother, Frank, George, Father, _____
    Actually arrangement (2) is NOT allowed due to condition 1, and neither of these arrangements are permitted by condition 3. This, logic leads one to eliminate Frank as an eligible candidate to sit next to George. Either Ida or Helen (CHOICE C) may sit next to George since the final arrangement can be:
    Ida, Mother, Frank, Helen, Father, George; or
    Helen, Mother, Frank, Ida, Father, George

    (Answer C)

16. For the purposes of abbreviation, the letters A, E, M, P, R, and S will be used to refer to each department. V means vacancy.
    CHOICE A is not accurate since one possible arrangement could be: P, A, E, S, V, V, R, M (other arrangments also exist).
    CHOICE B can be shown incorrect by this arrangement: R, A, P, V, S, E, V, M. The arrangement E, A, P, V, S, R, V, M shows
    CHOICE C to be false.
    CHOICE D is correct. Suppose Sales is not assigned to the 5th floor. Then the first 4 floors would be E or R, A, P, S. Now, if no department is assigned to the 5th floor, then the 2 vacant floors would be the 5th and 6th or the 5th and 7th. But having the vacancies on the 5th and 7th floors would violate restriction 1. Thus, vacancies on the 5th and 6th floors represent 2 consecutive vacancies.
    CHOICE E places the Sales department on the 5th floor. But we could have vacancies on the 3rd and 4th floors so that the final arrangement is: P, A, V, V, S, E, R, M. Thus 3 departments are located on higher floors than Sales.

    (Answer D)

17. CHOICE I violates no restriction, and can be completed for floors 5 through 8 as:
    Research, Engineering, Advertising, Vacant.
    CHOICE II violates restriction 1.
    CHOICE III violates restriction 5.

(Answer A)

18. CHOICE I violates restriction 5.
    CHOICE II is acceptable and the 1st through 4th floors could be occupied by Marketing, Advertising, Personnel, Sales.
    CHOICE III is also acceptable and here the first 4 floors could be Engineering, Personnel, Vacant, Vacant.
    CHOICE IV is not correct due to restriction 2.

(Answer C)

19. The pair 1, 2 is eliminated because of restrictions 3 and 4.
    The pair 4, 5 is eliminated because of restriction 5.
    The pair 2, 4 would create a violation of restriction 1.
    The pair 6, 8 also violates restriction 1.
    However, the pair 5, 6 can be both vacant. The completed arrangement must have Personnel on the 1st or 2nd floors and Sales on the 4th floor.

(Answer E)

20. Since Sales must be located on either the 4th or 5th floor, Research cannot be located on floor 5, and thus we have narrowed the selection to floors 1, 2, 3, or 4. But Personnel must occupy floor 1, since it is below all other departments (Recall, the 1st floor cannot be vacant). Also, Research must be higher than Engineering, so floor 2 cannot be occupied by Research. Either floors 3 or 4 are possible as shown by the following schemes: P, E, R, S, V, V, A, M or P, E, V, R, S, A, M, V (for example).

(Answer B)

21. Stipulation 1 eliminates selection I. Selections II and III are both permissible. Recognize that stipulation 2 does not preclude H from being chosen when B is not chosen.

(Answer D)

22. For seats 2, 3, 4, the four possibilities are: (1) D, H, K; (2) E, H, D; (3) E, H, J; and (4) E, H, K. Note that H MUST be selected due to stipulation 2.

(Answer B)

23. Once C is chosen for saxophone, only A or B are left as eligibles for trumpet. Now H has been eliminated, and thus stipulation 2 precludes B from playing. Thus CHOICE A is correct.
    In CHOICE B, the final selection could be C, E, G, _____, where any of D, J, or K may play drum. Thus A need not be chosen.
    In CHOICE C, selections exist for which A, B, or C will play trumpet.

(Answer A)

24. The final selection could be A, D, H, K and so none of the statements A, B, C need necessarily be correct.

(Answer E)

25. In CHOICE A, combinations exist where either G or H may play saxophone. Examples are: A, D, G, K and A, E, H, K.
In CHOICE B, once D is selected for trombone, only J and K remain eligible for drum. However, stipulation 1 forces K to be selected.
In CHOICE C, we could have A, D, G, K.
In CHOICE D, again, the selection of A, D, G, K is possible.
Thus, only CHOICE B is accurate.

(Answer B)

EXAMINATION SECTION
TEST 1

DIRECTIONS: Each question or incomplete statement is followed by several suggested answers or completions. Select the one that BEST answers the question or completes the statement. *PRINT THE LETTER OF THE CORRECT ANSWER IN THE SPACE AT THE RIGHT.*

QUESTIONS 1-5.

Questions 1-5 refer to the following factual conditions.

A person has five animals to care for. They are a dog, cat, alligator, horse, and rabbit. These animals will be kept in an area with 5 joining compartments, numbered 1 through 5 from left to right. Only 1 animal is allowed per compartment. Two other conditions must be met:
1. The dog and cat must not be kept in adjacent compartments unless the horse is kept in a compartment adjoining either one of them, since the horse's temperament is a stabilizing factor.
2. The horse is the only animal which is not afraid of the alligator. Thus, no other animal may be placed next to the alligator.

1. Which of the following is NOT possible concerning the arrangement of the animals in the last 3 compartments?
   I. dog, horse, alligator
   II. dog, horse, cat
   III. cat, dog, rabbit

   The CORRECT answer is:

   A. I *only*
   B. II *only*
   C. III *only*
   D. Exactly two choices of I, II, III
   E. All three choices of I, II, III

2. If the alligator is placed in compartment 4, which arrangement is MOST proper?

   A. The cat is placed in compartment 1
   B. The horse is placed in compartment 5
   C. The rabbit is placed in any compartment except 2
   D. No arrangement is possible
   E. The horse is placed in either compartments 3 or 5

3. Which of the following is a complete and accurate list of the compartment(s) which may be occupied by the rabbit?

   A. Any compartment B. 1, 2, and 3
   C. 5 *only* D. 2 and 4 *only*
   E. Any compartment but 3

4. If the horse is placed in compartment 2, in how many ways can the dog and cat be placed in the other compartments?

   A. 2   B. 3   C. 4   D. 5   E. 6

5. If the cat is not placed in compartment 3, which of the following is a complete list of animals which could occupy compartment 3?

   A. horse, dog
   B. rabbit
   C. alligator, dog
   D. rabbit, dog
   E. dog

QUESTIONS 6-11.

Questions 6-11 refer to the following factual conditions.

Six people are standing in a line at a movie theater, one behind the other. The individuals are numbered 1 through 6 from front to back. The theater is showing three movies entitled W, X, and Y. It is known that each of the six people has a ticket for exactly one of these movies. Also, the following conditions are known:
1. The 4th person has a ticket for either X or Y.
2. There is one individual standing between the two people who have tickets for X.
3. For the 3 people who have a ticket for W, exactly 2 of them are standing one behind the other. The third person with a ticket for W is standing neither directly in front of nor directly behind either of the other two.

6. Which of the following is an acceptable arrangement of the movie selections corresponding to the first 4 people?

   A. XWXY   B. WWWX   C. WXWY   D. XWWX   E. XYXW

7. Which of the following is(are) acceptable as position numbers for the individuals holding a ticket for X?

   I. 2, 4
   II. 4, 6
   III. 1, 3

   The CORRECT answer is:

   A. I only
   B. II only
   C. III only
   D. Exactly 2 choices of I, II, III
   E. All three choices of I, II, III

8. Which of the following is the most complete and accurate group of numbered positions of people who can hold a ticket for Y?

   A. 4   B. 2, 4   C. 1, 4   D. 1, 3, 4   E. 1, 2, 4

9. If the third person in line has a ticket for W, then which of the following must be true?

   A. The 4th person holds a ticket for Y
   B. The 4th person holds a ticket for X
   C. The 5th and 6th persons both hold the other 2 tickets for W

D. The 2nd person holds a ticket for X
E. The 1st person holds a ticket for W

10. Assuming that the 1st person does NOT have a ticket for W, then the 2nd person will have a ticket for

   A. W *only*
   B. X *only*
   C. Y *only*
   D. Either W or X
   E. Either X or Y

11. If the 5th and 6th individuals have tickets for X and W respectively, in how many ways can the other people be arranged?

   A. 1   B. 2   C. 3   D. 4   E. at least 5

QUESTIONS 12-18.

Questions 12-18 refer to the following factual conditions.

The Racing Secretary of Hoofbeats Raceway is about to assign eight horses their respective post positions (numbered 1 through 8) in today's feature race. The horses' names are: Applesauce, Bologna, Celery, Derma, Edible, Fruit Cup, Green Bean, and Honey Pie. The following restrictions apply:
1. Neither Applesauce nor Celery may be assigned to Post 1 or Post 8.
2. Derma must race from an even numbered post.
3. Bologna and Fruit Cup must both be assigned odd numbered posts.
4. Green Bean's post number must be smaller than that of Honey Pie.
5. Edible's post number must be higher than that of Honey Pie, but smaller than that of Fruit Cup.

12. Which of the following is a complete and accurate list of who may race from Post 1?

   A. Bologna, Fruit Cup, Honey Pie
   B. All but Applesauce and Celery
   C. Bologna, Green Bean
   D. only Green Bean
   E. Bologna, Derma, Fruit Cup, Green Bean

13. To what post numbers may Green Bean be assigned?

   A. 1, 2
   B. 1, 2, 3
   C. 2, 3, 4
   D. 1, 2, 3, 4
   E. 1, 2, 3, 4, 5

14. If Applesauce is assigned to post 3 and Celery is assigned to post 4, which of the following horses cannot be assigned to post 5?

   A. Green Bean   B. Bologna   C. Fruit Cup
   D. Honey Pie   E. Edible

15. How many different horses would be eligible to be assigned to post 8?

   A. 1   B. 2   C. 3   D. 4   E. 5 or 6

16. All of the following are acceptable arrangements of the horses assigned to posts 2, 3, and 4 respectively EXCEPT:

    A. Applesauce, Bologna, Celery
    B. Honey Pie, Fruit Cup, Edible
    C. Celery, Green Bean, Honey Pie
    D. Green Bean, Honey Pie, Edible
    E. Honey Pie, Applesauce, Edible

17. Which of the following gives the complete list of horses which CANNOT race from post 7?

    A. Derma, Edible, Fruit Cup, Green Bean
    B. Celery, Derma, Edible, Green Bean
    C. Derma, Edible, Green Bean, Honey Pie
    D. Derma, Edible, Fruit Cup, Green Bean, Honey Pie
    E. Bologna, Celery

18. Which restriction(s) could be removed WITHOUT affecting the solutions to the preceding questions?

    A. 1 and 3   B. 2 and 5   C. 1   D. 2   E. 5

QUESTIONS 19-22.

Questions 19-22 refer to the following factual conditions.

The work assignments are rather peculiar for the five employees of the Frozen prices Supermarket. Following are the work conditions:
1. Jack can only work on Mondays and Saturdays.
2. Lisa can work any days except Saturdays and Sundays.
3. Melanie can work on any days, provided at least one of the other four employees is also working on those days.
4. Nancy will only work on days when no one else is assigned.
5. Otto can work any days except Wednesdays. Also, since he cannot tolerate Lisa, he will not work on any day that she is assigned.

19. The MAXIMUM number of workers who can be assigned Tuesdays is

    A. 1   B. 2   C. 3   D. 4   E. 5

20. If the manager decides to assign 3 workers for Saturday, which of the following group(s) could be assigned?

    A. Jack, Melanie, Otto
    B. Nancy, Otto, Jack
    C. Jack, Lisa, Melanie
    D. Exactly two selections of A, B, and C
    E. None of the above

21. During one particular week (Sunday through Saturday), the manager decides to have Lisa work on only 2 days, which must be consecutive. Otto will be unable to work on Saturday, but he will also only work on 2 consecutive days. Nancy is assigned to work only on Monday.
On which 2 consecutive days can Lisa work?

   A. Monday, Tuesday
   B. Tuesday, Wednesday
   C. Thursday, Friday
   D. Friday, Saturday
   E. Sunday, Monday

   21.____

22. Refer to the situation in the previous question. If Jack is assigned to work only 1 day, what is the MAXIMUM number of days on which Melanie can work (during that week)?

   A. 3   B. 4   C. 5   D. 6   E. 7

   22.____

QUESTIONS 23-25.

Questions 23-25 refer to the following factual conditions.

A child is about to color in 4 pages of a coloring book, using only one color on each page. The available colors are yellow, red, and green; but not every color is required to be used. Certain conditions will also apply:
1. The number of pages colored in green cannot exceed the number of pages colored in red.
2. The 3rd page must be colored in yellow or red.
3. No two consecutive pages will have the same color.

23. If page 2 is colored red, which one(s) of the following arrangements is(are) possible for pages 1 through 4, respectively?

   A. Yellow, red, yellow, green
   B. Yellow, red, yellow, red
   C. Yellow, red, green, red
   D. Exactly 2 selections of A, B, and C
   E. All of the above

   23.____

24. If page 1 is colored green, how many different coloring arrangements are possible for the other pages?

   A. 0   B. 1   C. 2   D. 3   E. 4

   24.____

25. For which of the following conditions is it possible that NO page will be colored green?

   A. Page 1 is red
   B. Pages 1 and 3 are different colors
   C. Pages 1 and 4 are both yellow
   D. All selections of A, B, C
   E. None of A, B, C

   25.____

KEY (CORRECT ANSWERS)

1. B
2. D
3. E
4. C
5. E
6. A
7. E
8. D
9. B
10. D
11. B
12. C
13. D
14. A
15. A
16. B
17. C
18. D
19. B
20. A
21. B
22. C
23. D
24. C
25. A

SOLUTIONS TO PROBLEMS

1. CHOICE I can be allowed no matter how the cat and rabbit are arranged.
   CHOICE II is impossible, since whether the alligator is placed in the first or second compartments, condition 2 will be violated.
   CHOICE III is allowed provided that the first compartment is occupied by the alligator and the second one by the horse.

   (Answer B)

2. Once the alligator is placed into compartment 4, two other animals must occupy adjacent compartments. This situation violates condition 2.

   (Answer D)

3. If the horse is placed in compartment 4 with the alligator in compartment 5, then the rabbit can be put in either compartments 1 or 2. Similarly, by placing the alligator and horse in compartments 1 and 2 respectively, the rabbit can be put in compartments 4 or 5. Recognizing that the alligator must be put in compartments 1 or 5, if the rabbit were placed in compartment 3, we would have alligator, _____, rabbit, _____, _____ or _____, _____, rabbit, _____, alligator. In either situation, the horse must be placed between the rabbit and alligator. But then condition 1 will be violated.

   (Answer E)

4. Following are the only allowable arrangements:
   1. alligator, horse, cat, rabbit, dog
   2. alligator, horse, cat, dog, rabbit
   3. alligator, horse, dog, rabbit, cat
   4. alligator, horse, dog, cat, rabbit

   (Answer C)

5. It is already known that the alligator must be in compartments 1 or 5 and that the rabbit cannot be in compartment 3. Thus, only the horse and dog are left as candidates. But in order not to violate condition 2, the horse will have to be placed in compartment 2 or 4. Thus, only the dog can occupy compartment 3.

   (Answer E)

6. We know that 1 person has a ticket for Y, 2 have tickets for X, and 3 have tickets for W.
   CHOICE A would read as: XWXYWW, and thus all conditions are satisfied.
   CHOICE B violates condition 3.
   CHOICE C also violates condition 3.
   CHOICE D violates condition 2.
   CHOICE E violates condition 1.

   (Answer A)

7. CHOICES I, II, III can be shown as respectively WXYXWW, YWWXWX, and XWXYWW.

   (Answer E)

8. The solutions given above for problem #7 show Y in positions 1, 3, and 4. If Y were placed in position 2, this would force X into position 4 (by condition 1). However, by condition 2, we would then have to place X also in position 6. The three remaining slots would be filled by W's but would violate condition 3. A similar contradiction would occur if Y were in position 5. (Note that position 6 WOULD be a legal place for Y.)

   (Answer D)

9. If the 4th person had a ticket for Y, then condition 2 could not be satisfied no matter which two people have tickets for X. By condition 1, the 4th person must have a ticket for X. The arrangement of YWWXWX shows that choices C, D, and E need not be true.

   (Answer B)

10. If the 1st person has a ticket for X, then so must the 3rd person also have a ticket for X. This implies that the 4th person has a ticket for Y (by condition 1) and that the remaining people (including the 2nd person) have tickets for W. However, if the 1st person has a ticket for Y, then the 4th person has a ticket for X. At this point, the 2nd individual could also have a ticket for X, so that the 3rd, 5th, and 6th persons have tickets for W.

    (Answer D)

11. We know that of the other 4 people, 2 have tickets for W, 1 has a ticket for X, and 1 has a ticket for Y. In order to satisfy all three initial conditions of the problem (given in the paragraph preceding question 6), the arrangement of tickets must be WWXYXW. But the 2 people who have tickets for W (besides the 6th person) can be interchanged.

    (Answer B)

12. Restrictions 1 and 2 eliminate Applesauce, Celery, and Derma from post 1. Restriction 4 implies that Honey Pie must race from a post 2 or higher. Restriction 5 implies that both Edible and Fruit Cup must have post numbers higher than 2. Thus, only Bologna and Green Bean are candilates for post 1.

    (Answer C)

13. From restrictions 4 and 5, Green Bean, Honey Pie, Edible, and Fruit Cup must have post numbers in ascending order. This would normally imply that Green Bean's post number could be as high as 5. But, by restriction 3, Fruit Cup cannot have a post number higher than 7. Thus, Green Bean's highest post number could only be 4.

    (Answer D)

14. The explanation to question #13 provides the rationale for Green Bean not possibly being assigned to post 5. The only other horse not allowed post 5 would be Derma (restriction 2).

    (Answer A)

15. Restriction 3 eliminates Bologna and Fruit Cup from post 8. Restriction 5 implies that the post numbers assigned to both Edible and Honey Pie must be less than Fruit Cup's. Thus, neither of them is eligible for post 8. Question #13 removes Green Bean from consideration, while restriction 1 eliminates both Applesauce and Celery. Only Derma may race from post 8.

    (Answer A)

16. CHOICE B violates restriction 5, CHOICES A, C, D, and E could be satisfied with the following corresponding complete arrangements (using the first letters of the first name to abbreviate):
    For CHOICE A: GABCHEFD
    For CHOICE C: BCGHEAFD
    For CHOICE D: BGHEFACD
    For CHOICE E: GHAEBCFD

    (Answer B)

17. Restriction 2 could have been deleted, since we discovered from question #15 that Derma must race from post 8.

    (Answer C)

18. The highest post number for Fruit Cup is 7. By restriction 5, Edible's and Honey pie's post numbers must be less than that of Fruit Cup. Derma must be assigned post 8. Restriction 4 implies that Green Bean's post number must also be less than 7.

    (Answer D)

19. Both Lisa and Melanie could be assigned. Restriction 1 eliminates Jack, restriction 4 precludes Nancy, and by restriction 5, Otto will not work when Lisa is assigned. Note that both Melanie and Otto could be assigned, too.

    (Answer B)

20. CHOICE A violates no restrictions.
    CHOICE B is eliminated by restriction 4.
    CHOICE C is eliminated by restriction 2.
    Since only one choice among A, B, and C is correct, CHOICES D and E must be incorrect.

    (Answer A)

21. CHOICES D and E are not applicable due to restriction 2. Since Nancy is assigned to work on Monday, restriction 4 would prohibit Lisa from also working on Monday. Thus, CHOICE A is eliminated. By deduction, the only 2 consecutive days for Otto to work are Thursday and Friday. Thus Lisa must work Tuesday and Wednesday, due to restriction 5.

    (Answer B)

22. Since Nancy is already working on Monday, the only day left for Jack to work is Saturday. By restriction 3, Melanie will not be able to work on Sunday, and restriction 4 prevents her from working on Monday. Thus, she can work for 5 days maximum.

    (Answer C)

23. The arrangements for CHOICES A and B are acceptable. However, CHOICE C violated restriction 2. Thus, CHOICE D is correct.

    (Answer D)

10 (#1)

24. For pages 2 through 4, the only acceptable arrangements are red, yellow, red and yellow, red, yellow.   24._____

   (Answer C)

25. If page 1 is red, the sequence of all 4 pages could be red, yellow, red, yellow. If pages 1 and 3 were different, the third color would have to be used on page 2 (restriction 3). Finally, if pages 1 and 4 were both yellow, page 3 must be red. This would result in the same situation as described above in the second sentence.   25._____

   (Answer A)

EXAMINATION SECTION
TEST 1

DIRECTIONS: Each question or incomplete statement is followed by several suggested answers or completions. Select the one that BEST answers the question or completes the statement. *PRINT THE LETTER OF THE CORRECT ANSWER IN THE SPACE AT THE RIGHT.*

QUESTIONS 1-7.

Questions 1-7 refer to the following information:

Seven individuals attended a picnic at Majestic View Park. No two of these people are the same age. The following information is also known:
    I. Jack's age is exactly one-third of Ken's age and Jack is younger than Paula.
    II. Oliver is 8 years older than Paula.
    III. Laura's age plus Nancy's age equals Jack's age, but this sum is less than Mary's age.
    IV. Ken's age is exactly double that of Paula's.
    V. None of the seven individuals is younger than 10 years old nor older than 100 years old.
    VI. Laura is not the youngest person.
    VII. Mary's age is the average of Paula's age and Ken's age.

1. The OLDEST person is

    A. Laura   B. Mary   C. Ken
    D. Nancy   E. none of these

2. The LOWEST age that Jack could be is

    A. 12   B. 15   C. 18
    D. 21   E. 24

3. The HIGHEST age that Oliver could be is

    A. 58   B. 62   C. 66
    D. 70   E. 74

4. The individual who is *older* than 3 people and also *younger* than 3 people is

    A. Laura   B. Mary   C. Oliver
    D. Jack   E. none of these

5. How many individuals are *older* than Mary?

    A. 0   B. 1   C. 2
    D. 3   E. 4

6. If Jack were 30 years old, then Paula could be

    A. 33   B. 34
    C. 35   D. any of the above
    E. none of the above

7. Which of the following *correctly* lists the individuals by age in *ascending* order?

    A. Laura, Nancy, Paula, Oliver, Jack, Mary, Ken
    B. Nancy, Jack, Paula, Laura, Oliver, Ken, Mary
    C. Laura, Jack, Nancy, Paula, Ken, Mary, Oliver
    D. Paula, Laura, Jack, Mary, Oliver, Ken, Nancy
    E. Nancy, Laura, Jack, Paula, Oliver, Mary, Ken

QUESTIONS 8-14.

Questions 8-14 refer to the following information.

Rose, Sue, Ted, Viola, and William went bowling at the Roll-E-Z Bowling Alley, where they each bowled one game. Although none of the bowlers revealed his/her score, the following is known:
   I. No two bowlers had the same bowling score.
   II. A female bowled the lowest score, and she bowled last.
   III. Ted did NOT bowl the highest score, and he bowled third in the order.
   IV. William bowled before Ted, and he (William) bowled a better score than two bowlers.
   V. Viola's bowling score was better than Ted's score, and she bowled after Sue but before Rose.
   VI. Sue bowled after William.
   VII. In conditions V and VI, the expressions "bowled after" and "bowled before" do NOT necessarily mean "bowled directly after" or "bowled directly before."

8. The *second* bowler in the order was

    A. Viola   B. Sue
    C. either Sue or William   D. William
    E. Viola, Sue, or William

9. Rose bowled _____ in the order and scored _____.

    A. first; second best   B. next to Last; second lowest
    C. last; lowest   D. last; second lowest
    E. first; best

10. The CORRECT listing of bowlers from *first* to *last* is

    A. Sue, William, Ted, Rose, Viola
    B. William, Viola, Ted, Rose, Sue
    C. Rose, William, Ted, Viola, Sue
    D. William, Sue, Ted, Viola, Rose
    E. Sue, Viola, Ted, Rose, William

11. Who bowled the highest score?

    A. William or Sue   B. Sue or Viola
    C. William or Viola   D. Rose or Viola
    E. Rose or William

12. Ted's score was better than that of _____ other bowler(s).

    A. 1   B. 3   C. 4
    D. either 3 or 4 E. either 1 or 3

13. If Sue bowled better than Ted, which one(s) of the following is (are) necessarily TRUE?   13._____
    I. Sue bowled worse than Viola.
    II. Ted bowled worse than William.
    III. Viola bowled the best.

    A. I only
    B. II only
    C. III only
    D. Exactly two of the above
    E. All of the above

14. How many individuals bowled *after* William but *before* Sue?   14._____

    A. 0
    B. 1
    C. 2
    D. 0 or 1
    E. 1 or 2

QUESTIONS 15-25.

Questions 15-25 refer to the following information:

Amy, Bob, Carl, Donna, Ellen, and Florence are six individuals whose professions are: artist, bookkeeper, counselor, doctor, engineer, and fashion designer, though not necessarily in that order. They earn six different annual salaries, each one of which is a multiple of $5000. Also:
   I. The fashion designer is a female, but earns neither the lowest nor the highest salary.
   II. Carl and the engineer are bowling partners with the doctor, the latter of whom earns the highest salary. None of the other individuals bowl.
   III. The artist earned two degrees from State University, which she attended during the same time that Amy was attending that school. Currently the artist earns more than two of the other five people, including Donna.
   IV. Donna earns the least. Her steady boyfriend is the counselor, although she used to date the doctor.
   V. The fashion designer and the engineer were Ellen's guests at the latter's wedding reception recently.
   VI. The fashion designer earns more than the artist but less than the engineer.
   VII. Only the doctor earns more than Florence.
   VIII. The second highest income is $80,000 per year.
   IX. If the annual incomes were arranged in ascending order, the largest difference between any two consecutive salaries is $15,000.
   X. The fourth highest income is exactly double the lowest salary.
   XI. Each person's annual salary exceeds $25,000.
   XII. The second lowest income is exactly one-third of the highest income.

15. The artist is   15._____

    A. Amy
    B. Bob
    C. Carl
    D. Donna
    E. Ellen

16. _____ earned the HIGHEST salary and _____ earned the SECOND TO LOWEST salary.   16._____

    A. Bob; Carl
    B. Amy; Donna
    C. Ellen; Florence
    D. Bob; Ellen
    E. Amy; Florence

17. Amy's annual salary is

    A. $60,000
    B. $65,000
    C. between $65,000 and $80,000
    D. between $60,000 and $80,000
    E. between $60,000 and $75,000

18. The doctor's MINIMUM salary is

    A. $80,000
    B. $85,000
    C. $90,000
    D. $95,000
    E. none of these

19. _____ earns $40,000.

    A. Bob
    B. Carl
    C. Ellen
    D. Donna
    E. none of these

20. The dollar difference between the counselor's and the artist's salary is

    A. $10,000
    B. $15,000
    C. $20,000
    D. $25,000
    E. none of these

21. The individual whose salary CANNOT be determined exactly is the

    A. bookkeeper
    B. doctor
    C. fashion designer
    D. engineer
    E. artist

22. Donna is the

    A. artist
    B. bookkeeper
    C. counselor
    D. engineer
    E. none of these

23. The engineer earns more than _____ individual(s).

    A. 0
    B. 1
    C. 2
    D. 3
    E. 4

24. The individuals who do NOT bowl are

    A. Donna, Bob, Florence
    B. Donna, Bob, Ellen
    C. Donna, Amy, Ellen
    D. Amy, Bob, Florence
    E. Amy, Florence, Donna

25. The CORRECT listing of the six individuals arranged from LOWEST salary to HIGHEST salary is

    A. Ellen, Amy, Carl, Donna, Bob, Florence
    B. Donna, Carl, Ellen, Amy, Florence, Bob
    C. Amy, Ellen, Florence, Carl, Donna, Bob
    D. Donna, Florence, Carl, Bob, Ellen, Amy
    E. Ellen, Donna, Carl, Amy, Bob, Florence

KEY (CORRECT ANSWERS)

1.	C	11.	B
2.	D	12.	E
3.	A	13.	B
4.	E	14.	A
5.	B	15.	E
6.	E	16.	A
7.	E	17.	D
8.	B	18.	B
9.	C	19.	E
10.	D	20.	D

21. C
22. B
23. E
24. C
25. B

SOLUTIONS

For questions 1-7, let the ages corresponding to each person be represented by the first letter of the person's name(O for Oliver, for example). The seven conditions given yield the following equations: $J = 1/3K$, $J < P$, $O = P + 8$, $J < M$, $L + N = J$, $L + N < M$, $K = 2P$, $10 \leq$ each person ≤ 100, $M = (P + K)/2$.

We recognize that Ken must be older than Jack and Paula. Also, since Jack is older than both Laura and Nancy, Ken is also older than Laura and Nancy. From the last equation, $M = (P + K)/2$, we know that Mary's age is between Paula's age and Ken's age; thus Ken is also older than Mary. Suppose Ken were younger than Oliver (i.e.: $K < O$). Since $K = 2P$ and $O = P + 8$, we would get $2P < P + 8$ r $P < 8$. This, however is not possible, since each person is at least 10 years old.

1. Self-explanatory from the above paragraph.
   (ANSWER C).

2. We determine that since $L + N = J$, Jack is older than both Laura and Nancy, but further analysis reveals that he is younger than the other four people. It is given that Laura is not the youngest; thus Nancy must be. Now, the lowest age for anyone is 10, and since no two people have the same age, if Nancy were 10, then the lowest age for Laura would be 11. Thus Jack would be 21.
   (ANSWER D).

3. If Ken (who is the oldest) were 100 years old, Paula would be 50. By condition II, Oliver would be 58.
   (ANSWER A).

4. We already know that $P < M < K$, from the statements $M = (P + K)/2$ and Ken is the oldest. We want to know if Oliver is younger than Mary. (By condition II, we know that Oliver is older than Paula.) If $O < M$, consider the fact that M is the average of P and K of P and 2P, which is $3P/2$. This implies that $O < 3P/2$. But $O = P + 8$. Thus $P + 8 < 3P/2$, implying that $P > 16$, which is certainly true. Had $O > M$, then $P < 16$, which is impossible since Paula is older than Jack and J 2:21. Thus Paula is the individual younger than 3 people.
   (ANSWER E).

5. Only Ken is older than Mary.
   (ANSWER B).

6. If $J = 30$, $K = 90$, then $P = \frac{1}{2} K = 45$.
   (ANSWER E).

7. Evident from information given in above explanations.
   (ANSWER E).

For 8-14 the following three matrices are possible. First letters of names are used.

Matrix 1

Score \ Bowling Order	1	2	3	4	last
Lowest					R
2			T		
3	W				
4		S			
Highest				V	

Matrix 2

Score \ Bowling Order	1	2	3	4	last
Lowest					R
2		S			
3	W				
4			T		
Highest				V	

Matrix 3

Score \ Bowling Order	1	2	3	4	last
Lowest					R
2			T		
3	W				
4				V	
Highest		S			

8. Only Sue could bowl second.
   (ANSWER B).

9. Rose will bowl last and score lowest.
   (ANSWER C).

10. Evident by reading the names from left to right in any of the three matrices.
    (ANSWER D).

11. Sue has the highest score in matrix 3; Viola is highest in matrices 1 and 2.
    (ANSWER B).

12. For matrix 1 or 3 Ted's score beat Rose's score, but in matrix 2, Ted scored second highest.
    (ANSWER E).

13. If Sue bowled better than Ted, then matrix 1 or 3 applies, and William bowled better than Ted. Matrix 3 does not support statements I and III.
    (ANSWER B).

14. If matrix 1 applies, the answer is 0. The answer is also 0 if matrix 2 or 3 applies.
    (ANSWER A).

8 (#1)

For 15-25, the following matrix applies.

Salary Profession	Lowest	5th	4th	3rd	2nd	Highest
Artist			Ellen			
Bookkeeper	Donna					
Counselor		Carl				
Doctor						Bob
Engineer					Florence	
Fashion Designer				Amy		

15. Evident from the above matrix.
    (ANSWER E).

16. Evident from the above matrix.
    (ANSWER A).

17. Amy's salary is the 3rd highest and the 2nd highest is $80,000 by condition VIII. Now condition IX assures us that Amy's salary can be no lower than $65,000.
    (ANSWER D).

18. In the opening introductory paragraph for problems 15-25, we find that all salaries are multiples of $5000. Coupled with condition VIII, the minimum salary higher than 80,000 is 85,000.
    (ANSWER B).

19. By using conditions VII through XII, we can determine the following: Lowest salary = $30,000; 5th highest = $35,000; 4th highest = $60,000; 3rd highest = $65,000 or $70,000 or $75,000; 2nd highest = $80,000; highest = $105,000. Thus, no one earns $40,000.
    (ANSWER E).

20. The difference is $60,000 - $35,000 = $25,000.
    (ANSWER D).

21. The 3rd highest salary cannot be determined exactly, and this corresponds to the fashion designer.
    (ANSWER C).

22. Evident from the matrix.
    (ANSWER B).

23. Evident from the matrix.
    (ANSWER E).

24. From condition II, only Carl, the engineer (Florence), and the doctor (Bob) bowl.
    (ANSWER C).

25. Evident from the matrix.
    (ANSWER B).

EXAMINATION SECTION
TEST 1

DIRECTIONS: Each question or incomplete statement is followed by several suggested answers or completions. Select the one that BEST answers the question or completes the statement. *PRINT THE LETTER OF THE CORRECT ANSWER IN THE SPACE AT THE RIGHT.*

QUESTIONS 1-7.

Questions 1-7 pertain to the following.

Five people, named Alice, Bob, Conrad, Diane, and Elaine are applying for jobs at the EZ Manufacturing Company. When they arrive at the personnel office, each will be assigned to a room to take a written test. The available rooms are numbered 1 through 6 and are arranged in numbered sequence from left to right along one side of a corridor. Certain restrictions shall apply.
1. A maximum of 2 people may occupy the same room.
2. Two females may NOT occupy the same room, except Alice and Elaine.
3. Two men must NOT occupy adjacent rooms, nor may they occupy the same room.
4. Alice and Bob used to be husband and wife. Thus, they refuse to be assigned to either the same room or to adjacent rooms.
5. Conrad and Diane are engaged and want to be assigned to either the same room or to adjacent rooms.
6. There must be at least 1 vacant room next to Elaine's room.

1. If each person is assigned to a different room, which of the following is(are) acceptable arrangement(s) for rooms 1 through 6 respectively?
   I. Alice, Diane, Bob, Conrad, Elaine, Vacant
   II. Vacant, Elaine, Bob, Diane, Conrad, Alice
   III. Bob, Elaine, Vacant, Conrad, Alice, Diane
   The CORRECT answer is:

   A. I only   B. II only   C. III only
   D. None   E. I, II, and III

2. Suppose Diane and Elaine are taking the same test and are directed to rooms 1 and 6 respectively.
   If Bob is assigned to room 3, which of the following is TRUE?

   A. Alice can be assigned to room 4
   B. Conrad can be assigned either to room 1 or to room 2
   C. Alice and Conrad will share adjacent rooms
   D. Room 4 must be vacant
   E. Conrad must be assigned to room 1

3. Consider the conditions presented in the previous question. Which of the following is a complete and accurate list of the room(s) which could be simultaneously vacant?

   A. Room 2 *only*   B. Rooms 2 and 4   C. Room 5 *only*
   D. Rooms 4 and 5   E. Rooms 2, 4, and 5

4. Suppose the first room is occupied by Conrad and Diane, the second room is vacant, and the third room is occupied by Elaine.
   If the fourth room is not vacant, then which of the following situations MUST be false?

   A. The fifth room is vacant
   B. Bob is assigned to the sixth room
   C. Alice is assigned to the fourth room
   D. Bob is assigned to the fifth room
   E. None of the above

5. Alice is assigned to room 1, Elaine to room 3, and Bob to room 4.
   In how many different ways can Diane and Conrad be assigned to rooms?

   A. 1   B. 2   C. 3   D. 4   E. 5 or more

6. Based on the conditions in the previous question, which room(s) must be vacant?

   A. Room 2   B. Rooms 5 and 6   C. Room 5 or room 6
   D. Room 6   E. Rooms 2 and 5

7. If Bob is assigned to room 5, which of the following is a complete list of people who CANNOT be assigned to room 6?

   A. Alice and Elaine   B. Diane and Elaine
   C. Diane and Conrad   D. Diane, Conrad, and Elaine
   E. Alice, Diane, and Elaine

QUESTIONS 8-12.

Questions 8-12 pertain to the following conditions.

Four people, Ginny, Harry, Ike, and June, are running in a one mile race along a straight roadway. After exactly 2 minutes, a photograph of all 4 runners is taken. We find out that
1. Ginny is 20 yards ahead of Harry.
2. Harry and Ike are 10 yards apart.
3. June is 5 yards behind Ike.

8. Who must be in *second* place?

   A. Either Harry or Ike   B. Either Harry or June
   C. Ike   D. June
   E. Either Ike or June

9. What is the MINIMAL distance, in yards, between Ginny and the runner immediately behind her?

   A. 5   B. 10   C. 15
   D. 20   E. it cannot be determined

10. The distance between the 3rd and 4th place runners must be

    A. less than 5 yards
    B. 5 yards
    C. more than 5 yards but less than 10 yards
    D. 10 yards
    E. more than 10 yards

11. The distance between the 2 females is _____ yards. 11.____

    A. 10   B. 15   C. Either 15 or 30
    D. Either 10 or 30   E. More than 30

12. The longest distance separates which 2 *consecutive* runners? 12.____

    A. Harry and Ike
    B. Harry and June or Ike and June
    C. Harry and June
    D. Ike and June or Ginny and Ike
    E. Ginny and Harry or Ginny and Ike

QUESTIONS 13-19.

Questions 13-19 pertain to the following conditions.

From the Happy Landing Airport, 3 different airlines operate; Algebraic Airlines, Calculus Airlines, and Geometric Airlines. These airlines have flights both into and out of the airport. Assume that a plane is always available for each airline when needed. Certain restrictions apply.

1. The airport is open continuously except between 11:05 PM and 1:55 AM, inclusive.
2. Algebraic planes leave from landing strip 1 and arrive at strip 3.
3. Calculus planes depart from strip 2 and arrive at landing strip 1.
4. Geometric planes leave from strip 3 and can arrive at either strip 2 or strip 3.
5. In the interest of safety, no 2 planes may either arrive at or depart from the same landing strip unless their times are at least 10 minutes apart.
6. If 2 planes are utilizing 2 different landing strips, their times of either arrival or departure must be at least 10 minutes apart.
7. For Algebraic Airlines, planes leave once an hour at 10 minutes after the hour. Their arriving planes reach the airport 4 times each day. Arrival times are 3:00 AM, 6:00 AM, 9:00 AM and 12:00 Noon.
8. Calculus planes leave twice an hour -- at 5 minutes after and before the hour. Arrivals are at 2:00 AM, 10:00 AM, and 6:00 PM.
9. Geometric planes leave randomly but must depart 3 times each hour, counting from on the hour. Their planes arrive randomly once every 2 hours counting from on the hour, when the airport is first opened each day.

13. Between 3:05 PM and 5:05 PM inclusive, what is the number of planes which either arrive at or leave from strip 3 that belong to Geometric Airlines? 13.____

    A. 8   B. 9   C. More than 8
    D. At most 8   E. More than 9

14. Between 3:05 AM and 6:05 AM inclusive, how many arriving planes are there at landing strip 3? 14.____

    A. 1   B. 2   C. At most 2
    D. 2 or 3   E. More than 3

15. Which airline utilizes all 3 landing strips?

    A. Algebraic
    B. Geometric
    C. Calculus
    D. Exactly 2 of the airlines
    E. None of the airlines

16. A Calculus plane has just landed in the early evening. What is the number of Calculus planes which will depart from the airport between 6:00 PM and 6:55 PM, inclusive?

    A. 1   B. 2   C. 3   D. 4   E. 5

17. What is the MAXIMUM number of planes which may depart between 1:20 PM and 2:30 PM, inclusive?

    A. 4   B. 5   C. 6   D. 7   E. 8

18. It is now 5:17 PM. A traffic controller has noticed that since 5:00 PM, exactly two Geometric planes have departed. He also has noticed that the next Geometric plane is due to arrive at strip 3 at 5:58 PM.
    What is the latest time, of the following, before 6:00 PM, when another Geometric plane will depart?

    A. 5:20 PM   B. 5:25 PM   C. 5:30 PM   D. 5:45 PM   E. 5:55 PM

19. A plane has departed from landing strip 2 exactly 15 minutes ago.
    What is the MINIMUM time that must elapse before a Geometric plane can arrive at the airport?

    A. 10 minutes   B. 15 minutes   C. 30 minutes
    D. 45 minutes   E. 1 hour

QUESTIONS 20-25.

Questions 20-25 pertain to the following conditions.

> There are four people standing on a flight of 4 steps. The following restrictions apply:
> 1. No more than two people may stand on any one step.
> 2. Allen and David can neither be on the same step nor on 2 adjacent steps.
> 3. Beth and Connie must be either on the same step or on 2 adjacent steps.
> 4. David MUST not occupy the same step with anyone.
> 5. Allen will never occupy step 4.

20. If Allen is on step 1 and David is on step 3, in how many different ways can Beth and Connie be assigned to the steps?

    A. 2   B. 3   C. 4   D. 5   E. 6

21. Which of the following conditions would imply that each person occupies a different step?

    A. David is on step 4; Beth, Allen, Connie are on different steps
    B. Beth is on step 2; Connie is on step 3
    C. Allen is on step 3; Connie is on step 2
    D. Allen and Beth are on different steps
    E. Neither Beth nor Connie is on step 4

22. Which of the following conditions is NOT allowed? 22.____

    A. Allen on step 1
    B. Allen and Beth both on step 1
    C. Step 1 being vacant
    D. Connie on step 4
    E. David on step 2

23. Which of the following conditions would imply that step 2 is vacant? 23.____

    A. Beth and Connie both on step 4
    B. Allen and Beth both on step 3
    C. Allen and Connie both on step 4
    D. David on step 1
    E. None of the above

24. If Beth and Connie choose to be on different steps, which numbered step(s) could be vacant? 24.____

    A. Steps 1 and 4   B. Steps 2 and 3   C. Only step 2
    D. Any 2 steps   E. Any 2 step

25. What is the complete list of individuals who are eligible to occupy step 1 if step 3 must be vacant? 25.____

    A. Allen, David
    B. Allen, Beth, Connie
    C. Beth, Connie, David
    D. Beth, Connie
    E. Allen, Beth, Connie, David

KEY (CORRECT ANSWERS)

1. B   11. C
2. E   12. E
3. E   13. D
4. D   14. D
5. B   15. E

6. A   16. B
7. D   17. E
8. A   18. D
9. B   19. A
10. B   20. C

21. A
22. E
23. A
24. E
25. B

SOLUTIONS TO PROBLEMS

1. Selection I violates conditions 3 and 5. Selection III violates condition 5.

(Answer B)

2. Alice would have to be assigned to room 6, so as not to violate any conditions. Room 5 must remain vacant in order to comply with condition 6. By condition 3, Conrad may not occupy rooms 2, 3, or 4, But condition 5 then implies that Conrad be assigned to room 1.

(Answer E)

3. Room 5 is already vacant. Rooms 2 and 4 can also be vacant by the following assignment: Conrad and Diane to room 1, Bob to room 3, Alice and Elaine to room 6.

(Answer E)

4. Choices A, B, and C could be true with the assignment of Alice and Bob to the 4th and 6th rooms respectively. However, if Bob were placed in room 5, there would be no place to put Alice without violating condition 4.

(Answer D)

5. By condition 6, room 2 must be vacant. Condition 3 forces Conrad to be assigned to room 6. Since Diane and Conrad must be either in the same room or in adjacent rooms, she can be in room 5 or room 6. Thus, either Diane and Conrad are both in room 6, or they are in rooms 5 and 6, respectively.

(Answer B)

6. As described above, room 5 may be vacant, But not necessarily if Diane is in room 5 and Conrad in room 6. Only room 2 MUST be vacant.

(Answer A)

7. Condition 6 prohibits Elaine from being assigned to room 6. By condition 3, Conrad could only be assigned to rooms 1, 2, or 3. Condition 5 would thus restrict Diane to rooms 1, 2, 3, or 4.

(Answer D)

8. The photograph will show one of 2 scenes for the identity of the runners in 1st through last place respectively.
Scene 1: Ginny, Ike, June, Harry.
Scene 2: Ginny, Harry, Ike, June.
Thus, either Harry or Ike is in 2nd place.

(Answer A)

9. For scene 1, the distances between the 1st and 2nd runners, 2nd and 3rd, 3rd and 4th are 10 yards, 5 yards, and 5 yards respectively. The corresponding distances for scene 2 are 20 yards, 10 yards, and 5 yards respectively. Thus, scene 1 shows only a distance of 10 yards separating Ginny and the 2nd place runner (Ike).

7 (#1)

(Answer B)

10. For either scene, 5 yards separate the 3rd and 4th place runners.

(Answer B)

11. In scene 1, Ginny and 3rd place June are 15 yards apart. But in scene 2, June is in last place, and now is 30 yards behind Ginny.

(Answer C)

12. For scene 1, the biggest gap is between Ginny and Ike. In scene 2, the largest gap is the 20 yards between Ginny and Harry.

(Answer E)

13. By condition 9, a total of 7 Geometric planes will depart from strip 3: 3 between 3:05 and 4:00, 3 between 4:00 and 5:00, and 1 plane between 5:00 and 5:05. Now, from 3:00 to 5:00, 1 Geometric plane must leave. Also, it is IMPOSSIBLE that a Geometric plane will leave between 5:00 and 5:05 under the condition that 1 plane has already arrived during this interval. This would conflict with restriction 5. Thus, at most 8 Geometric plane are involved.

(Answer D)

14. 1 Algebraic plane will arrive at 6:00 AM and 1 Geometric plane must arrive between 3:00 and 5:00. Additionally, one more Geometric plane must arrive at either strip 2 or 3 between 5:00 and 7:00; thus, it could arrive at strip 3 by 6:05.

(Answer D)

15. By inspecting the given conditions, each airline is found to be using exactly 2 airstrips.

(Answer E)

16. The 2 Calculus planes will leave at 6:05 PM and 6:55 PM.

(Answer B)

17. An Algebraic plane will depart at 2:10. 3 Geometric planes will depart between 1:20 and 1:50 and 2 more Geometric planes can leave at 2:20 and 2:30. Now, 2 Calculus planes will depart at 1:55 and 2:05. Note that due to restriction 6, no more Geometric planes may be allowed to depart. Total of 8 planes maximum.

(Answer E)

18. A Geometric plane could depart as late as 5:45 but no later, since a Calculus plane will leave at 5:55.

(Answer D)

19. Conditions 5 and 6 both require that a minimum of 10 minutes must elapse between arrival/departing times of any planes.

(Answer A)

20. The 4 possibilities are:
    1. Beth and Connie both on step 2.
    2. Beth on step 1, Connie on step 2.
    3. Beth on step 2, Connie on step 1.
    4. Beth and Connie both on step 4.

    (Answer C)

21. Since David shares his step with no one, CHOICE A yields the arrangement of Allen, Beth, Connie, David (Beth and Connie may be interchanged). For CHOICE B, it can be refuted by placing Allen on step 2. CHOICE C can be refuted with Beth and Connie both on step 2, David on step 1, and Allen on step 3. Also, CHOICES D and E can be refuted by the arrangement mentioned in the last sentence.

    (Answer A)

22. With David on step 2, there is no place left for Allen, since condition 2 forbids Allen from steps 1, 2, or 3 and condition 5 forbids him from step 4.
    CHOICES A, B, C, and D are permissible.

    (Answer E)

23. If Beth and Connie are both on step 4, then Allen and David are BOTH restricted to steps 1, 2, and 3 (Condition 1). Since the two men cannot be on adjacent steps or the same step, one of them will occupy step 1 and the other will occupy step 3.

    (Answer A)

24. For step 1 vacant: Allen and Beth on step 2, Connie on step 3, David on step 4.
    For step 2 vacant: David on step 1, Allen and Connie on step 3, Beth on step 4
    For step 3 vacant: Connie on step 1, Allen and Beth on step 2, David on step 4.
    For step 4 vacant: David on step 1, Beth on step 2, Allen and Connie on step 3.
    Note that no 2 steps could be vacant simultaneously.

    (Answer E)

25. Possible arrangements are: 1. Beth and Connie on step 1, Allen on step 2, David on step 4; 2. Allen on step 1, Beth and Connie on step 2, David on step 4; David would not be allowed on step 1, since there is no place to put Allen.

    (Answer B)

EXAMINATION SECTION
TEST 1

DIRECTIONS: Each question or incomplete statement is followed by several suggested answers or completions. Select the one that BEST answers the question or completes the statement. *PRINT THE LETTER OF THE BEST ANSWER IN THE SPACE AT THE RIGHT.*

QUESTIONS 1-5.

Questions 1-5 pertain to the following.

The Know-Z Marketing Company is interested in determining the major sports preferences of a large city. A total of 100 people are sent a questionnaire on which the sports of baseball, basketball, and football are listed. Each respondent is asked to place a check mark next to each sport he likes. When the 100 responses were received, the following results emerged:

1. Five individuals showed a preference for all 3 sports.
2. Some individuals liked no sport.
3. Ten people liked basketball and football, but not baseball.
4. A total of 40 individuals checked off football.
5. Eighteen people showed a preference for only basketball.
6. A total of twenty-four people checked off exactly 2 sports.
7. A total of 50 people showed a preference for only one sport.

1. How many people checked off *both* basketball and football? 1._____
   A. 5   B. 10   C. 15   D. 20   E. 25

2. If 16 people preferred only football, how many people preferred baseball and basketball, but NOT football? 2._____
   A. 5   B. 10   C. 15   D. 20   E. 25

3. Suppose no responses were received on which both baseball and basketball but not football were checked off. How many individuals did NOT check off basketball? 3._____
   A. 30   B. 46   C. 53   D. 67   E. 72

4. Suppose 6 people checked off baseball and football, but not basketball. How many respondents checked off *both* baseball and basketball? 4._____
   A. 8   B. 10   C. 13   D. 15   E. 18

5. What is the MINIMUM number of people who checked off basketball? 5._____
   A. 5   B. 10   C. 18   D. 23   E. 33

QUESTIONS 6-11.

Questions 6-11 pertain to the following.

The Liftweight elevator is capable of carrying up to and including 550 lbs. The six individuals who use this elevator, and their respective weights are: Adam, 200 lbs.; Bonnie, 125 lbs.; Cathy, 150 lbs.; David, 175 lbs.; Eva, 100 lbs.; and Frank, 250 lbs.
The following restrictions exist:
1. Frank will not ride alone.
2. Bonnie will only ride the elevator if either Cathy or Eva is also a passenger. However, Bonnie will not ride with both of these ladies simultaneously.
3. David will either ride alone or with at least one of the ladies.
4. Adam will ride the elevator only if the total weight of the other passenger(s) is between 100 lbs. and 200 lbs, inclusive.

6. If Adam is on the elevator, which of the following is(are) permissible?
   I. David is the only other passenger.
   II. Cathy is the only other passenger.
   III. Frank is the only other passenger.
   The CORRECT answer is:

   A. I only
   B. II only
   C. III only
   D. I, II only
   E. I, II, and III

7. Frank, Bonnie, and Eva are currently on the elevator, heading toward the first floor. On the way down, the elevator stops at the second floor, where David is waiting to board. Which one of the following actions is NOT allowed?

   A. Bonnie steps out and David steps into the elevator
   B. Eva steps out and David steps into the elevator
   C. Frank steps out and David steps into the elevator
   D. Both Frank and Bonnie step out and David does not step into the elevator
   E. Frank, Bonnie, and Eva step out and David steps into the elevator

8. How many of these 6 individuals can ride alone?

   A. none   B. 1   C. 2   D. 3   E. 4 or more

9. Adam and Eva are riding the elevator as it approaches the 5th floor, and neither of them intends to exit at that floor. If the other 4 people are waiting on the 5th floor, how many combinations exist for those who may join Adam and Eva as passengers?

   A. none
   B. 1 or 2
   C. 3 or 4
   D. 5 or 6
   E. more than 6

10. Which of the following is the MOST complete and accurate list of passengers who may NOT share the elevator ride with both Eva and Bonnie simultaneously?

    A. David
    B. Cathy and Frank
    C. Adam
    D. Frank and David
    E. Adam and Cathy

11. If it is known that the weight of all individuals on the elevator is exactly 400 lbs. and if none of the original 4 restrictions existed, how many combinations of individuals could ride the elevator?

    A. 1   B. 2   C. 3   D. 4   E. 5

QUESTIONS 12-16.

Questions 12-16 pertain to the following:

A blue box weighs one-half of a red box.
A green box weighs 3 lbs. more than a blue box.
A yellow box weighs the average of the weights of a green and red box.

12. Which color box is the heaviest? 12.____
    A. Blue   B. Green   C. Red or yellow
    D. Yellow or green   E. Green or red

13. Which color box is the lightest? 13.____
    A. Blue   B. Green   C. Red or blue
    D. Yellow or green   E. Green or red

14. If the blue box is 15 lbs. how much does the yellow box weigh? 14.____
    A. 12 lbs.   B. 18 lbs.   C. 21 lbs.   D. 24 lbs.   E. 30 lbs.

15. Suppose the red box is the 2nd lightest box. 15.____
    Then the green box must weight

    A. more than 6 lbs.
    B. more than 3 lbs.
    C. 3 lbs.
    D. between 3 lbs. and 6 lbs. inclusive
    E. less than 6 lbs.

16. If the yellow box weighs more than the green box, and the red box weighs 20 lbs., which 16.____
    of the following conclusions can be drawn about the yellow box? It weighs

    A. between 10 lbs. and 13 lbs. not inclusive
    B. between 13 lbs. and 20 lbs. not inclusive
    C. more than 20 lbs.
    D. less than 13 lbs.
    E. none of the above

QUESTIONS 17-22.

Questions 17-22 pertain to the following.

At the Studymore High School, a student is required to sign up for 6 classes during the 7 period school day. (No two classes may be taught during one period.) The following restrictions apply:
1. Language must be scheduled during an odd numbered period.
2. History must be scheduled during period 4, 5, or 6.
3. Mathematics must be scheduled at least 2 periods later than a Language class.
4. Science may only be scheduled between a Language class and a History class.
5. Economics can be scheduled for any even numbered period, but must not precede a mathematics class.
6. Art must be scheduled during period 1, 2, 6, or 7.
7. No more than 4 classes may be scheduled consecutively.

17. What is the complete list of periods which could be vacant?

    A. 3 only   B. 4 only   C. 3 or 5   D. 4 or 5   E. 3, 4, or 5

18. If art is scheduled during period 6, then which course could be scheduled during period 7?

    A. Language   B. Science   C. Economics
    D. History   E. None of these

19. What is the complete list of courses which may NOT be offered during period 1?

    A. Language, History, Economics. Science
    B. Mathematics, History, Science, Economics, Art
    C. Language, Science, History, Mathematics
    D. Mathematics, Science, Economics
    E. Mathematics, History, Science, Art

20. If period 4 is vacant, which is the CORRECT sequence of classes for periods 1, 2, and 3 respectively?

    A. Language, Art, Science   B. Language, Art, Mathematics
    C. Art, Science, Language   D. Language, Science, Mathematics
    E. Art, Science, Mathematics

21. If History is scheduled for period 4, in how many ways can the other 5 courses be scheduled?

    A. 1   B. 2   C. 3   D. 4   E. at least 5

22. If Mathematics is offered during period 3, then period 6 will be scheduled with

    A. Science   B. Science or History
    C. Economics   D. Economics or Science
    E. Economics or History

QUESTIONS 23-25.

Questions 23-25 pertain to the following:

The town of Petville allows each household to own a maximum of 2 dogs, 4 cats, and 5 birds.

23. If the Adams family has at least 2 of each of these 3 types of pets, how many different combinations of numbers of each type of pet would there be?

    A. 3   B. 6   C. 12   D. 20   E. 40

24. The Smith family has no dogs, but has more cats than birds. What is the MAXIMUM number of pets in this household?

    A. 9   B. 7   C. 6   D. 4   E. 3

25. The Jones family has fewer cats than either dogs or birds. Also, the number of birds does not exceed the number of birds in the Smith family in the preceding question. What is the MAXIMUM number of pets in the Jones family?

    A. 10   B. 9   C. 8   D. 7   E. 6

KEY (CORRECT ANSWERS)

1. C
2. A
3. B
4. C
5. E

6. B
7. B
8. D
9. A
10. E

11. B
12. E
13. A
14. D
15. E

16. B
17. E
18. E
19. B
20. D

21. A
22. E
23. C
24. B
25. E

SOLUTIONS TO PROBLEMS

For Questions 1-5 consider this diagram:

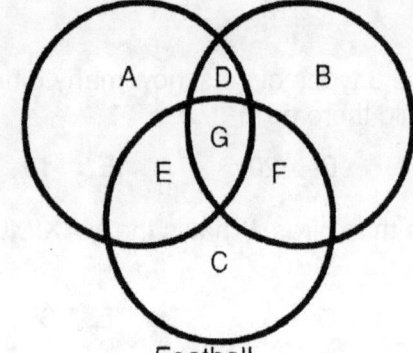

Baseball   Basketball

The letters represent number corresponding to those areas.

Football

Using the information in conditions 1, 3, and 5, we know: G=5, F=10, and B=18.

Condition 2 implies that A + B + ... + G < 100.
Condition 4 implies C + E + F + G = 40 or C + E = 25.
Condition 6 implies D + E + F = 24 or D + E = 14.
Condition 7 implies A + B + C = 50 or A + C = 32.

1. We seek F + G = 10 + 5 = 15

(Answer C)

2. Since we are given that C = 16, condition 4 would result in E = 9. Finally, condition 6 gives D + 9 = 14, or D = 5.

(Answer A)

3. Supposing D = 0, we can find A + C + D + E by adding the equations for conditions 6 and 7. (Note that D = 0 does not affect the answer.)

(Answer B)

4. Since E = 6, condition 6 gives D = 8. Thus D + G = 8 + 5 = 13.

(Answer C)

5. Regardless of the value of D, B + F + G = 18 + 10 + 5 = 33.

(Answer E)

6. If David and Adam were the only passengers, condition 3 would be violated. If Frank and Adam were passengers, condition 4 would be violated. Only Cathy may be the other passenger.

(Answer B)

7. If the elevator contained Frank, Bonnie, and David, then condition 2 would be violated.

(Answer B)

8. Only Cathy, Eva, or David could ride alone. If any of the others rode alone, restriction 1, 2, or 4 would be violated.

(Answer D)

9. Restriction 4 restricts the weights of the other passengers to a limit of 200 lbs. When Eva stays on as a passenger, only 100 more lbs. would be allowed. However, all other riders exceed 100 lbs.

(Answer A)

10. If Adam joins Eva and Bonnie, the 4th condition is out. If Cathy joins the 2 ladies, condition 2 is violated.

(Answer E)

11. The two combinations would be: a) Eva, Bonnie, David; and b) Bonnie, Frank.

(Answer B)

For Questions 12-16, the increasing order of weights is either blue, green, yellow, red or blue, red, yellow, green.

12. Self explanatory from above sentence.

(Answer E)

13. Self explanatory from above sentence.

(Answer A)

14. The red box is 30 lbs., green box is 18 lbs., and the yellow box is the average of 18 and 30, which is 24 lbs.

(Answer D)

15. This implies that the green box is the heaviest. If x = weight of the blue box, $2x$ = weight of the red box, $x + 3$ = weight of the green box, then we must have $2x < x + 3$ or $x < 3$ (i.e., blue box is less than 3 lbs.) Thus, the green box will be less than 6 lbs.

(Answer E)

16. The order is blue, green, yellow, red (increasing weight). We know the blue box is 10 lbs. (half the red box), and the green box is 3 lbs. more than the blue box or 13 lbs. Finally, the yellow box must be the average of 13 and 20 or 16 1/2 lbs.

(Answer B)

For Questions 17-22, the original schedule might appear as follows (using the L = Language, M = Mathematics, H = History, E = Economics, A = Art, S = Science).

Period #	1	2	3	4	5	6	7
	L		L		L		L
		M		M	M	M	M
				H	H	H	
		S	S	S			
				E		E	
	A	A				A	A

When all restrictions have been considered, certain options drop out and the final distribution appreas as:

Period #	1	2	3	4	5	6	7
	L	S	M	M	M	M	A
				H	H	H	
				E		E	

(Keep in mind that one period will be vacant.)

17. If any of periods 1, 2, 6, or 7 were vacant, restriction 7 is out.

(Answer E)

18. By the first diagram above and all restrictions considered, all periods 1 through 6 would have to have the classes Language, Science, Mathematics, Economics, History, Art, Vacant. Again, restriction 7 is being violated.

(Answer E)

19. The 2nd diagram shows only language being offered in period 1.

(Answer B)

20. Answer is evident from 2nd diagram.

(Answer D)

21. The only single combination is: Language, Science, Mathematics, History, Vacant, Economics, Art.

(Answer A)

22. The combinations allowed, where _____ = vacant are:
    a) L, S, M, _____, H, E, A; or
    b) L, S, M, E, _____, H, A.

(Answer E)

23. The family has 2 dogs, either 2, 3, or 4 cats and either 2, 3, 4, or 5 birds. The number of combinations = the product of the number of different numbers of each pet. Thus 1 x 3 x 4 = 12. As an example, one combination for dogs, cats, and birds would be 2, 2, and 4 respectively. Another might be 2, 4, 3 respectively. There are 12 such arrangements.

(Answer C)

24. Maximum would be: 0 dogs, 4 cats, 3 birds = 7 pets.

(Answer B)

25. Since the maximum number of dogs is 2, the maximum number of cats is 1. Since the Smith Family had a maximum of 3 birds, the same goes for the Jones Family.
Now 2 + 1 + 3 = 6 pets maximum.

(Answer E)

EXAMINATION SECTION
TEST 1

DIRECTIONS: Each question or incomplete statement is followed by several suggested answers or completions. Select the one that BEST answers the question or completes the statement. *PRINT THE LETTER OF THE CORRECT ANSWER IN THE SPACE AT THE RIGHT.*

QUESTIONS 1-5.

Questions 1-5 refer to the following:

The cruising speed of all of the following automobiles is in a number ending in the digit 5 or 0.
1. Ford has a cruising speed 15 m.p.h. above a Plymouth.
2. Chevy has a cruising speed 20 m.p.h. above a Ford.
3. Datsun has a cruising speed exactly one-half as great as a Ford, but is only 10 m.p.h. below a Plymouth.
4. Toyota has a cruising speed between that of a Plymouth and that of a Chevy, but greater than that of a Ford.

1. Which of the following is the CORRECT order of cruising speeds from *fastest* to *slowest*?   1.____

   A. Chevy, Ford, Plymouth, Toyota, Datsun
   B. Chevy, Toyota, Ford, Plymouth, Datsun
   C. Ford, Plymouth, Chevy, Toyota, Datsun
   D. Plymouth, Toyota, Chevy, Datsun, Ford
   E. Chevy, Ford, Toyota, Datsun, Plymouth

2. What is the cruising speed of a Chevy?   2.____

   A. Under 50 m.p.h.
   B. More than 50 m.p.h. but less than 65 m.p.h.
   C. 65 m.p.h.
   D. More than 65 m.p.h. but less than 70 m.p.h.
   E. 70 m.p.h.

3. In order for the Toyota's cruising speed to be *exactly* halfway between that of a Ford and that of a Chevy, it must be _____ m.p.h. faster than a Datsun.   3.____

   A. 15   B. 25   C. 35   D. 50   E. 60

4. If the cruising speed of a Plymouth were increased to twice its current speed, it would then exceed how many other autos?   4.____

   A. 2   B. 3   C. 4   D. 1   E. 0

5. Assume that the cruising speed of a Buick ends in the digit 0 or 5.   5.____
   If that speed is less than 3 times that of a Plymouth but at least 4 times that of a Datsun, then the Buick's speed is m.p.h.

   A. Either 105 or 110   B. 105 *only*
   C. 100 *only*   D. 110 *only*
   E. More than 110

QUESTIONS 6-10.

Questions 6-10 refer to the following.

In Deep Creek High School, Physical Education meets on Monday, Wednesday, and Friday during first period; and, Tuesday and Thursday during last period. Assume that first period is in the morning and that last period is in the afternoon. In order for a student to be excused from a Physical Education class, he must get a note from the School Nurse, bring an approval from a School Doctor, and obtain a permission of excusal from the Vice Principal. Certain additional restrictions apply:
1. The School Doctor is only available on Tuesday before school and on both Wednesday and Thursday after school.
2. The School Nurse is available on Monday and Wednesday before school but will not issue a note without the doctor's signature.
3. The Vice Principal is available only after school and only on days when the nurse is not available.
4. The Vice Principal will issue a permission for excusal only if both an approval from the doctor and a note from the nurse are also submitted.

6. On Monday morning, little Jimmy doesn't feel well.
   When is the earliest time that he can get excused from Physical Education class?

   A. Tuesday morning
   B. Tuesday afternoon
   C. Wednesday morning
   D. Thursday afternoon
   E. Friday morning

7. Referring to the facts in the preceding question, if the rule about seeing the Vice Principal were waived, when would be the earliest time for excusal?

   A. Tuesday morning
   B. Tuesday afternoon
   C. Wednesday morning
   D. Wednesday afternoon
   E. Thursday afternoon

8. Early Wednesday morning before school, Bobby becomes ill. The School Nurse is not in, but the nurse's aide is willing to give him a note. However, the doctor refuses to issue an approval until the following week.
   The earliest time that Bobby can be excused from Physical Education class under these circumstances is _____ of the following week.

   A. Monday morning
   B. Tuesday morning
   C. Tuesday afternoon
   D. Wednesday morning
   E. Wednesday afternoon

9. Johnny has just received a signed note from the Vice Principal, which will excuse him from Physical Education class. On this particular day, he did not receive a doctor's note or nurse's note, but he had received these two notes earlier in the week.
   This implies that Johnny received the Vice Principal's note _____.

   A. Wednesday
   B. Thursday
   C. Friday
   D. either Wednesday or Thursday
   E. either Thursday or Friday

10. If a student becomes ill on Monday after school, he could miss a Physical Education class as early as _____ if the 3 notes are received in ANY order.

   A. Tuesday morning
   B. Tuesday afternoon
   C. Wednesday morning
   D. Wednesday afternoon
   E. None of the above

10.____

QUESTIONS 11-15.

Questions 11-15 refer to the following:

On the radio dial of the newest type of radio, 100 AM corresponds to 150 FM, and 125 AM corresponds to 200 FM. Station W is to the left of station X, and are both on AM. Stations V, Y, and Z are all on FM, with Z lying between V and Y. It is also known that the call number for X is lower than the call number (station number) for Z. The call number for Y lies between the call numbers for W and X.

11. If a station had call number 110 AM, it would correspond to _____ FM.

   A. 160
   B. 170
   C. 180
   D. 190
   E. none of these

11.____

12. What is the CORRECT *ascending* order of stations with regard to their associated numbers? (Disregard whether AM or FM)

   A. WYXZV
   B. WXYZV
   C. WYZXV
   D. WYZVX
   E. WXZVY

12.____

13. If W is call number 105 and Y is call number 120, what call number describes X?

   A. Higher than 115
   B. Lower than 125
   C. Higher than 120
   D. Between 100 and 125
   E. Lower than 115

13.____

14. Suppose X is call number 100 and Z is call number 180. Thus, when moving the dial from left to right, we can be certain that the AM call number correspnding to the location of V is _____.

   A. higher than 115
   B. lower than 125
   C. higher than 100
   D. between 100 and 125
   E. lower than 115

14.____

15. Suppose that, in moving the dial from left to right, the first 3 stations reached are Y, Z, and W, respectively. A new FM station P corresponds to the location of station W. If the call number for P is double that of Z, then the call number for W is _____.

   A. double that of Y
   B. double that of Z
   C. 10 less than that of X
   D. 25 more than that of Z
   E. more than double that of Y

15.____

QUESTIONS 16-19.

Questions 16-19 refer to the following:

At a business luncheon, there were four guest speakers: Robert, Sam, Ted, and Vic. Each speaker provided at least one business tip on how to be successful. It is also known that:

1. Robert spoke before Sam, but after Vic.
2. Ted was not the last speaker, but spoke after Robert.
3. Robert gave less than twice as many tips as Ted, but only one-third as many as Vic.
4. Ted did not give the fewest number of tips, but gave five fewer tips than Robert.
5. Sam gave exactly one-fourth as many tips as Rober.

16. The CORRECT order of speakers from *last to first* is:

    A. Vic, Ted, Robert, Sam
    B. Sam, Robert, Ted, Vic
    C. Sam, Ted, Robert, Vic
    D. Vic, Robert, Ted, Sam
    E. Robert, Sam, Ted, Vic

17. How many tips did Robert give?

    A. 8   B. 9   C. 10   D. 11   E. At least 12

18. Which of the following numbers could NOT represent the number of tips Vic gave?

    A. 33   B. 36   C. 39   D. 42   E. 45

19. If Vic had actually given *fewer* than 50 tips, then Ted would have given _____ tips.

    A. 15
    B. 20
    C. 25
    D. 30
    E. none of these

QUESTIONS 20-25.

Questions 20-25 refer to the following:

A dentist by the name of Dr. Toothclean has six patients in the waiting room with different appointment times. There are two men and four ladies. Unfortunately, he has misplaced his appointment book; but he does remember certain facts:
1. Each individual's appointment is either exactly on the hour or half-hour.
2. Mr. Pain's appointment is later than 1:00 PM but earlier than Miss Root's.
3. Mrs. Cavity's appointment is halfway between Miss Root's and Mr. Molar's.
4. Miss Novocaine's appointment is at 1:30 PM.
5. The time of Miss Injection's appointment is half as close to Miss Novocaine's as it is to Mr. Pain's time.
6. Mr. Molar's appointment is later than Mr. Pain's time.

20. What is the EARLIEST possible time for Miss Injection's appointment?

    A. 12:30 PM
    B. 1:00 PM
    C. 1:30 PM
    D. 2:00 PM
    E. 2:30 PM

21. Of these 6 patients, who will be the THIRD patient to be attended to? 21.____
    A. Miss Novocaine
    B. Miss Novocaine or Mr. Pain
    C. Miss Novocaine or Mr. Molar
    D. Mr. Pain
    E. Mrs. Cavity

22. How many individuals have appointments before 1:00 PM? 22.____
    A. 0   B. 0 or 1   C. 1   D. 1 or 2   E. 2

23. How many possible arrangements of the order in which the six patients are taken are possible? 23.____
    A. 1   B. 2   C. 3   D. 4   E. 5 or more

24. Mrs. Cavity must be the _____ patient to be taken. 24.____
    A. 2nd   B. 3rd   C. 4th   D. 5th   E. 6th

25. If Miss Root's appointment is not last, what is the EARLIEST time she can be taken? 25.____
    A. 1:00 PM
    B. 2:00 PM
    C. 3:00 PM
    D. 4:00 PM
    E. None of these

KEY (CORRECT ANSWERS)

1. B   11. B
2. E   12. A
3. C   13. C
4. B   14. A
5. C   15. D

6. E   16. C
7. B   17. E
8. D   18. A
9. E   19. E
10. C 20. B

21. D
22. B
23. D
24. D
25. E

SOLUTIONS TO PROBLEMS

For Questions 1-5, let the speeds corresponding to each auto be represented by the first letter of that auto. Then, since F = speed of a Ford, we can determine P = F - 15; C=F+20; D = $\frac{1}{2}$ F and D = P - 10; T > F. Thus, $\frac{1}{2}$ F = P - 10 and P = F - 15, which yields P = 35 m.p.h. and F = 50 m.p.h. Furthermore, C = 70 m.p.h., D = 25 m.p.h., and T > 50 m.p.h. Also, we know that T < 70 m.p.h.

1. Self-explanatory from the values obtained above.

   (Answer B)

2. Self-explanatory.

   (Answer E)

3. Since F = 50 m.p.h. and C = 70 m.p.h., therefore T = 60 m.p.h. (to be halfway between the speeds of a Ford and a Chevy). But, D.= 25, so that a Toyota is 35 m.p.h. faster than a Datsun.

   (Answer C)

4. By doubling P, we get 70 m.p.h., it would exceed the speed of a Toyota, Ford, and Datsun.

   (Answer B)

5. In symbols, B < 3P and B 4D. Thus 100 m.p.h. $\leq$ B < 105 m.p.h. Since the Buick's speed ends in a 0 or 5, its speed must be 100 m.p.h.

   (Answer C)

For Questions 6-10 use the following matrix to show the availability of the nurse, doctor, and Vice Principal. Also, depict the times of Physical Education (P.E.) class.

	Before School	1st Period	Lunch	Last Period	After School
Monday	Nurse	P.E.			
Tuesday	Doctor			P.E.	Vice Principal
Wednesday	Nurse	P.E.			Doctor
Thursday				P.E.	Vice Principal, Doctor
Friday		P.E.			Vice Principal

6. The earliest time he (Jimmy) can get a doctor's note is Tuesday before school. Note that Jimmy could not get any written note from the nurse on Monday before school due to restriction 2. But by restriction 4, the Vice Principal cannot give a permission of excusal on Tuesday afternoon. After the nurse writes out a note on Wednesday before school, the next time the Vice Principal is available (Thursday after school), Jimmy can finally get an approval from the Vice Principal. Thus, by Friday 1st period, he can be excused from Physical Education class.

N.B. Recognize that the order in which any student will receive the approval notes is: Doctor, Nurse, Vice Principal.

   (Answer E)

7. By Tuesday, last period, Jimmy would have secured both the Doctor's note and the Nurse's note.

   (Answer B)

8. By the following Tuesday before school, Bobby will have the two required notes before the Vice Principal can issue an excuse note. The Vice Principal can issue this note on Tuesday after school and thus Bobby can get excused from the 1st period P.E. class on Wednesday.

   (Answer D)

9. Evident from the matrix.

   (Answer E)

10. The student could see the Doctor on Tuesday before school, the Vice Principal on Tuesday after school, and the Nurse on Wednesday before school. Thus, he would miss P.E. on Wednesday 1st period.

    (Answer C)

    For Questions 11-15, the following diagram is useful:

    Notice that since the call number for Z is greater than that of X and the call number for Y is less than that of X, Z's number is greater than Y's.

11. The equation FM = (2)(AM) - 50, will convert any AM station number to an FM station number and vice versa. Thus, if the call number is 110 AM, then the FM = (2)(110) - 50 = 170.

    (Answer B)

12. From all information given, the order must be WYXZV.

    (Answer A)

13. Since X > Y, and Y = 120, then X > 120.

    (Answer C)

14. In the equation FM = 2(AM) - 50, since Z = 180, the corresponding number on the AM dial is 115. Now, V > Z, so the corresponding AM number is > 115.

    (Answer A)

15. Using the basic equation: FM = 2(AM) - 50, we know P = 2W - 50 where P, W are the call numbers of their respective stations. Also, P = 2Z. Thus, 2Z = 2W - 50 and so W = Z + 25.

(Answer D)

QUESTIONS 16-19.

By using the first letters of the names of each speaker, Restriction 1 implies that the order of speaking was V, R, S. Restriction 2 implies that the order for all speakers was V, R, T, S, from first to last. Letting R = # of Robert's tips, T = # of Ted's tips, V = # of Vic's tips, and S = # of Sam's tips, you can deduce the following from restrictions 3, 4, and 5: R < 2T, R = 1/3V, T = R - 5, S = $\frac{1}{4}$R. Also, since Ted did not give the fewest number of tips, Sam gave the fewest number.

16. The reverse order of speakers must be S, T, R, V.

(Answer C)

17. Using R < 2T and T = R - 5, we get R < 2(R - 5), which gives R > 10. However, S = $\frac{1}{4}$R, so that the smallest R value allowable is 12. (If R were 11, S = $\frac{1}{4}$(11) ≠ a whole number).

(Answer E)

18. Since R ≥ 12 and R = 1/3V, V ≥ 36. Thus, 33 is not allowed.

(Answer A)

19. We know that T + 5 = 1/3V. Now 1/3V must be a whole number and if V < 50, V could be no higher than 48. This implies that T + 5 ≤ 1/3(48) = 16. Now, T ≤ 11. None of the choices given is correct.

(Answer E)

QUESTIONS 20-25.

Using a time line, four possibilities exist:

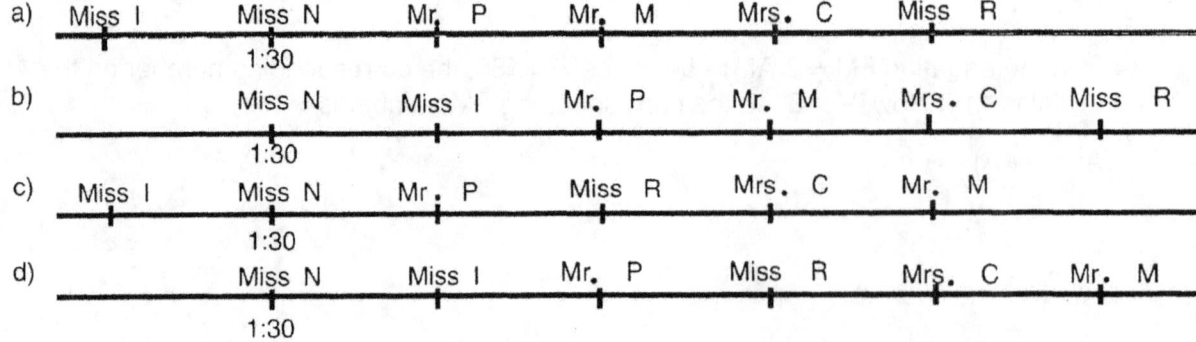

20. Since Mr. Pain's appointment is after 1:00 PM, the earliest it could be is 2:00 PM. Now condition 5 implies that Miss Injection's appointment could be no earlier than 1:00 PM. In this way Miss Injection's appointment is $\frac{1}{2}$ hour away from Miss Novocaine's, and 1 hour away from Mr. Pain's.

    (Answer B)

21. Evident from the above time lines.

    (Answer D)

22. If Mr. Pain's appointment is 2:30 PM or later, Miss Injection's appointment could be earlier than 1:00 PM (using possibility a) or c) above).

    (Answer B)

23. Evident from the above time lines.

    (Answer D)

24. Evident from the above time lines.

    (Answer D)

25. Using time line c) above, Mr. Pain's appointment could be as early as 2:00 PM. Thus Miss Root's appointment could be as early as 2:30 PM. None of the given answers corresponds to this time.

    (Answer E)

LOGICAL REASONING

Logical reasoning questions test the ability to understand, analyze, and evaluate arguments. Some of the abilities tested by specific questions include recognizing the point of an argument, recognizing assumptions on which an argument is based, drawing conclusions from given premises, inferring material missing from given passages, applying principles governing one argument to another, identifying methods of argument, evaluating arguments and counterarguments, and analyzing evidence.

Each question or group of questions is based on a short argument, generally an excerpt from the kind of material graduate students are likely to encounter in their academic and personal reading. Although arguments may be drawn from specific fields of study such as philosophy, literary criticism, social studies, and the physical sciences, materials from more familiar sources such as political speeches, advertisements, and informal discussions or dialogues also form the basis for some questions. No specialized knowledge of any particular field is required for answering the questions, however, and no knowledge of the terminology of formal logic is presupposed.

Specific questions asked about the arguments draw on information obtained by the process of critical and analytical reading described above.

The following strategies may be helpful in answering logical reasoning questions:

> The passage on which a question (or questions) is based should be read very carefully with close attention to such matters as (1) what is said specifically about a subject, (2) what is not said but necessarily follows from what is said, (3) what is suggested or claimed without substantiation in what is said. In addition, the means of relating statements, inferences, and claims - the structure of the argument- should be noted. Such careful reading may lead to the conclusion that the argument presented proceeds in an unsound or illogical fashion, but in many cases there will be no apparent weakness in the argument. It is important, in reading the arguments given, to attend to the soundness of the method employed and not to the actual truth of opinions presented.
>
> It is important to determine exactly what information the questtion is asking for; for instance, although it might be expected that one would be asked to detect or name the most glaring fault in a weak argument, the question posed may actually ask for the selection of one of a group of other arguments that reveals the same fault. In some cases, questions may ask for a negative response, for instance, a weakness that is NOT found in an argument or a conclusion that CANNOT be drawn from an argument.

LOGICAL REASONING

SAMPLE QUESTIONS

DIRECTIONS: The questions in this section require you to follow or evaluate the reasoning contained in brief statements or passages. In some questions, each of the choices is a conceivable solution to the particular problem posed. However, you are to select the one that answers the question *best,* that is, the one that does not require you to make what are, by common-sense standards, implausible, superfluous, or incompatible assumptions. After you have chosen the best answer, print the letter of the correct answer in the space at the right.

Questions 1-2.

Despite their progress in civilization, men have not yet outgrown the chicken coop. Man, too, has his "pecking order," and those who have been victims will require victims.

1. The paragraph would be *most appropriately* used in an argument

   A. for industrial progress
   B. against the evils that result from progress
   C. against rigid class sytems
   D. for humane treatment of animals
   E. for more effective military tactics

2. Which of the following assumptions underlie(s) the paragraph?
   I. Men cannot avoid behaving as their animal ancestors did.
   II. Progress in civilization is possible.
   III. Those who are victimized by one fear all.
   The *CORRECT* answer is:

   A. I only   B. II only   C. III only
   D. I and III   E. I, II, and III

3. All ice creams are delicious.
   No delicious dishes are wholesome.
   This dish is sauerkraut.
   Given the premises above, which of the following could *NOT* be true?
   I. The sauerkraut is both wholesome and delicious.
   II. The sauerkraut is either wholesome or delicious.
   III. The sauerkraut is neither wholesome nor delicious.
   The *CORRECT* answer is:

   A. I only   B. II only   C. III only
   D. I and II   E. I and III

4. All members of the advisory committee, appointed by each mayor to serve during his term, must belong to registered political parties.
   The only registered political parties in town are the Progressive and Monarchist parties.
   The present mayor is a Monarchist noted for his strong party bias.
   On the basis of the evidence stated above, which of the following conclusions is *most likely* to be *TRUE?*

A. The present mayor has been a Monarchist all of his life.
B. All members of the advisory committee have usually belonged to the party to which the mayor belonged.
C. The present mayor's advisory committee has some Monarchists appointed to serve only during his term.
D. Everyone in town professes loyalty to either the Progressive or the Monarchist party.
E. The Progressive and Monarchist parties recommend to the mayor candidates for the advisory committee.

KEY (CORRECT ANSWERS)

1. C
2. B
3. A
4. C

LOGICAL REASONING

EXAMINATION SECTION
TEST 1

DIRECTIONS: Each question or incomplete statement is followed by several suggested answers or completions. Select the one that BEST answers the question or completes the Statement. *PRINT THE LETTER OF THE CORRECT ANSWER IN THE SPACE AT THE RIGHT.*

QUESTIONS 1-3.

For questions 1-3 an initial argument is presented. Of the five given choices, select the one that MOST closely resembles the argument.

1. A stove is usually hot. One often reads about a child who burns his hands by touching a stove.

    A. The weather is probably cool. I see several people wearing jackets.
    B. A science course is often difficult. One usually hears a high school student complain about science exams.
    C. High school football is sometimes dangerous. Players often do not take proper precautions.
    D. A person can learn to appreciate art. However, not all people will become artists.
    E. Bowling alleys are normally crowded. Yet some people enjoy waiting several hours in order to bowl.

2. Joseph lives in New Jersey. Newark is located in New Jersey. Therefore, Joseph lives in Newark.

    A. The letter A is a vowel. Vowels are part of the alphabet. Therefore, the letter A is part of the alphabet.
    B. Susan enjoys bowling. John enjoys tennis. Therefore, Susan and John are not compatible.
    C. Bob goes to Central High School. Mathematics is taught at Central High School. Therefore, Bob is taking mathematics.
    D. Jane play field hockey. Field hockey is considered a dangerous sport. Therefore, Jane plays a dangerous sport.
    E. All mammals drink water. Tables do not drink water. Therefore, tables are not mammals.

3. Not all libraries have phone directories. If they did, there would be less room to stock books.

    A. Some baseball umpires are honest. If they were not, it would be impossible to have baseball games.
    B. Some chemicals are poisonous. All labels on bottles indicate whether the contents are poisonous.
    C. All flags have stripes. If they did not, they would not be considered flags.
    D. Some restaurants do not have booths. If they had booths, there would not be ample space for counter seats.
    E. No city is safe. If they were, there would be no more crime.

QUESTIONS 4-11.

Questions 4-11 pertain to the following.

A college student has four vertical shelves mounted in his dorm. Each shelf is assigned a subject title, corresponding to each of the four subjects he is taking. Those subjects are math, English, chemistry, and history. Also it is known that:

1. There is AT LEAST one book on each shelf.
2. The shelf for English books is two slots above the shelf for math books, but adjacent to the slot for chemistry books.
3. The shelf for chemistry books is NOT the top shelf.
4. The number of English books is three times the number of chemistry books.
5. The number of math books is five less than the number of English books, but more than the number of chemistry books.
6. The number of history books is more than the number of math books, but less than the number of English books.
7. The number of books on the third shelf does not exceed 20.

4. There are _____ chemistry books.

    A. at least 2
    B. at most 6
    C. between 3 and 5 inclusive
    D. between 3 and 6 inclusive
    E. either 4 or 5

5. The MINIMUM total number of books is

    A. 20   B. 21   C. 22   D. 23   E. 24

6. Math books are found on the _____ shelf.

    A. 1st or 2nd   B. 2nd or 3rd   C. 3rd
    D. 2nd   E. 1st

7. Which subject(s) will have NO books on neither the top nor bottom shelves?

    A. math   B. English
    C. chemistry and English   D. chemistry
    E. math and history

8. The MAXIMUM number of books on the fourth shelf is

    A. 16   B. 18   C. 20
    D. 22   E. more than 22

9. Which pair of subject books CANNOT lie on adjacent shelves?

    A. English and chemistry   B. chemistry and history
    C. history and English   D. history and math
    E. math and chemistry

10. In how many different ways can the subject titles be assigned to the four shelves?   10.____

    A. 1 B. 2 C. 3
    D. 4 E. at least 5

11. Which of the following could NOT be the number of history books?   11.____

    A. 15   B. 12   C. 9   D. 6   E. 3

QUESTIONS 12-16.

Questions 12-16 pertain to the following.

Lucky Charlie visited his favorite racetrack yesterday. There were a total of four races; in each race there were only six horses, numbers 1 through 6. The names of the winning horses were Lucky Molly, Mister Class, Super Power, and Great Lady. Also, it is known that:

1. The number of the winning horse of each race was lower than the number of the winner of any previous race.
2. The number 5 horse did not win the second race.
3. An even numbered horse won the third race.
4. Great Lady won the fourth race.
5. Super Power's number is twice Lucky Molly's number.

12. What number did Great Lady have?   12.____

    A. 1   B. 2   C. 3 or 4   D. 5   E. 6

13. If Super Power won his race directly before Lucky Molly won her race, then Super Power's number is   13.____

    A. 1 or 2   B. 2 or 4   C. 4   D. 4 or 6   E. 6

14. How many different possibilities exist for the winning numbers for all four races?   14.____

    A. 1 B. 2 C. 3
    D. 4 E. at least 5

15. Mister Class won the _____ race and his number was _____.   15.____

    A. second, 2   B. third, 1   C. third, 4
    D. fourth, 4   E. first, 6

16. If the number 3 horse won the second race and Lucky Molly won the third race, then the CORRECT order of the winning horses in races 1, 2, 3, and 4 respectively is   16.____

    A. Super Power, Mister Class, Lucky Molly, Great Lady
    B. Mister Class, Great Lady, Lucky Molly, Super Power
    C. Great Lady, Super Power, Lucky Molly, Mister Class
    D. Mister Class, Super Power, Lucky Molly, Great Lady
    E. Super Power, Great Lady, Lucky Molly, Mister Class

QUESTIONS 17-19.

Questions 17-19 pertain to the following:

1. If A is true, then C is false.
2. If A is false, then B is true.
3. Either D is false or C is true.
4. It is possible that both D is false and C is true.

17. If B is true, then _____.

    A. A is false
    B. D is true
    C. A is true
    D. C is true
    E. no conclusion can be reached about A, C, or D

18. At least one of _____ or _____ is true.

    A. A, B
    B. A, D
    C. B, opposite of C
    D. D, opposite of C
    E. C, D

19. If D is true, then _____ is (are) true.

    A. C *only*
    B. B *only*
    C. both A and B
    D. both B and C
    E. both A and the opposite of B

QUESTIONS 20-25.

Questions 20-25 pertain to the following:

Alice has invented a word game in which each letter A through J is assigned one number from 1 through 10. It is possible, however, that two or more letters are assigned to the same number. In fact, the three vowels correspond to the same odd number. The letters B, D, and F correspond to three different even numbers. Each consonant, with one exception, has a higher numerical value than any vowel. Exactly one letter is worth 1. All consonants, except G, have an even numerical value. The value of C is higher than that of F, but lower than that of D. The value of J is 4 and no other letter has this value. The value of A is one half that of F. The value of H is higher than that of C.

20. How many letters have a value of 5?

    A. none
    B. 1
    C. 2
    D. 3
    E. at least 4

21. B has the same value as

    A. C
    B. D
    C. E
    D. G
    E. H

22. Which letter has a value of 6?

    A. none
    B. A
    C. F
    D. G
    E. H

23. The value of I is

    A. 1
    B. 3
    C. 5
    D. 7
    E. 9

24. The value of J is _____ the value of D.

    A. 1/4 B. 1/2 C. 1/3
    D. 2/3 E. none of these

25. Which pair of letters has values which are consecutive numbers?

    A. A, C   B. F, G   C. D, H   D. B, D   E. I, J

KEY (CORRECT ANSWERS)

1. B
2. C
3. D
4. D
5. B

6. A
7. D
8. B
9. B
10. B

11. E
12. A
13. D
14. D
15. E

16. A
17. E
18. C
19. D
20. A

21. A
22. C
23. B
24. E
25. E

SOLUTIONS TO PROBLEMS

1. The first sentence states a general conclusion, which is substantiated by information that an individual might have read or heard about. Only choice B presents that same type of logic pattern.

   (ANSWER B).

2. The logic presented here is faulty, since two facts may imply a third fact without implying each other. In choice C, the conclusion is structured as one of two statements implying the other simply because they are both related to a third statement.

   (ANSWER C).

3. A statement is given, followed by a justification in terms of "what-if". Note that the first statement takes the form of "not all," which can be interpreted as "some" or "at least one". Choice D is most closely structured in this way.

   (ANSWER D).

4. Let x = number of chemistry books. Then $3x$ = number of English books and $3x - 5$ = number of math books. It is also known that $3x$ > number of history books > $3x - 5$. It can be determined that the correct order of subjects from the first through fourth shelves is: history, math, chemistry, English, or math, chemistry, English, history. Thus $3x \leq 20$, so $x \leq 6$. Since the number of math books has to be at least 2, $3x - 5 \geq 2$, which means $x \geq 3$ (whole numbers only). Thus $3 \leq$ number of chemistry books ≤ 6.

   (ANSWER E).

5. Since 3 is the least number of chemistry books, the least number of English, math, and history books are 9, 4, and 5 respectively. The total is 21.

   (ANSWER B).

6. Refer to explanation for #4.

   (ANSWER A).

7. Refer to explanation for #4.

   (ANSWER D).

8. Since only English or history books may appear on the fourth shelf, and the number of English books would be greater, we find the maximum value for $3x$. Since $x \leq 6$, $3x \leq 18$.

   (ANSWER B).

9. Either chemistry and history books will lie on the third and first shelves (respectively) or on the second and fourth shelves (respectively).

   (ANSWER B).

10. Refer to explanation in #4.

    (ANSWER B).

11. In question 5, we established that the actual least number of math books is 4; thus, the number of history books must *exceed* 4.

    (ANSWER E).

12. Only four possibilities exist for the numbers of the winning horses in races 1 through 4 respectively.
    Possibility 1: 6, 4, 2, 1   Possibility 2: 6, 3, 2, 1
    Possibility 3: 5, 4, 2, 1   Possibility 4: 4, 3, 2, 1
    Since Great Lady won the fourth race, her number was 1.

    (ANSWER A).

13. Since Super Power's number is twice Lucky Molly's number, only the first three possibilities listed in #12's explanation could exist. Thus Super Power's number could only be 4 or 6.

    (ANSWER D).

14. Refer to explanation for #12.

    (ANSWER D).

15. If possibility 1 is true then Mister Class had to win the first race and his number was 6. If possibility 2 is true, Mister Class had to win the third race and his number was 2. If possibility 3 is true, Mister Class had to win the first race and his number was 5. Finally, if possibility 4 is true, then Mister Class won the second race and his number was 3.

    (ANSWER E).

16. Only possibility 4 would be correct, so that the winning numbers of the four races are 4, 3, 2, 1 respectively. Since Super Power's number is twice Lucky Molly's number, their numbers are 4 and 2 respectively. Great Lady's number is 1; thus Mister Class' number is 4.

    (ANSWER A).

17. Since B and D cannot both be true, and B is true, then D must be false. By Statement 3, C can be true or false.

    (ANSWER E).

18. Exactly one will happen: Either B being true or C being false. By Statement 2, if B were false, A would be true (contrapositive). Then, Statement 1 says that C is false.

    (ANSWER C).

8 (#1)

19. By Statement 3, if D is true, C must be true. Then, the contrapositive of statement 1 says that A is false. Furthermore, by Statement 2, B must be true.

(ANSWER D).

For questions 20-25, the following chart shows the allowable letter(s) for each number 1 through 10:

1 = G	6 = F
2 = none	7 = none
3 = A, E, I	8 = B, C
4 = J	9 = none
5 = none	10 = D, H

Note that all questions 20-25 can be answered based on the above chart. In #24 choice E is correct since the ratio of values of J and D is 4/10 or 2/5..

EXAMINATION SECTION
TEST 1

DIRECTIONS: Each question or incomplete statement is followed by several suggested answers or completions. Select the one that BEST answers the question or completes the statement. *PRINT THE LETTER OF THE CORRECT ANSWER IN THE SPACE AT THE RIGHT.*

QUESTIONS 1-4.

Questions 1-4 refer to the following information.

A recent study shows that of the 1000 graduates of Learnmore High School, 40% claimed that they smoked during their high school years, 30% said they started smoking before entering high school and continued smoking during high school years. Of the people who didn't smoke at all during their high school year, 70% claim that they have no medical problems. However, only 10% of those who did smoke during their high school years reported no medical problem.

1. What percent of all these graduates claim they have NO medical problem?   1.____

   A. 30 B. 42
   C. 60 D. 70
   E. None of the above

2. How many non-smokers have had at LEAST one medical problem?   2.____

   A. 70   B. 180   C. 280   D. 350   E. 450

3. What is the MAXIMUM number of people who began smoking before entering high school, and have had NO medical problems?   3.____

   A. 10   B. 30   C. 40   D. 100   E. over 100

4. Counting only individuals who have experienced at least one medical problem, what is the ratio of those who didn't smoke during high school years to those who did smoke during that time period?   4.____

   A. 3:2   B. 1:2   C. 1:3   D. 2:3   E. 3:1

5. If John enjoys the taste of pineapple, he'll like the taste of all fruit. The preceding statement is MOST similar to which of the following?   5.____

   A. If a dog has a liking for human food, he'll like all dog food
   B. If a person can understand algebra, he can understand all mathematics
   C. If a Chevrolet gets good gas mileage, then so will a Datsun
   D. If Sue's favorite color is red, then she won't buy a green dress
   E. If Bob can fix any electrical item, then he can fix a toaster

6. Only a few people who are heavy smokers will live past the age of 90. Since Eve is a 30-year-old non-smoker, she will probably live beyond the age of 90.
The argument is MOST similar to which of the following?   6.____

A. Only a few cities like Cleanville have a low crime rate. Thus, if a person lives in a low crime rate city, that city must be Cleanville.
B. Only birds have feathers. Thus, some birds have morefeathers than other birds.
C. All weight-lifters are light sleepers. Since Bob is a heavy sleeper, he doesn't lift weights.
D. Not many individuals who worry a lot can get a good night's rest. Since John does not worry at all, he can probably get a good night's rest.
E. Some mathematicians enjoy all sports. Since William is a mathematician, he may not enjoy any sports.

7. Since Jack is left-handed, he is an excellent tennis player. Assuming that the preceding statement is true, from which one(s) of the following can this quoted statement be logically deduced?
    I.   All tennis players are left-handed.
    II. None of the excellent tennis players is right-handed.
    III. Either Jack is right-handed or he is an excellent tennis player.

    A. I only B. II only C. III only
    D. II and III E. I, II, and III

8. Gamblers are boisterous individuals. Yesterday, I went to the racetrack and there was a lot of shouting after every race. The above argument assumes:
    I.   Gamblers frequent racetracks.
    II. Noisy people are gamblers.
    III. Quiet people don't go to racetracks.

    A. I only B. II only C. III only
    D. I, III E. I, II, III

QUESTIONS 9-14.

Questions 9-14 refer to the facts below. It is to be assumed that it is the month of July, the first day of which is a Monday.

The Ail-Weather appliance store sells televisions, radios, toasters, and refrigerators. Certain conditions govern this store:

   I.   The store is open only Monday through Friday every month. Thus, all purchases and deliveries can only be made Monday through Friday.
   II. TV's and radios are only delivered on even numbered days.
   III. Refrigerators are delivered only on Tuesdays and Thursdays.
   IV. Toasters are delivered on any date of the month which can be divided evenly by 3 or 5.
   V.   A customer may purchase a radio or a toaster on the day of delivery.
   VI. Since refrigerators and TV's are more expensive items, they are immediately inspected on the day of delivery. However, a customer may not purchase these items until 3 business days after delivery.

9. Which item(s) could be neither delivered nor purchased on Wednesdays?

    A. TV's and radios   B. TV's, radios, and refrigerators
    C. Refrigerators and toasters   D. Refrigerators *only*
    E. Toasters *only*

10. On how many days during this month can toasters be purchased? 10._____

   A. At least 4 but fewer than 7 B. 9
   C. 11 D. More than 11
   E. None of the above

11. During the first week, on which dates may a TV either be purchased or delivered? 11._____

   A. 2nd, 3rd, 4th B. 2nd, 4th, 5th C. 3rd, 4th, 5th
   D. 2nd, 5th, 6th E. 2nd, 3rd

12. On how many days during this month can TV's be delivered? 12._____

   A. Fewer than 6 B. 8 C. 9
   D. 10 E. 11

13. What is the *earliest* date on which both a TV and toaster can be purchased? 13._____

   A. 3rd B. 5th C. 7th D. 9th E. 11th

14. Which appliance(s) has(have) exactly 2 delivery dates on Fridays? 14._____

   A. Toasters, radios, TV's B. Toasters, TV's
   C. TV's, radios D. Toasters, radios
   E. Only toasters

15. If a person studies hard, he can pass any high school course. 15._____
    This statement can be logically deduced from which of the following?

   A. Some people study while others don't study.
   B. A person who has passed a particular high school course must have studied hard.
   C. A high school course can be passed if a person is willing to study hard.
   D. If a person doesn't study, he can't expect to pass a high school course.
   E. Some high school courses require more studying than do other courses.

QUESTIONS 16-17.

Questions 16 and 17 are to be answered on the basis of the following.

The most dangerous sport in the world is thoroughbred horseracing, since more participants per thousand are killed than in any other sport. Hang-gliding is the second most dangerous sport. By contrast, boxing ranks tenth on the list of most dangerous sports.

16. The author of the above paragraph is *most likely* trying to convey the message that: 16._____

   A. Most sports are dangerous
   B. Hang-gliding is popular despite its danger
   C. Only ten sports are considered dangerous
   D. The most number of injuries occur in horseracing
   E. Boxing is not the most dangerous sport

17. The author would *probably* be opposed to: 17.____

    A. Any dangerous sport
    B. A ban on boxing
    C. Amateur boxing
    D. Horseracing
    E. A ban on horseracing

QUESTIONS 18-22.

Questions 18-22 are to be answered on the basis of the following.
The Expanding Food Company has outlet stores on each of First Ave., Second Ave., Third Ave., Fourth Ave., and Fifth Ave. Also, it is known that:

   I.   There is at least one store on each avenue.
   II. The number of stores on Fifth Ave. equals the sum of the number of stores on First Ave. plus those on Second Ave.
   III. The number of stores on Second Ave. is double the number of stores on Third Ave.
   IV. The number of stores on Fourth Ave. is greater than the number of stores on Fifth Ave.
   V.   There are an even number of stores on First Ave.

18. What is the *fewest* number of stores that must exist on Fourth Ave.?   18.____

    A. 2   B. 3   C. 4   D. 5   E. 6

19. Which avenue has the MOST stores?   19.____

    A. Fifth Ave.   B. Fourth Ave.
    C. Third Ave.   D. All of the above
    E. None of the above

20. Suppose NO avenue has *more* than 7 stores. Find the total number of stores on all 5   20.____
    avenues.

    A. 16 or 19   B. 20
    C. 21   D. 16, 19 or 20
    E. 16, 20 or 21

21. The number of stores on Fifth Ave   21.____

    A. must be even
    B. must be odd
    C. could equal the number of stores on First Ave.
    D. could equal the number of stores on Second Ave.
    E. none of the above

22. Suppose it is known that there are 4 stores on Third Ave. and that there are *more* than 4   22.____
    stores on First Ave.
    Find the *minimum* number of stores on all 5 avenues.

    A. 45   B. 49   C. 46   D. 48   E. 47

QUESTIONS 23-25.

Questions 23 through 25 are to be answered on the basis of the following.

In a particular group of 21 people, each individual is one of three professions: doctor, engineer, or teacher. Half the number of people who smoke are engineers. One-third of the number of non-smokers are doctors. The number of engineers who smoke equals the number of non-smokers who are not doctors.

23. How many of the non-smokers are doctors? 23.____

    A. 2   B. 3   C. 5   D. 6   E. 9

24. If all the teachers are smokers, and there are only 2 doctors who smoke, then the teachers represent _____ Percent of the entire group. 24.____

    A. 19   B. 25   C. 29   D. 33   E. 40

25. Using the information from the preceding question, *how many* engineers are there in the entire group? 25.____

    A. 3   B. 6   C. 9   D. 12   E. 15

KEY (CORRECT ANSWERS)

1.	E	11.	B
2.	B	12.	E
3.	C	13.	B
4.	B	14.	A
5.	B	15.	C
6.	D	16.	E
7.	C	17.	B
8.	A	18.	D
9.	D	19.	B
10.	E	20.	E

21. A
22. E
23. B
24. A
25. D

SOLUTIONS

1. $(.70)(.60) = .42$ of all the graduates didn't smoke and didn't have any medical problems, whereas $(.10)(.40) = .04$ of all the graduates did smoke but yet didn't experience any medical problems. Thus, $.42 + .04 = .46$ or 46% of all graduates claimed they had no medical problems.

   (ANSWER E).

2. $(.30)(.60) = .18$ of the population were non-smokers and yet had at least one medical problem. Now $(.18)(1000) = 180$.

   (ANSWER B).

3. $(.10)(.40) = .04$ indicates the number of people who did smoke during their high school years and had no medical problem. Of the .04, it is not possible to determine what fraction actually started smoking before entering high school. So, $(.04)(1000) = 40$.

   (ANSWER C).

4. $(.30)(.60) = .18$ of the non-smokers had at least one medical problem, whereas $(.90)(.40) = .36$ of the smokers had at least one medical problem. Then $.18/.36 = 1:2$ ratio.

   (ANSWER B).

5. The original statement uses the truth of a specific item in order to imply the truth of a general item containing that specific item. Only choice B illustrates that kind of reasoning.

   (ANSWER B).

6. The original statement can be written: "If A, then B. If not A, then not B." This argument is not necessarily valid, but choice D resembles it most closely.

   (ANSWER D).

7. Statement I is false, since we can assume that there exist both left-handed and right-handed players. Statement II is also false, because there may be excellent right-handed players. Statement III is true, since Jack is not right-handed and thus would have to be an excellent tennis player.

   (ANSWER C).

8. The only valid implication is Statement I, since one can assume that gamblers do visit racetracks. (This statement could be false, since it is only an assumption). Statement II is not valid since many types of people are noisy. Statement III is also invalid since one can assume that both noisy and quiet people frequent racetracks.

   (ANSWER A).

QUESTIONS 9-14.

Questions 9-14 see calendars below showing days of receiving and purchasing of each of the 4 different appliances. Note that for question #10, the actual answer is 10.

7 (#1)

Radio Delivered / TV Delivered

Sun	Mon	Tu	Wed	Th	Fri	Sat
	1	(2)	3	(4)	5	6
7	(8)	9	(10)	11	(12)	13
14	15	(16)	17	(18)	19	20
21	(22)	23	(24)	25	(26)	27
28	29	(30)	31			

Toaster Delivered

Sun	Mon	Tu	Wed	Th	Fri	Sat
	1	2	(3)	4	(5)	6
7	8	(9)	(10)	11	(12)	13
14	(15)	16	17	(18)	19	20
21	22	23	(24)	(25)	26	27
28	29	(30)	31			

Refrigerator Delivered

Sun	Mon	Tu	Wed	Th	Fri	Sat
	1	(2)	3	(4)	5	6
7	8	(9)	10	(11)	12	13
14	15	(16)	17	(18)	19	20
21	22	(23)	24	(25)	26	27
28	29	(30)	31			

Radio Purchased

Sun	Mon	Tu	Wed	Th	Fri	Sat
	1	(2)	3	(4)	5	6
7	(8)	9	(10)	11	(12)	13
14	15	(16)	17	(18)	19	20
21	(22)	23	(24)	25	(26)	27
28	29	(30)	31			

8 (#1)

Radio Purchased

Sun	Mon	Tu	Wed	Th	Fri	Sat
	1	②	3	④	5	6
7	⑧	9	⑩	11	⑫	13
14	15	⑯	17	⑱	19	20
21	㉒	23	㉔	25	㉖	27
28	29	㉚	31			

Toaster Purchased

Sun	Mon	Tu	Wed	Th	Fri	Sat
	1	2	③	4	⑤	6
7	8	⑨	⑩	11	⑫	13
14	⑮	16	17	⑱	19	20
21	22	23	㉔	㉕	26	27
28	29	㉚	31			

TV Purchased

Sun	Mon	Tu	Wed	Th	Fri	Sat
	1	2	3	4	⑤	6
7	8	⑨	10	⑪	12	13
14	⑮	16	⑰	18		20
21	22	㉓	24	㉕	26	27
28	㉙	30	㉛			

Refrigerator Purchased

Sun	Mon	Tu	Wed	Th	Fri	Sat
	1	2	3	4	⑤	6
7	8	⑨	10	11	⑫	13
14	15	⑯	17	18	⑲	20
21	22	㉓	24	25	㉖	27
28	29	㉚	31			

9. (ANSWER D).

10. (ANSWER E).

11. (ANSWER B).

12. (ANSWER E).

13. (ANSWER B).

14. (ANSWER A).

15. The original statement follows logically from choice C, since it implies that studying hard is a prerequisite to passing any high school course.

(ANSWER C).

16. Although the general public perceives boxing as the most dangerous sport(or at least one of the most dangerous), the author is relying on a certain type of statistic to illustrate that there are nine other sports which could be considered more dangerous than boxing.

(ANSWER E).

17. The author, by his argument, appears to be defending any ban on the sport of boxing. He does not make any case for or against another sport.

(ANSWER B).

18. Let x, $2y$, y, w, z be the number of stores respectively on First, Second, Third, Fourth, and Fifth Avenues. Also, $z = x + 2y$, $w > z$, and x must be an even number. Since the smallest values for x and y are 2 and 1 respectively, the minimum value of $z = 2 + (2)(1) = 4$. Now w = the number of stores on Fourth Ave., and since $w > z$, then $w > 4$. Thus, 5 is the minimum value of w.

(ANSWER D).

19. Since $z = x + 2y$, $z > x$ and $z > y$. But $w > z$, so that w is the variable with the highest value. We know that w = the number of stores on Fourth Ave.

(ANSWER B).

20. Assume $z = 7$. Then there are two e possible combinations of numbers associated with the number of stores on First, Second, Third, Fourth, and Fifth Avenues respectively. The 1st combination is 2, 4, 2, 7, 6; the 2nd combination is 4, 2, 1, 7, 6; the 3rd combination is 2, 2, 1, 7, 4. Thus, only 16, 20, or 21 are the possible totals.

(ANSWER E).

21. Since $z = x + 2y$ and x must be even, then z must also be an even number. Note that $2y$ is already even. Thus, even number + even number = even number.

(ANSWER A).

22. Since Third Ave. has 4 stores, Second Ave. has 8 stores. We also know that First Ave. has more than 4 stores; thus it must have a minimum of 6 stores (even number). Fifth Ave. has $6 + 8 = 14$ stores at minimum, and 15 = the minimum stores on Fourth Ave. Thus, the number of stores on all 5 avenues (minimum) = $6 + 8 + 4 + 14 + 15 = 47$.

(ANSWER E).

23. Let x = # of smokers, so that $21 - x$ = # of non-smokers. Then $1/2x$ = # of smokers who are also engineers. This number must equal the number of non-smokers who are not doctors. We can infer that 2/3 of the non-smokers (i.e. $2/3 [21 - x]$) are not doctors. Thus, $1/2x = 2/3 (21 - x)$. So, $x = 12$ and $21 - x = 9$. This implies that there are a total of 9 non-smokers. Since 1/3 of this number are doctors, there are 3 non-smoking doctors.

(ANSWER B).

24. Since 1/2 of the smokers are engineers, this translates to (1/2)(12) = 6 people. Only 2 doctors smoke, so the number of teachers who smoke = 12 - 6 - 2 = 4. (All teachers are smokers). Now 4/21 = .1905 or approximately 19%.

(ANSWER A).

25. The non-smokers must consist of only doctors and engineers. Of the 9 non-smokers, 3 are doctors. Thus 6 non-smokers are engineers. We already know that there are 6 engineers who smoke, so that there are a total of 12 engineers.

(ANSWER D).

EXAMINATION SECTION
TEST 1

DIRECTIONS: Each question or incomplete statement is followed by several suggested answers or completions. Select the one that BEST answers the question or completes the statement. *PRINT THE LETTER OF THE CORRECT ANSWER IN THE SPACE AT THE RIGHT.*

Questions 1-7.

DIRECTIONS: Questions 1 through 7 are to be answered based on the following set of facts.

The four towns of Alpha, Beta, Gamma, and Delta lie in a straight line from left to right, but not necessarily in that order. Each town has a different maximum speed limit, and each maximum speed limit ends in 0 or 5. Delta lies to the east of Beta. Alpha lies east of Beta, but west of Delta. The distance between Beta and Alpha equals the distance between Alpha and Delta. Alpha and Gamma are adjacent towns. Gamma and Delta are 50 miles apart. The distance between Alpha and Gamma is less than 10 miles.

Concerning the maximum speed limits, Beta's is one-third that of Alpha's, Delta's is higher than Alpha's by 10 m.p.h., and Gamma has the highest. No town's maximum speed limit exceeds 80 m.p.h. nor is less than 20 m.p.h.

1. Which of the following is the CORRECT order of towns from west to east?   1.____

   A. Beta, Delta, Gamma, Alpha   B. Beta, Alpha, Gamma, Delta
   C. Delta, Alpha, Gamma, Beta   D. Gamma, Alpha, Beta, Delta
   E. Delta, Gamma, Alpha, Beta

2. What is Gamma's MAXIMUM speed limit in m.p.h.?   2.____

   A. 65   B. 70   C. Over 70
   D. 60   E. Under 60

3. What is the ratio of Beta's MAXIMUM speed limit to that of Delta?   3.____

   A. 4:15   B. 1:3   C. 1:4   D. 3:5   E. 2:7

4. Suppose that next year Beta's maximum speed limit is tripled, and Alpha's is reduced by 5 m.p.h.   4.____
   What would be the CORRECT order of towns from lowest to highest maximum speed limit?

   A. Delta, Alpha, Beta, Gamma   B. Beta, Delta, Alpha, Gamma
   C. Alpha, Delta, Beta, Gamma   D. Alpha, Beta, Delta, Gamma
   E. Beta, Alpha, Gamma, Delta

5. What is the distance, in miles, between Delta and Alpha?   5.____

   A. Between 50 and 55 inclusive   B. Under 50
   C. Over 55 but under 65   D. Over 50 but under 60
   E. Over 60

6. The distance between Beta and Delta must be less than _____ miles.

   A. 50   B. 65   C. 75   D. 90   E. 120

7. For which towns can the EXACT maximum speed limit be determined?

   A. Alpha and Gamma
   B. Alpha, Beta, and Delta
   C. Beta, Delta, and Gamma
   D. Beta and Gamma
   E. All four towns

Questions 8-14.

DIRECTIONS: Questions 8 through 14 are to be answered based upon the following set of facts.

Johnny Quicksale sells three types of books: biographical, novels, and statistical. Each type of book comes in three different versions: condensed, regular, and expanded. For each type of book, the order of cost from least expensive to most expensive is condensed, regular, and expanded. Each type has a different price, and the pricing between books is somewhat involved. Condensed statistical books cost more than both regular novels and regular biographies, but less than expanded novels. Expanded biographies cost less than regular novels, but more than condensed novels. Condensed biographies are the cheapest. Expanded statistical books are not the most expensive. The price for each condensed and regular book is a multiple of $5, whereas the price of each expanded book is a multiple of $25. Each book sells for less than $95. A regular statistical book costs less than $45.

8. The CORRECT sequence of the first three books (in increasing price) starting from the cheapest is:

   A. Condensed biography, regular biography, consensed novel
   B. Condensed novel, condensed biography, condensed statistical
   C. Condensed statistical, condensed novel, condensed biography
   D. Condensed novel, condensed biography, regular novel
   E. Condensed biography, condensed novel, regular biography

9. How many books cost over $10?

   A. 3   B. 4 or 5   C. 6   D. 7 or 8   E. all 9

10. If just the expanded versions were listed in correct order from the most expensive to the cheapest, that order would be:

    A. Novel, statistical, biography
    B. Statistical, biography, novel
    C. Biography, novel, statistical
    D. Statistical, novel, biography
    E. Biography, statistical, novel

11. How many books cost under $30?

    A. 2   B. 3   C. 4   D. 5   E. 6 or more

12. For which type(s) of books are the prices arranged so that the regular version could be the average in price of the prices of the condensed and expanded versions?   12._____

    A. Only novels
    B. Only biographies
    C. Only statistical
    D. Exactly 2 types
    E. All 3 types

13. For which type(s) of books are the prices arranged so that the condensed version costs MORE than the expanded version?   13._____

    A. All 3 types
    B. Exactly 2 types
    C. Only biographies
    D. Only novels
    E. None

14. Suppose that next year the cost of the condensed statistical book doubled, but all other prices remained the same.   14._____
Which statement(s) is(are) CORRECT?
    I. The condensed statistical book would be the most expensive.
    II. The price of the condensed statistical book would equal the price of the expanded novel book.
    III. The price of the condensed statistical book would exceed that of the expanded statistical book.

The CORRECT answer is:

    A. I *only*
    B. II *only*
    C. III *only*
    D. None of the above
    E. Exactly 2 of the above

Questions 15-22.

DIRECTIONS: Questions 15 through 22 are to be answered on the basis of the following set of facts.

Ann, Beth, Carol, Diane, and Eve have entered a local beauty contest in which Mr. Brown, Mr. Smith, and Mr. Jones are the judges. The point system to be used is 0, 1, 2, 3, and 4, where 4 is the highest. Each judge will rank each applicant exactly once, and no judges may assign the same ranking to two or more applicants. The girl with the highest total wins the contest. Brown and Jones both ranked Diane the same, and this ranking matched the score that Smith gave to Carol. Smith's ranking for Ann was exactly double Jones' ranking for Ann, but less than the score Brown assigned to Ann. Brown ranked Eve higher than Ann. Carol accumulated the same number of points as Ann. Carol and Ann were the only applicants who received three different rankings from the three judges.

15. Who won the contest?   15._____

    A. Ann   B. Beth   C. Carol   D. Diane   E. Eve

16. If the rules were adjusted so that for each applicant only the best two rankings given by the three judges would count, who would have the HIGHEST total?   16._____

    A. Ann   B. Beth   C. Carol   D. Diane   E. Eve

17. What is the complete list of applicants who did NOT receive any 0 rating?

   A. Ann, Carol, Diane
   B. Ann, Beth, Eve
   C. Beth, Carol, Eve
   D. Ann, Diane, Eve
   E. Beth, Carol, Diane

18. Who came in second place?

   A. Ann   B. Beth   C. Carol   D. Diane   E. Eve

19. Which judge(s) scored Diane the LOWEST?

   A. Only Brown
   B. Only Jones
   C. Only Smith
   D. Exactly 2 of them
   E. All 3 judges

20. Which judge(s) scored Ann the HIGHEST?

   A. Only Brown
   B. Only Jones
   C. Only Smith
   D. Exactly 2 of them
   E. None of them

21. How many applicants earned the HIGHEST ranking at least once?

   A. All 5   B. 4   C. 3   D. 2   E. 1

22. Which is(are) correct?
   I. Ann's total + Diane's total = Carol's total
   II. Beth's total + Diane's total = Ann's total
   III. Carol's total + Diane's total = Beth's total

   The CORRECT answer is:

   A. I only
   B. II only
   C. III only
   D. All of them
   E. None of them

Questions 23-25.

DIRECTIONS: Questions 23 through 25 are based on the following paragraph.

There are 200 correctional facilities nationwide. Exactly 75% of all inmates with the disease AIDS are housed in correctional facilities in just three states: New Jersey, New York, and Pennsylvania. Also, 4% of the entire nation's correctional institutions have 72% of all the inmate AIDS cases; 50% of all such institutions are totally free of the disease.

23. How many AIDS-infected inmates are housed *outside* the states of New York, New Jersey, and Pennsylvania?

   A. 8   B. 25   C. 50   D. 75   E. 100

24. If one could find a total of 216 inmates with AIDS in just eight institutions, then the LEAST number of AIDS-infected inmates nationwide would be

   A. 240   B. 270   C. 300   D. 330   E. 360

25. It is a certainty that exactly _____ correctional facilities combined would contribute 28% of the total number of inmates with AIDS, where none of these institutions are disease-free. 25.____

   A. 46   B. 50   C. 72   D. 92   E. 100

KEY (CORRECT ANSWERS)

1. B
2. C
3. E
4. D
5. D

6. E
7. B
8. E
9. D
10. A

11. C
12. B
13. E
14. C
15. E

16. E
17. B
18. B
19. D
20. E

21. D
22. C
23. C
24. C
25. D

SOLUTIONS TO PROBLEMS

For Questions 1 through 7, the order of towns from west to east are: Beta, Alpha, Gamma, Delta, and would be arranged mileage wise as:

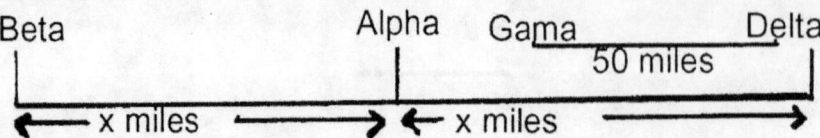

The present maximum speed limits are:
- Beta = 20 m.p.h.
- Alpha = 60 m.p.h.
- Delta = 70 m.p.h.
- Gamma = 75 m.p.h. or 80 m.p.h.

For Questions 8 through 14, the correct sequence in order of increasing price would be:

Condensed biography, condensed novel, regular biography, expanded biography, regular novel, condensed statistical, regular statistical, expanded statistical, expanded novel.

There are three possible sets of solutions for the prices:

1st solution:	$5,	$10,	$15,	$25,	$30,	$35,	$40,	$50,	$75
2nd solution:	$5,	$10,	$20,	$25,	$30,	$35,	$40,	$50,	$75
3rd solution:	$5,	$15,	$20,	$25,	$30,	$35,	$40,	$50,	$75

Note that the differences occurred only in the lowest three prices.

For Questions 15 through 22, the scoring by each judge and for each applicant appears as:

	Ann	Beth	Carol	Diane	Eve
Brown	3	1	2	0	4
Jones	1	3	4	0	2
Smith	2	3	0	1	4

23. 100% - 75% = 25% of AIDS-infected inmates are located outside the 3 states of New York, New Jersey, and Pennsylvania. (25%)(200) = 50. (Ans. C)

24. Eight institutions could represent the 4% of the entire nation's correctional facilities which have 72% of all inmate AIDS cases (200 times 4% = 8). If 216 represents 72% of all such infected inmates, then the total number of AIDS-infected inmates is 216 ÷ 72% = 300. (Ans. C)

25. 100% - 4% - 50% = 46%, which could contribute 28% of the total number of inmates with AIDS. This 46% figure would represent the fraction of institutions outside the 4% and outside the 50% (which have no such cases). (46%)(200) = 92. (Ans. D)